GW00656490

A Most Respectable
Meeting of Merchants

A Most Respectable
Meeting of Merchants

A Most Respectable Meeting of Merchants

Dublin Chamber of Commerce: A History

Enda MacMahon

LONDUBH BOOKS

First published in 2014 by Londubh Books

18 Casimir Avenue, Harold's Cross, Dublin 6w, Ireland

www. londubh. ie

1 3 5 4 2

Cover by bluett; design and layout by David Parfrey

Printed by Gráficos Castuera, Navarra, Spain

ISBN: 978-1-907535-43-7

A NOTE ON THE TYPE

This book is set in the typefaces Garamond Premier Pro,
Hoefler Text and Optima.

LONDUBH BOOKS

This book is dedicated to Dublin's business community.

Contents

FOREWORD

Dublin Chamber of Commerce, which was founded in 1783, is one of the oldest chambers in the world. Today, more than two hundred and thirty years later, as CEO and President of Dublin Chamber, we are honoured to lead the organisation, which continues to hold a unique position among businesses and influencers throughout the Dublin city region.

History is important for all of us; it is through remembering the past that we form the future and aspire to greatness beyond our present situation. Dublin is no exception to that rule. Enda MacMahon's expertly researched history of Dublin Chamber chronicles the development of this capital city region and explores Chamber's role in its growth as a great place to work, to live in and to visit. Dublin has reinvented itself many times, sometimes by design and sometimes in response to external or domestic events, and Chamber has played a central role, promoting the business of business and acting as advocate for the critical part the economy plays in the life of Dublin.

A Most Respectable Meeting of Merchants recalls members past and present, businessmen and women, and those who came together to form Dublin Chamber under the first president, Travers Hartley. It celebrates centuries of volunteerism by business people as Chamber members and the work of the executive staff, past and present, all of which has contributed to making Dublin Chamber such a success.

Today, Chamber provides a strong, respected and reasoned voice for business in the area, promoting a vision for Dublin as a global city region and a crucial driver of the Irish economy. Chamber is a key participant in dialogue with national and local government and a strong contributor to the national media on issues that have an impact on our society and our economy.

Chamber has an extensive programme of activity, delivering learning, business development and networking. In 2014, more than 10,000 people will connect through Chamber's extensive local and international business network and online via its expanding digital platform. Chamber's premises in 7 Clare Street, Dublin 2, are home to its staff of twenty-five professionals and host many networking events, while the members' lounge is open for members' use.

Chamber's vision is: 'helping your business succeed in a successful Dublin'. Providing Dublin's best business network, inspiring business learning and leadership is key to delivering this vision.

Chamber takes the lead in championing Dublin as a great place to do business. By fostering all aspects of a great city region – quality of life, jobs, education, connectivity and infrastructure, social supports and diversity – the organisation focuses on supporting Dublin business and promoting prosperity in the region, now and for centuries to come. It is through the generous support and participation of its member companies that Chamber plays this vital role in shaping Dublin's future.

Dublin Chamber of Commerce is proud to dedicate this history, *A Most Respectable Meeting of Merchants*, to all the business people of the city who contributed to Chamber's achievements over its first two hundred and thirty one years.

Martin Murphy, President
Gina Quin, Chief Executive
Dublin Chamber of Commerce
October 1914

INTRODUCTION

A most respectable meeting of merchants, traders, &c. took place yesterday at the Commercial Buildings, pursuant to public advertisement, for the purposes of forming a Chamber of Commerce. Randall McDonnell, esq., in the chair. Several resolutions were passed, and a number of the first mercantile signatures was placed on the subscription list.

The *Freeman's Journal*, 14 October 1820

This notice, from which the present book takes its title, announced the beginnings of the reconstituted Dublin Chamber of Commerce in 1820, two earlier attempts to establish a Chamber, in 1783 and 1805, having petered out. Since humankind discovered the benefits of trade, merchants have promoted commerce, with a natural tendency to operate within collectives.

According to Patrick L. Prendeville's history of Dublin Chamber of Commerce, chambers of commerce began in France, the first in Marseille in 1599. It was called 'Le Bureau de Commerce', later 'La Chambre du Commerce de Marseille' – hence the anglicised term 'Chamber' of Commerce. The raison d'être of the Bureau de Commerce was to protect marine trade, especially in the Mediterranean, from the depredations of pirates, as the forces of the crown had failed to do so in an era of religious wars and civil strife.

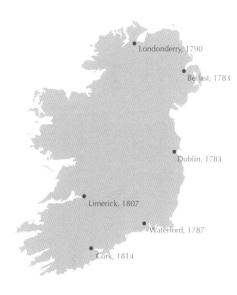

The location and founding dates of the early Irish chambers of commerce.

Report of the meeting of merchants to convene Dublin Chamber of Commerce in the Freeman's Journal, *14 October 1820.*

The first British chamber of commerce emerged in Jersey, one of the Channel Islands off the French coast, in 1767-8, and chambers of commerce began to develop in America at roughly the same time. They appeared in cities along the Eastern seaboard; New York in 1768, Charleston in 1773 and Boston in 1785. Merchants in Jamaica had their own chamber from 1778. It is no coincidence that most of the early chambers originated in coastal cities, both in America and in the British Isles, as merchants moved freely between these trading centres, sharing ideas. Joseph Wilson and John Duncan, early presidents of Dublin Chamber of Commerce, had both been in business in America.

Mediaeval trade guilds were the first commercial combinations in Ireland, introduced by the Norman conquerors to the major towns they controlled. They worked in collaboration with and were essentially part of the city's administration, regulating and restricting business for the benefit of members. By the late 18th century the guilds' restrictions had become an impediment to innovation and the expansion of trade. Following the example of the trading cities – Manchester and Liverpool in 1774 and London in 1782 – in 1783 merchants in Dublin as well as in Belfast, Glasgow and Birmingham established chambers of commerce, reflecting more sophisticated business requirements, particularly in the areas of law, debt and insurance, that required greater oversight.

The late 18th century was a period of new ideas, in business as well as in politics and philosophy, that were more readily accessible than before through widespread dissemination of printed material. The founding of the first Dublin Chamber of Commerce coincided with the achievement of substantial legislative independence for the parliament in Dublin and the beginning of the relaxation of the Penal Laws against Catholics and dissenters. It was an era in which prosperous merchants began to challenge the supremacy of the landed and titled classes. The American War of Independence, which began in 1776, had disrupted colonial trade and the British government imposed heavy duties on commerce to fund it. Early chambers advocated a reduction in state interference in their activities, promoting laissez-faire or liberal economics, unlike their predecessors, the merchant guilds, which were protectionist. Much of the focus of Dublin Chamber in its early years was on opposing impositions and restrictions on export trade.

Other Irish cities were not slow to follow Dublin and Belfast in forming their own chambers: Waterford in 1787, Londonderry in 1790, Limerick in 1807 and Cork in 1814. By 1819 there were nineteen chambers of commerce operating in Britain and Ireland, a figure that had risen to twenty-four by 1850 and more than ninety by 1900. The first British federation, the Association of Chambers of Commerce, began in 1860 and included the Irish chambers. Since independence, Chambers in southern Ireland have been members of their own association. This body is now called Chambers Ireland and has forty-four member chambers.

The production of a book like this depends on the efforts of many people and I would like to acknowledge their contributions. The idea of writing a new history of Dublin Chamber of Commerce came from its CEO, Gina Quin, and Chamber was unstinting in giving me access and information. Sandra Houlihan as liaison was always efficient and most helpful in arranging access, providing particulars and sourcing images for the book. Chamber

'The late 18th century was a period of new ideas, in business as well as in politics and philosophy.'

has kept good written records of its affairs, and research for this book also involved visits to Dublin's main historical repositories: the Royal Irish Academy, the National Archives, the National Library and Dublin Civic Archives. As always, the staff of these institutions readily gave support. I talked to a number of former Chamber presidents who were most helpful: I would especially like to thank Desmond Miller and Tom Hardiman for their time and observations. Thanks too to Donal de Buitléir for information about Dublin Junior Chamber and Roger Kirker of the National Maritime Museum for his efforts to answer my queries about the flag of the HMS *Dublin* and for providing an image of the flag.

Sourcing the images for this book required the assistance of many people, among them: Conor McCabe, photographer; Sophie Evans; Amy Hughes, Royal Irish Academy; Colm Lyon; Paul Flanagan; the helpful staff in the Mansion House; Margaret Sweeney; Desmond Miller; Kieran Tobin; Sarah Connolly; Carol Quinn, Pernod Ricard; Bernie Murphy and Lesley-Anne Carey, Christ Church Cathedral; Chris Harbidge, the National Museum; Bertie Kelly, National College of Ireland; Alice Boardman and the staff in City Hall; Conal O'Flanagan, Dublin Port Company.

I appreciate the work of Jo O'Donoghue of Londubh Books who did a wonderful job of editing my manuscript, David Parfrey for his efforts on the layout and Syd Bluett for the cover. Finally I thank my own personal source of Chamber presidential information, my wife, Imelda Reynolds.

I

THE TRINITY GUILD OF MERCHANTS

Next march the Guild, who plow the frothy main
In depth of Winter for the hopes of gain,
To distant climes our beef and wool convey,
And barter wholesome food for silk and tea;
Fearless of rocks, they seek the unknown shore,
And bring from thence the glit'ring, tempting ore.

From a poem by Bartholomew Corcoran, Inn's Quay, printed in 1767

In 1767 members of Dublin's twenty-five guilds lined up behind the Lord Mayor and sheriff in a colourful parade for 'the riding and perambulating of the franchises, liberties, meares and bounds of the city', as they had done since the Middle Ages. Bartholomew Corcoran's poem celebrating the event includes a description of the Merchants' Guild. As this was the city's premier guild, its masters and wardens followed directly behind the Lord Mayor, high sheriffs and their retainers on horseback, all wearing the blue and yellow of the guild; next was a cart displaying the guild's produce, with brothers, journeymen and apprentices coming then on foot. Drummers and trumpeters and shield- and armour-bearers accompanied the parade. In modern times the parade at the start of the Palio in Siena, northern Italy, which includes that city's guilds, gives a good sense of what the Dublin procession must have looked like.

The merchants' arms illustrated on Charles Brooking's 1728 map of Dublin, along with those of twenty-three other guilds. Richard Carney, Ulster King at Arms, had confirmed them in 1687.

timeline

1169
Norman Invasion of Ireland
under Strongbow.

1172
Henry II grants first charter to
Dublin.

1190
Large parts of Dublin destroyed
by fire.

1205
Foundations of
Dublin Castle laid.

1348
Plague thought to have taken
14,000 lives in Dublin.

1364
Rebuilding of St Patrick's
Cathedral after a fire.

1494
Poyning's Law greatly
reduces the power of the Irish
parliament.

The ritual of 'riding the franchise' took place every three years. It was expensive for the guilds to participate – for example, 60 per cent of the Stationers' Guild outgoings for 1728 were spent on the procession – but all members were obliged to attend on pain of being fined. The practice gradually waned with the weakening power of the guilds and the last riding of the franchise, in 1785, was abandoned after rioting occurred as it passed through the Coombe, resulting in three deaths. To this day Dublin City Council maintains one part of the ancient ritual when the Lord Mayor takes a boat out on the River Liffey and throws a dart into the river to mark the franchise boundary.

When the Normans arrived in Ireland in 1169 they brought merchants and traders from England and Wales, as well as more advanced commercial systems. They settled initially on the east coast and Dublin became their capital and commercial centre. Henry II gave the city its first charter in 1172 and twenty years later Richard II granted a charter that permitted the formation of guilds to regulate city trade. The Merchants' Guild was the first to be established and its membership roll for the years 1192-1265 is still extant, showing that the enrolment included not just importers and exporters but all sorts of traders and manufacturers who later formed their own guilds. From the outset the guilds had a religious aspect: each gave devotion to a particular saint and worshipped in a specific church or chapel within a church. Each appointed a chaplain whose role, it would appear, was solely to preach a sermon on the feast day of the guild's patron saint. The merchants' place of worship was Trinity Chapel in Christ Church and their sermon was given on Trinity's Eve. (Trinity Sunday, the first Sunday after Pentecost, falls fifty-seven days after Easter Sunday.) Trinity Chapel was next to Strongbow's tomb and brethren of the guild were entitled to be buried in its vault. (The chapel did not survive a collapse of the south wall in 1562 and was not reinstated in the renovation of the cathedral in 1878.) In 1451 the guild received a new charter from Henry VI, which directed that two masters and two wardens be elected each year to effect its business. It granted the masters the power to imprison, under the common seal of the guild, those who did not comply with its regulations. The guild also employed two clerks and a beadle or constable, who issued summonses and made arrests. As well as merchants, members of the Holy Trinity Guild included woollen and linen drapers, mercers, haberdashers, grocers, tobacconists and timber merchants.

The guild was a trading as well as a regulatory body that bulk-purchased goods, often by the shipload, on behalf of its members, thereby reducing and controlling prices. A charter granted by Queen Elizabeth in 1577 gave the Merchants' Guild sole authority to buy in wholesale for the city. Members of guilds, or corporations as they were sometimes known, made up the city assembly. Dublin had twenty-five guilds, of which the last to be established was the apothecaries', which seceded from the barbers and surgeons in 1747. The system encouraged exclusiveness by allowing only guild members to trade; however, the common council of the city assembly acted to control the guilds to ensure that they did not abuse their monopoly to the detriment of the citizens.

After the Reformation, the guilds conformed to the established church. Some of their property, which had been was used for religious purposes, was seized by the crown. Sectarian rules were introduced by both the common council and the guilds: these were reinforced after the Cromwellian War and extended with the introduction of the Penal Laws following the Williamite

1534
Henry VIII declares himself Head of the Church of England under the Act of Supremacy. Religious land reverts to the crown.

1591
Trinity College founded by Queen Elizabeth; opens two years later.

1649
Cromwell arrives in Dublin.

1661
Smock Alley Theatre opens.

1665
Dublin appoints its first Lord Mayor.

1672
The Lord Lieutenant, the Earl of Essex, introduces new rules for the better government of the city.

1683
Building of Dublin's new Tholsel.

War. The Dublin Assembly Rolls of 1699 commented 'that severall Papists have been and are imployed in the citty service, to the great scandall of the city and the prejudice of poore Protestants, who might get a livelyhood by the said imployments' and ordered that they were to take the oath or be dismissed. Catholics could not be guild members or apprentices. These discriminatory rules would ultimately be a factor in the demise of the guild system.

At the beginning of the 18th century the population of Dublin was estimated at 50,000. The city had developed slowly over the previous centuries but the 18th century saw unprecedented growth, mainly due to an influx of Catholics from rural Ireland. Dublin had been predominantly a Protestant city but by the middle of the century the balance had changed. In 1798 Reverend James Whitelaw carried out a detailed survey of the city, parish by parish, and calculated the population of Dublin as 191,000 – nearly four times what it had been at the beginning of the century. The largest proportion of the new citizens were Catholic; furthermore, the numbers of people professing membership of the established church were falling. They were replaced by dissenters: Presbyterians, Quakers and Huguenots. The Penal Laws discriminated against dissenters as well as Catholics but impediments in commerce were less restrictive than those relating to the professions or land ownership. Gradually dissenters were admitted to the guilds: Huguenots (Protestant refugees from Catholic France who arrived in Ireland in the late 17th century) received favourable treatment under an act of 1692 and were admitted to the guilds, whether conforming or non-conforming, Quakers were admitted

The procession of guilds, showing the bricklayers' guild, which precedes the Palio in Siena – a contemporary reminder of the triennial procession of guilds held in Dublin.

THE GUILDS OF DUBLIN

Guild	Patron	Date of Charter	Colours	Number on Council
Merchants	Holy Trinity	1192	Blue & yellow	31
Tailors	St John the Baptist	1418	Saxon blue & white	4
Smiths	St Loy	1474	Black & white	4
Barbers and Surgeons	St Mary Magdalen	1577	Purple, cherry & white	2
Bakers	St Clement & St Anne	1478	Orange, cherry & lemon	4
Butchers	The Virgin Mary	1569	Red & white	3
Carpenters	The Blessed Virgin Mary & House of St Thomas	1508	Red & white	3
Shoemakers	The Blessed Virgin Mary	1465	Red, blue & green	4
Saddlers	The Blessed Virgin Mary	1558	Crimson, white & green	3
Cooks	St James the Apostle	1444	Orange & black	2
Tanners	St Nicholas	1688	Blue, white & yellow	2
Tallow Chandlers	St George	1585	Blue & sky	2
Glovers and Skinners	St Mary	1476	Green & brick	2
Weavers	St Philip & St James	1446	Orange & blue	3
Sheermen and Dyers	St Nicholas	–	Blue & white	2
Goldsmiths	All Saints	1637	Red, yellow & white	4
Coopers	St Patrick	1666	White & green	2
Feltmakers	–	1667	White hats with sky	2
Cutlers, Painters, Stainers & Stationers	St Luke	1670	Crimson, lemon & sky	3
Bricklayers	St Bartholomew	1670	Blue & orange	2
Hosiers	St George	1688	White, blue & copper	2
Curriers	St Nicholas	1695	Yellow, red & black	2
Brewers	St Andrew	1696	Buff & blue	4
Joiners	The Blessed Virgin Mary	1700	Green, yellow & white	2
Apothecaries	St Luke the Evangelist	1747	Purple & orange	2

from the 1720s and finally Presbyterians from the 1740s. Catholics, denied membership, would trade outside the guild, so to deal with this reality the guild created a membership category known as a 'quarter brother'. Quarter brothers paid a fee each quarter day and were expected to comply with the rules of the guild but had no say in its administration; nor were they afforded the franchise. By the second half of the 18th century most Dublin guilds had more quarter brothers than full members. For instance, Bartholomew Corcoran, author and printer of the poem quoted at the beginning of this chapter, was a Catholic and a quarter brother in the stationers' guild, paying 1s/6d per quarter. There were few benefits in quarterage and Catholics eventually succeeded in having them declared illegal in a ruling from the King's Bench in 1759, thereby permitting a regularisation of trading outside the guilds. This period of great development in Dublin coincided with the gradual demise of the guilds, which were restrictive rather than expansionist in their philosophy.

The guilds' remaining influence was political. Dublin had a mayor from 1229, elevated to a Lord Mayor from 1665. The city council was bicameral. The aldermanic chamber, from which the Lord Mayor (who was also the chief city magistrate) was elected, chose its own members for life. There were twenty-four aldermen: within days of an alderman's death his replacement was chosen from among those in the lower house, or common council, who had served as sheriff. The common council comprised up to a hundred and forty-four members. Every three years ninety-six of these were elected by the twenty-five guilds in proportion to their size. The Merchants' Guild, being the largest, elected thirty-one members, while the other twenty-four guilds had two, three or four seats each. The remaining members of the common council were the two high sheriffs, elected from among its

James Malton's drawing of the Tholsel shortly before it was demolished in 1809.

members, and a variable number of men who had previously served as high sheriff – the second most important position in the city administration. The Merchants' Guild dominated the aldermanic chamber and the choice of Lord Mayor. In a Corporation Reform Act of 1760 the power of aldermen to veto guild representatives was removed and members of the common council were given the power to veto the selection of mayor.

Guild members who were freemen of the city elected the guild representatives on the common council; they also constituted the electorate for the two parliamentary seats in Dublin. Freedom of the city could be acquired in several ways – sons and daughters of freemen by birth; by marriage to the daughter of a freeman; by service or an apprenticeship of seven years in a guild; by payment of a fine to the city treasury; by 'grace especial' for dignitaries or

The Tholsel

The word 'Tholsel' derives from the old English form of 'toll stall' a structure in which traders paid tolls upon entering the city. A number of Irish tholsels survive, principally Kilkenny's and Drogheda's, but Dublin's is long gone. The first Tholsel in Dublin was erected in the early 14th century in Skinner's Row (now Christ Church Place), pretty much the highest point in the city, at the junction of north-south and east-west roads. In 1683 the original Tholsel was demolished and a larger building erected. The new Tholsel incorporated a covered exchange on the ground floor for the merchants to display their wares. On the first floor there were two large rooms: the merchants' guildhall and the city council chamber. The building also contained courtrooms for lesser criminal offences and civil actions.

The Tholsel was built on soft ground and suffered subsidence toward the end of the 18th century. About two-thirds of the building had to be demolished in 1809 and the remainder was removed by 1820.

All that remains of the Tholsel today are the statues of King Charles II and his brother, the Duke of York, the future King James II, and the royal crest, which are held in the crypt of Christ Church Cathedral.

Courtesy of Christ Church Cathedral

those trained outside the city; or by an Act of Parliament which was passed in 1661 to 'encourage Protestant strangers and others to inhabit and plant in the Kingdom of Ireland'.

It was this franchise that latterly attracted applications for guild membership. Many individuals in professions that were not covered by the guild paid for a freedom from a guild, thereby acquiring a vote. Indeed when the master of the bricklayers' guild was asked shortly after the Act of Union to advise the government on the state of a building, he declined to do so as he was 'only an attorney'. The awarding of freedoms provided the guild with an income.

However, the sectarian elephant in the room remained: Catholics were refused admittance on a ballot of members. The guilds were to the fore in opposing Catholic relief. The Relief Act of 1793 which removed most of the Penal Laws (save for the right to stand for parliament) should have opened up the guilds' membership and soon afterwards the Merchants' Guild did admit eleven Catholic brothers, but no further Catholics were allowed to become members. As late as 1822 an attempt to admit twenty leading Catholic merchants – many of them on the Council of Dublin Chamber – to the Merchants' Guild failed at the ballot. Thomas Ellis, one of the city's MPs, led the opposition and was praised for supporting 'the constitution and maintaining the honour and character of the guild'. In 1828, when Catholic Emancipation was imminent, the Merchants' Guild drew up a petition against further concessions to Catholics, which was prefixed by an 'enlightened, talented, and constitutional exposé of the papists' association and the machinations of the Italian sect'.

In 1835 the Commission on Municipal Corporations in Ireland noted that there were nine hundred brothers and one sister in the Merchants' Guild and 'the majority are not connected with commerce, and cannot be truly described as "merchants".' The report continued that 'the vast majority of Dublin merchants are not members of the guild. It is generally understood that not only Roman Catholics, but also Protestants, professing political opinions at variance with those of the corporation, have been, and are, studiously excluded' and that 'in fact the commons are totally distinct from the mercantile body of the city, and nothing can more clearly illustrate the position than the facts that the Council of the Chamber of Commerce, the committee of the Commercial Buildings, the directors of the Corn Exchange, and the committee of the Linen Hall, the principal commercial institutions of the city, do not contain a single alderman, sheriff's peer or member of commons.' Indeed, of the first group of members of Dublin

Merchants' Hall, also known as Merchants' Arch, today.

Merchants' Arch

The Merchants' Guildhall on Wellington Quay, more commonly called Merchants' Arch, was designed by Frederick Darley Junior (1797-1872), and built by Edward Carolin & Sons in 1821. Darley may have been trained by Francis Johnston, designer of the GPO. He had a very extensive practice. The Merchants' Guildhall appears to have been his first work: others include the library in King's Inns, Straffan House, County Kildare, and the Central Model Schools in Marlborough Street.

The guildhall is described as a three-bay granite palazzo. It incorporates a ground-floor passage from the Halfpenny Bridge (Wellington Bridge, erected in 1819) to Temple Bar. The building has an oval cantilevered granite staircase to the rear leading to the assembly hall on the first floor, overlooking the river. The guild occupied the building for only twenty years before its demise and it was subsequently used for various commercial purposes.

A drawing of Christ Church Cathedral by George Petrie before it was substantially renovated in 1878 to the designs of George Edmund Street. The Merchants' Guild, or Guild of the Holy Trinity, had a chapel on the south wall to the left of the transept. It collapsed in 1562.

Courtesy of the National Library of Ireland

Chamber of Commerce from 1783 only about half were members of a guild. In its third manifestation in 1820, Chamber took a particular interest in objecting to a sole surviving levy that was in the gift of the Merchants' Guild, that of coal meter at the port.

In truth, throughout Europe the guild system was in decline. In Dublin the weakening of the guilds left an opening for bodies like the Chamber of Commerce that advocated free trade. The guilds' failure to be representative of all merchants, as well as their association with the city assembly, the source of many impositions on trade, were among the reasons for the formation of the Society of Merchants in 1761. The Ouzel Galley Society, which was founded at the beginning of the 18th century, had already embraced inclusive membership. In 1839 the writer of a letter to the *Freeman's Journal* disdainfully referred to: 'The knot of fools and bigots, commonly called the

Guild of Merchants, [who] had a meeting the other evening to deliberate upon – and devise the best means of upholding – the present state of the corporation.'

The Municipal Act of 1840 was the death knell of the guilds. Although the freemen remained enfranchised, the electorate was greatly enlarged by the inclusion of forty-shilling freeholders. Henceforth the corporation had a single chamber and candidates who topped the poll in each ward became the aldermen. The Merchants' Guild effectively ceased to exist in 1840, after more than six centuries, and in 1846 Chamber vigorously resisted an attempt by the Bricklayers' Guild to enforce its old by-laws by issuing threatening writs to contractors to prevent them from employing non-guild artisans. A law was passed at the end of the year effectively abolishing the guilds by restraining their interference. The goldsmiths' guild is the only one that might be considered to have a presence in Dublin today, through the Assay Office.

II

THE OUZEL GALLEY SOCIETY, 1705-1888

I...do swear that I will be Faithfull, and bear true allegiance to our sovereign Lord King George the 3rd and this gally intrusted to my command I will to the best of my power defend against all pyrates both by sea and land; The Rules and Orders established on board, I will see observed to the utmost of my power and justice administered to the crew and all who put any freight on board; I will continue to be a good fellow, and as long as I can Hearty and merry.

Oath of the Captain of the Ouzel Galley Society from 1748

Nothing has come more to symbolise Dublin Chamber of Commerce than the Ouzel Galley Society, although the society, which was founded in the first decade of the 18th century, sought little publicity for its activities. The legend of how it was founded is its best-known facet. The version of the story which has become standard was first published in 1904 by Caesar Litton Falkiner (great-great-grandson of Travers Hartley, an early captain of the Ouzel Galley Society and first president of Dublin Chamber), then enhanced and popularised in the *Dublin Historical Record* of 1940 produced by the Old Dublin Society. The author, Dr George A. Little, had a florid style and a penchant for imagination and embellishment.

According to this version the *Ouzel Galley*, captained by Eoghan Massey from Waterford and with a crew of forty, was chartered by Dublin merchants

An Ouzel Galley medal with Equity to the obverse. No examples of the early medals are to be found: John Parkes struck this in the 19th century.

timeline

1701

Erection of statue of William III in College Green, a bone of sectarian contention until its removal in 1929.

1704

Parliament passes the last of the Penal Laws, the Act to Prevent the Further Growth in Popery.

1707

Construction of Custom House at Essex Bridge begins.

Establishment of Ballast Board to manage the port of Dublin.

Act of Union between England and Scotland.

1714

Succession of the first Hanoverian king, George I.

1724

Publication of *Drapier's Letters* by Jonathan Swift.

1726

Opening of the Linenhall.

Ferris, Twigg and Cash to take woollen goods to Smyrna (now Izmir, in Turkey). The shippers took the precaution of insuring the ship and its cargo before she sailed from Dublin in the autumn of 1695. When the galley failed to return as expected a few years later, it was assumed lost: Ferris, Twigg and Cash successfully claimed against the insurers and it seemed the matter was closed. But in autumn 1700 the ship reappeared in the port, complete with the crew, a cargo of gold and jewels and a story to tell: of being captured by Algerian Corsairs on its way to the Mediterranean and the crew being forced to act for the pirates for a number of years before making good their escape from their sleeping captors and returning home. The insurers, unnamed in the story, claimed the ship and cargo as theirs as they had paid out on the policy, while Ferris, Twigg and Cash disputed their interest in the returned cargo as only the outbound merchandise had been insured.

The dispute went to court but after several years of argument there was no determination. It was agreed that a number of merchants would act as arbitrators and they decided to use the profits for the benefit of destitute members of the commercial community, a decision that proved popular. Thus it was resolved to institute a society of prominent merchants to act as arbitrators in similar disputes. Founded in 1705, it was named after the now famous ship ('ouzel' is an old English word for a blackbird) and, according to Little (but not Falkiner), Eoghan Massey was elected its first captain.

The narratives of Falkiner and Little seem to have their foundation in an adventure story, *The Missing Ship or the Log of the* Ouzel Galley, by a prolific Victorian children's novelist, W.H.G. Kingston, first published in 1877. The names Massey, Ferris, Twigg and Cash were all first used in Kingston's book. Kingston was a cousin of Sir John Kingston James, a member of the Ouzel

Galley Society from 1842, and he may have heard a story about the ship from him. His claim in the preface that he dined with the officers of the Ouzel Galley may be true but his other claim – that in Waterford he met an old friend, Captain Massey, a relative of Eoghan Massey, and was shown the original log of the galley – was probably pure fiction. Kingston's book differed from the versions of Falkiner and Little in that his galley, after being waylaid by pirates in the Caribbean, returns to Dublin without booty. Kingston's introduction to the story relates: 'A case arose regarding a vessel, which excited much controversy and legal perplexity, without being brought to any satisfactory decision. To put an end to this delay and expense, it was finally referred to the arbitration of several leading merchants of the city.' This is probably the account that most accurately sums up the events that led to the formation of the Ouzel Galley Society.

In all likelihood there was a ship called the *Ouzel Galley* that was the subject of some dispute, although the issue was probably more mundane. Irish ships were more likely to voyage to the West Indies than the Levant, although a series of navigation acts between 1663 and 1696 prohibited trade in English territories abroad by ships other than English ones. These acts were difficult to enforce and smuggling was widespread, so the source of the dispute might have been an illegal activity. Older reports do state that the *Galley* lay in Dublin port in 1700. The founding date of the society, 1705, may also have been a later invention – it is first mentioned in *Watson's Directory* for 1834 – as its log book entry for a dinner in December 1807 notes that 'after an evening spent with that harmony and good fellowship which has for almost a century uninterruptedly subsisted, the galley adjourned *sine die*.'

1729
Construction of Houses of Parliament on College Green begun; completed ten years later.

1731
Establishment of Dublin Society, (later Royal Dublin Society).

1741
Famine in Ireland, with an estimated 400,000 deaths.

1742
George Frederick Handel's *Messiah* first performed in Fishamble Street.

1746
The Battle of Culloden ends hopes of Stuart restoration in Scotland.

1752
Adoption of Gregorian calendar with the 'loss' of eleven days.

1756
Construction of the Grand Canal begins; not completed until 1805.

W.H.G. Kingston
(1814-80)

William Henry Giles Kingston was born in London, the son of Lucy Henry Kingston, a wine merchant whose business was based in Oporto. Kingston worked in his father's business and frequently sailed between England and Portugal, journeys that nurtured his interest in nautical matters.

Kingston published his first novel in 1844 and wrote one hundred and thirty books in all, mostly boys' adventure stories and travel books, many of which had a nautical theme and some with Irish characters. He also received a commission to translate the works of Jules Verne from French, although it is believed that his wife, Agnes Kinloch, did the actual translating. Although Kingston was a successful writer he found himself in financial difficulties and almost went bankrupt in 1868. He became reclusive in the last decade of his life and died at home in Willesden, Middlesex, three years after the publication of *The Missing Ship* in 1877.

Above: *W.H.G. Kingston.*

Below: *The cover of Kingston's novel,* The Missing Ship.

George Aloysius Little
(1899-1965)

The third and last son of Francis Little, a solicitor, George Aloysius Little was educated in Belvedere College, Clongowes Wood and the Royal College of Surgeons, where he qualified as a doctor in 1922. While still a student he was a medical officer for the First Dublin Brigade of the IRA during the War of Independence.

Interested in history and particularly that of Dublin, Little was a founder member of the Old Dublin Society and succeeded Tom Kelly as the society's president in 1942. He instigated the establishment of Dublin Civic Museum, which was opened by Éamon de Valera in the old Assembly Rooms in South William Street in 1953. Little wrote five books, including one on the Ouzel Galley, and had a medical practice in Rathgar Road. One of his daughters was the well-known newspaper agony aunt, Angela McNamara.

The earliest surviving records of the society date from 15 February 1748 (1749 in the new-style calendar), when it convened in the Phoenix Tavern in Werburgh Street to appoint a new captain. In all probability it had gone into abeyance for a decade, as the previous captain, Alderman John Porter (a merchant who traded with the West Indies), had died in 1739. Of the other officers, only Charles Howison, the boatswain, was still living, so the small cohort of remaining crew gathered to fill the officers' posts and replenish the society's numbers. Porter's brother-in-law, Alderman John Macarrell, a banker, was elected the new captain. The early Ouzel Galley Society had a strong link with the aldermanic class of Dublin Corporation and five further aldermen and a sheriff were among the twenty-one new members appointed that day. There was also strong Huguenot representation in the early society, as in the city's guilds: William Darquier, James Digges La Touche, John Vareilles and Peter Barre, as well as Porter and Macarrell. Alderman Macarrell commissioned a large painting of the *Ouzel Galley* by an unknown artist, which he presented to the Society in 1752 and which was initially kept in the tavern of John Morris in Chapelizod where the society then met. The log book includes a signed receipt: 'Received from John Macarrell esq., Capt. of the Ouzle Galley a large painted peice [*sic*] which is put up in the great room in my house, and I do hereby acknowledge that the said painted peice is the property of the said galley, and that I will deliver same when demanded by the said Capt. Macarrell, or the majority of the crew belonging to the said gally, [signed] John Morris.' After the society retrieved the painting from Morris – with some difficulty – in 1778, it hung in the Ouzel Galley rooms in Commercial Buildings and remained with Dublin Chamber of Commerce after the demise of the society.

1756
Establishment of the Catholic Association to agitate for relief from Penal Laws.

1757
Establishment of Dublin Wide Street Commissioners.

1759
Opening of Guinness brewery.

The obverse of the medal.

Macarrell attended only two Ouzel Galley meetings in the years before his death in 1757 but the society thrived, described as 'an ancient institution for determining Commercial Differences by Arbitration, where all Costs to the Parties are applied to charitable Purposes'. Among the statutes that were passed in 1698, during the reign of William III, was 'An Act for Determining Differences by Arbitration' which gave legal recognition to the principle of arbitration, and the ship's affairs may have been the catalyst for the foundation of the society. But the society's log books give the impression that its primary function was social. The members met for dinner about three times a year, generally in taverns such as the Rose and Bottle in Dame Street, the Phoenix Tavern in Werburgh Street and the Ship in Chapelizod. The first charitable purpose to be mentioned in the log was in 1754, when a donation of £10 was made to J. Haighton 'toward the loss he sustained by a mob having burned and destroyed some English Woollen Cloathes imported by him and lodged in his warehouse on Thomas Street.' (This was presumably the result of a protectionist riot.)

From the outset the society was structured like a ship's crew under the leadership of the captain. The boatswain's whistle, now in the National Museum, was provided by the carpenter in 1754 and used thereafter to summon the crew to dinner. In 1772 it was ordered that gold medals be struck portraying the ship on one face and 'Equity' on the other. Crew members had to wear the medals on orange ribbons at the society's dinners, on pain of a fine of a shilling.

Charles Howison replaced Macarrell as captain in the Rose and Bottle in June 1757 and under his captaincy a portion of the accounts was allocated to charitable purposes at each dinner. Generally small sums were given to

the widows and children of merchants, to merchants themselves or to port officials down on their luck. These, along with the cost of the dinners, were paid out of the society's funds. Until 1770 the members paid no subscription fee so it would appear that the society was in receipt of an income from arbitration. Unfortunately, although there is some mention of arbitration in the early log books, the arbitration books – listing nearly four hundred decisions – survive only for the years 1799 to 1884.

Membership of the society, which was limited to forty from 1768, was by nomination and the invitation of the captain. In the early days the crew, comprising merchants and bankers, was generally drawn from the city's corporation and belonged either to the established Church or the Huguenot community. A Quaker, Robert Jaffray, was admitted when the

The painting of the Ouzel Galley *that hung in Dublin Chamber after the Society started using Chamber's rooms in 1852. Chamber loaned the painting to the National College of Ireland in the IFSC in 2006 and it hangs there.*

One of the last acts of the Council of the Society in 1884 was to pay a picture restorer, John Tracey of Harrington Street, eight guineas to clean, restore and varnish the painting. Chamber had Tracey restore the painting again in 1905.

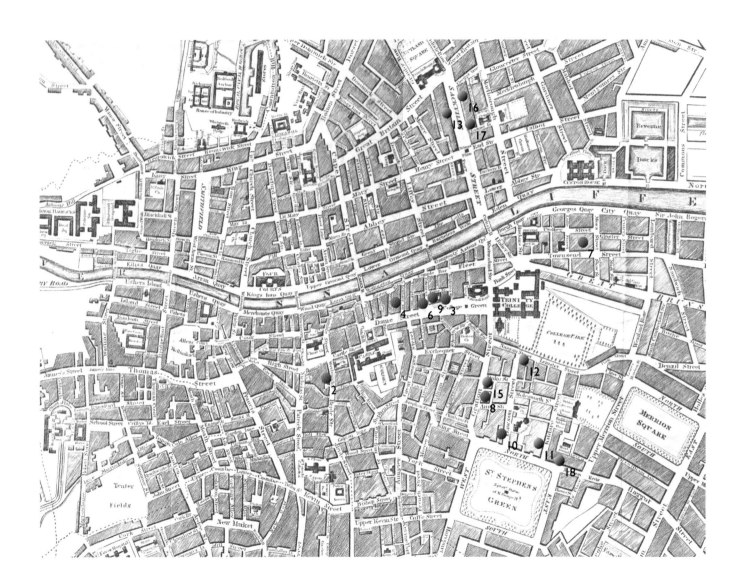

OUZEL GALLEY SOCIETY DINING VENUES

The Ouzel Galley Society held its annual dinners in these venues, 1748-1879.

The locations of numbers 1, 5 14 and 19 were outside the city; they are not shown on this map.

Taverns

1. Chapelizod, 1748-88, possibly The Ship owned by James Morris, visited occasionally.

2. Phoenix Tavern, in a lane just off Werburgh Street, 1754-69.

3. Rose and Bottle Tavern, 22 Dame Street, on the site of Commercial buildings, 1754-66, kept by Maurice Fenian.

4. Eagle Tavern, 3 Eustace Street, 1769-89.

5. Powers, Booterstown (once) 1776.

6. Ryans, Crow Street (once), 1783 (a John Ryan, vintner, 9 Fownes Street, is mentioned in *Watson's Directory*).

7. King's Arms, Townsend Street, 1786-8.

8. (James) Harrington's, 14 Grafton Street (a fashionable eating house), 1796-9.

9. Atwell's Commercial Buildings Tavern, Dame Street, 1800-6. Proprietor: Joseph Atwell.

10. Mail Coach Tavern, attached to the Mail Coach Hotel, 12 Dawson Street (once), 1806. Proprietor: Andrew Faulkner.

Hotels

11. Leech's (also Royal) Hotel, 41 Kildare Street, 1807-13. Proprietor: Thomas Leech.

12. Morrisson's Hotel, corner of Dawson & Nassau Streets, 1814-39. Proprietor: Arthur Morrisson.

13. Bilton's Hotel, 56 Upper Sackville Street, 1839-56. Proprietor: Lewis Heinikey.

14. Salthill Hotel, Salthill, Old Dunleary (occasionally), 1840-70. Proprietors: Messrs Lovegrove (1840-1), Daniel Jones (1847), William Parry (1868-70).

15. Jude's Hotel, 13 Grafton Street, (twice), 1853-4, (also called Royal Hotel). Proprietor: Horatio Thomas Jude.

16. Gresham Hotel, 20-21 Upper Sackville Street, 1857-8. Proprietor: Thomas Gresham.

17. Reynolds Hotel, 11-12 Upper Sackville Street, 1860-6. Proprietor: Mrs Kezia Reynolds.

18. Shelbourne Hotel, 27-31 St Stephen's Green, 1869-80. Proprietors: Jury, Cotton & Goodman.

19. Royal Marine Hotel, Gresham Terrace, Kingstown, (once), 1879. Manager: Thomas Lurring.

society was revived and a second, John Joshua Pim, in 1756. Travers Hartley, a Presbyterian, was selected in 1762. He was a member of the Committee of Merchants, founding president of Dublin Chamber of Commerce and, as captain of the Ouzel Galley Society in 1791, he nominated a Catholic, Valentine O'Connor, for membership. O'Connor took the (innocuous) oath but Anthony McDermott, another prominent Catholic merchant, who had been proposed in 1783, did not take the oath and never joined.

The Eagle Tavern, 3 Eustace Street, subsequently the site of a Quaker meeting house, was among the taverns that hosted the society's dinners. It was home to a number of clubs and also to the Duke of Leinster's regiment of Volunteers. In the mood of patriotic fervour that gripped the country prior to its achieving legislative independence in 1782 the Ouzel Galley Society strayed from its normal concerns of charity, arbitration and dining: in November 1780 'a respectable Deputation having waited on the Captain and crew of the Galley from his grace the Duke of Leinster and his Corps of Volunteers, informing them that they were drinking Health and Prosperity to the Galley', the Society's captain, Theophilus Thompson, ordered a return deputation to inform them that they were drinking 'Health and Prosperity to the Volunteers of Ireland'.

In April 1782 the Society issued what amounted to a political statement of support for the 'patriot' cause and had it published in the newspapers. While recognising the relationship between Great Britain and Ireland, it declared that the King and the parliament in Ireland were those 'solely competent' to make the laws for Ireland. The statement further declared 'that the captain, officers and crew of this galley will cooperate with their countrymen in every constitutional effort to support the just rights of Ireland and oppose the

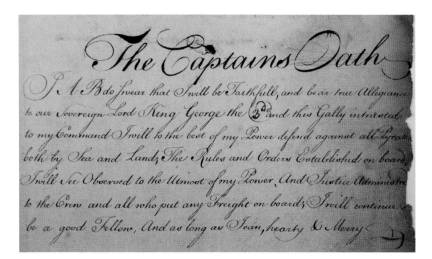

Right: The captain's oath at the beginning of the first Ouzel Galley Society log book.

interference of any other legislature.' The Eagle later became the Dublin home of the United Irishmen but by then the society had moved to the King's Arms in Townsend Street.

Requests for charitable donations came through members of the Galley. For instance, in 1777, William Byrne, 'a poor distressed sailor', received five guineas; the unnamed 'widow of a reputable merchant' received £5/13s/9d in 1780. One of the main recipients of charitable donations for a period of forty years from 1766 – £650 in all – was the Hibernian Marine Nursery, a school set up to care for orphans and, it was envisaged, prepare them for naval service. The school began in Ringsend before moving to purpose-built premises in Sir John Rogerson's Quay. This was one of several small Church of Ireland schools that combined to form Mount Temple Comprehensive in Clontarf in 1972.

By 1770 the society's income was unable to meet its charitable and refectory outgoings and a guinea was levied on all members. Thereafter an admission

CAPTAINS OF THE OUZEL GALLEY SOCIETY 1705-1888

It is interesting to note that all the Ouzel Galley captains died in office.

Those marked with an asterisk were also presidents of Dublin Chamber of Commerce.

1705–?	Captain Eoghan Massey	Most probably fictitious.
? – 1739	Alderman John Porter (d. 1739)	A Huguenot merchant, he was Lord Mayor 1723-4. His son, also John, was hanged for murder in St Stephen's Green in December 1730.
1748-57	Alderman John Macarrell (1695-1757)	Also a Huguenot and related to John Porter by marriage, he was Lord Mayor 1738-9 and MP for Carlingford 1741-57. A banker in the firm of Mitchell & Macarrell in Ormond Quay, Macarrell lived in Lissenhall in County Dublin.
1757-8	Charles Howison (d. 1768)	Described as a merchant 'of the strictest integrity', Howison lived in Mary's Lane. His son, Henry, was Lord Mayor of Dublin.
1768-72	Matthew Weld (1697-1772)	Merchant of Pill Lane.
1772-91	Theophilus Thompson (d. 1791)	Merchant of 20 William Street.
1791-96	*Travers Hartley (1723-96)	Initially a linen merchant but later a general wholesale merchant of 89 Bride Street, MP for Dublin and first president of Dublin Chamber of Commerce.
1796-99	Joseph Lynam (d. 1799)	Banker and alderman of Bachelor's Walk.
1799-1800	Henry Bevan (d. 1800)	Linen merchant of 5 Linenhall Street and alderman; Lord Mayor in 1776.
1800-02	Samuel Dick (1742-1802)	Also a linen merchant, of 13 Linenhall Street, and captain of the Linenhall Volunteer Corps. Much of his trade was with America and when he died he was estimated to be worth £400,000.
1803-22	*Joshua Pim (1748-1822)	A woollen and general merchant of 15 Usher's Island who had a strong trade with America.
1822-5	*Leland Crosthwait (1747-1825)	Substantial merchant of 63 Fleet Street, founder director and later governor of the Bank of Ireland. He lived in Dollymount.
1826-7	Joseph Pim (d. 1827)	Brother and partner of Joshua Pim. Like his brother he was unmarried. He lived in Brennanstown, Cabinteely.
1828-70	*Thomas Crosthwait (1782-1870)	Son of Leland Crosthwait. With his two brothers he ran the family milling and merchant business in 63 Fleet Street and Chapelizod. He lived in Fitzwilliam Square.
1870-87	George Pim (1801-87)	Nephew of Joshua and Joseph Pim, who inherited his uncles' wool exporting business in Usher's Island. He lived in Brennanstown, Cabinteely.

fee, also a guinea, was charged. Funds were still insufficient and in 1774 it was agreed that an annual subscription of a guinea apply, 'toward the ordinary ware and tare of the galley to commence from the 12 July next and to continue so long as the Captain and Officers shall think and that all the money that shall be received for determining differences be applied to charitable purposes.' The society clearly still had income from arbitration.

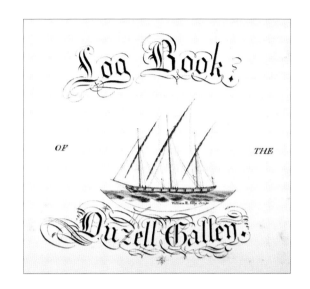

Many members of the Ouzel Galley Society were also shareholders in the Commercial Buildings Company. When the building was completed in 1799 it included a carved image of a sailing ship thought to represent the *Ouzel Galley* over the courtyard door to Dame Street (in 1821 the Society made its permanent home there). Also in 1799 the society decided to formalise its rules, including those for arbitration. (Most of the surviving records of the society extend from this period.) A council of officers was initiated that met several times during the year and the secretary, who had previously been unpaid (but received a stipend for attending arbitrations), was to receive twenty guineas a year for his service. Two sets of accounts were to be kept, the subscription fund for expenses and the charitable fund incorporating the income from arbitrations. About this time, also, the society appeared to receive a payment of £2 or £3 from several of the members, called a 'general average', on ships carrying merchandise to or from the port.

Above: Frontispiece of the second Ouzel Galley Society log book with a decorative title by William R. Elly, scrivener.

Below: The first Ouzel Galley logbook.

By permission of the Royal Irish Academy
© RIA

Dinners were still held three times a year, with the last of the year used for formal approvals of the council's decisions. The convivial dinners were generally well attended by between twenty and thirty crew members and part of the ritual was the use of the society's glass goblet or 'loving cup'

Above: Menu card, in French, for the last Ouzel Galley dinner, held in the Shelbourne Hotel on 1 June 1880. The nineteen members dined sumptuously on eight courses with appropriate wines for each course. The total cost was just under £21.

By permission of the Royal Irish Academy © RIA

Right: The Ouzel Galley goblet, a captain's glass or 'loving cup' dating from the early 19th century, which holds a half-pint or a third of a bottle of wine.

The Bank of Ireland held the goblet on the demise of the Ouzel Galley society and presented it to the National Museum (where it remains), although ownership of the goblet passed to Chamber.

for toasts 'with a full bumper and all due honours' – a full bumper is a glass filled to the brim. The cut-glass goblet had the words 'Ouzel Galley Society' and 'Atwell Commercial Building Tavern' engraved on it, as well as a frigate and the figure of equity. Presumably Joseph Atwell, whose premises, newly opened in Commercial Buildings, were favoured by the Galley from 1800 to 1806, gave the goblet to the Society. Initially the Society held its dinners in hostelries and inns in the city but after 1806 it patronised various Dublin hotels, including the Royal, the Gresham and the Shelbourne, where the last dinner was held in 1880. The cost of these meals was recorded in the 'Accompts Book', with a substantial proportion spent on wine.

In the early years of the 19th century the members of the Ouzel Galley adjudicated about thirty arbitrations a year: for each, the society was paid

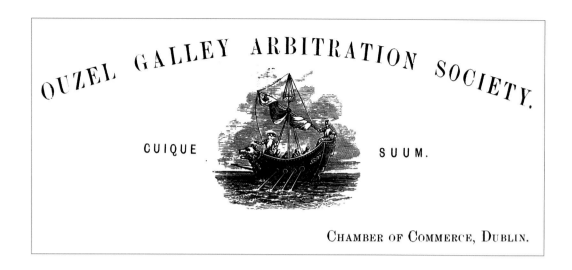

OUZEL GALLEY ARBITRATION SOCIETY.

CUIQUE • SUUM.

CHAMBER OF COMMERCE, DUBLIN.

anything between two and fourteen guineas, depending upon the complexity of the case and the time expended. The registrar or secretary was also paid for his services in calling meetings, keeping notes and issuing the award. The number of cases sent to arbitration fell off to single figures annually after 1815 and after 1850 there were many years with no arbitrations at all. The society kept its own rooms in the Commercial Buildings until 1832. Thereafter it sublet a room, known as the arbitration room, from Chamber at a lower rent. From this time on the society became increasingly associated with Chamber, unsurprising as, in 1848, all but four of the Galley members were also Chamber members, a third of them on Council.

From the early 19th century the society began to invest excess income in government stock and by 1888 it had £3000 in 3 per cent stock. But arbitrations had virtually ceased. In an attempt to increase business from 1873 the secretary of Chamber was employed to attend at Commercial Buildings each morning to take instructions on arbitrations. The name of the society was changed to 'Ouzel Galley Arbitration Society' and advertisements to this effect were placed in the daily papers but as there was little increase in uptake, they were discontinued three years later. The number of dinners also declined and vacancies in the crew remained unfilled.

The society's last recorded council meeting was held in the Bank of Ireland on 3 April 1886, presided over by the aged captain, George Pim. Only James C. Colvill and Edmund D'Olier attended and the main item on the agenda was their letters of resignation. Pim stated that he too wished to resign and when he died the following year he was not replaced. A statement the society's solicitors lodged with the Charity Commissioners reported that several further meetings were held in 1887, at which it was decided to close the society and distribute its assets, amounting to £3300, among six Dublin hospitals. In 1888 before Judge Chatterton of the Court of Chancery at the Four Courts the Ouzel Galley Society took a suit to administer its funds and was closed. Because of the Ouzel Galley Society's close association with Chamber the image of a galley has become a symbol of Chamber and appears on the president's chain of office.

III

THE SOCIETY OF MERCHANTS, 1761-83

Having long experience of the utter inattention of corporate bodies to the interests of trade, although the original purpose of their institution; and observing the generality of them entirely taken up in the contest for little distractions of pre-eminence among themselves, and largely engaged in the pursuit of honours or emoluments of magistracy.

Case printed by the merchants of Dublin

In 1761 a group of Dublin merchants, expressing dissatisfaction at the failure of 'corporate bodies' (the guilds) to look after the interests of trade, decided to form an association to be called the Society of Merchants. It was run by a committee of twenty-one wholesale merchants chosen from the group, in 'defence of trade against any illegal imposition'. This association was known as the Committee of Merchants.

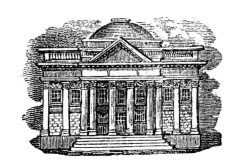

The Royal Exchange, monument to the success of the Society of Merchants, as depicted in Watson's Directory *of the era.*

There is a strong case for considering the Society of Merchants as a precursor to Dublin Chamber of Commerce, which was founded in 1783, as both organisations concerned themselves with the same commercial issues, although there were differences of structure and governance between them. Unlike Chamber, membership of the Society of Merchants was drawn from among wholesale merchants only but it was composed 'indiscriminately of

timeline

1763
The *Freeman's Journal* first published in Dublin.

1766
Death of James III, the Old Pretender.

1768
Passing of Octennial Act requiring parliamentary elections every eight years.

Captain Cook embarks on his voyage of discovery in HMS *Endeavour*.

1775
Outbreak of American War of Independence.

1778
First major repeal of the Penal Laws with the passing of Luke Gardiner's Relief Act.

Britain imposes a trade embargo on France, Spain and Holland.

all merchants who were willing to join in defraying the necessary expense of such an institution', irrespective of their beliefs. Two-thirds of those who served on its committee were members of the Ouzel Galley Society and two-thirds (although not the same two-thirds) were freemen of the guild. Significantly, however, only 40 per cent of committee members were city politicians and the society saw itself as being independent of the corporation, as indicated in its founding manifesto. The names of committee members from 1765 are available: most of these are likely to have been founding members. Christopher Deey, notary public, acted as secretary and meetings were convened in his office in Crampton Court off Dame Street (beside what is now the Olympia Theatre).

Minutes for committee meetings from 1767 are extant but some indications of the society's activities in its previous six years of existence can also be deduced: members petitioned parliament and the Lord Lieutenant on various issues of commercial concern, including the scarcity of halfpence, additional dues on spirits and a proposed bankruptcy law. In 1764 the Committee sought subscriptions to enable Bernard Scale and William Richards to prepare nautical charts of the area from Wicklow Head to Skerries, as 'the frequent Loss of Ships on the Coast, near the Entrance of the Bay of Dublin, has been considered as chiefly owing to the want of proper Charts'. These maps appeared in 1765.

The Committee rarely pronounced on political issues. It did, however, support a bill proposed by Charles Lucas (1713-71) in 1767 that parliament should hold elections every eight years rather than, as previously, only on the death of the king. In the same year it presented an address of welcome to Viscount Townshend, the new Lord Lieutenant, a ritual repeated many times by Chamber. In 1763 one Thomas Allen was appointed by patent to the lucrative sinecure of 'Taster of Wines and Surveyor of Outs'. He used this position to demand a duty of two shillings per ton on all wines and spirits imported into Dublin and members asked the Committee to take action against this illegal exaction. After an investigation into Allen's activities a number of merchants refused to pay the duty and Allen appealed to the Treasury to prosecute. The Committee of Merchants took up a general subscription in 1767 to defend the case and Allen lost when the case came to court in April 1768.

Merchants transacted most of their importing and exporting business through bills of exchange, promissory notes that facilitated payment by one party to another through a third party, such as a bank. These were traded at an exchange in the Tholsel, home of the Merchants' Guild, where the corporation held the city courts, 'occasioning a concourse of the meanest and most vicious people, whilst from beneath issue the steams of kitchens, reeking with preparations of city "entertainments".' In 1757 an Act of Parliament was passed for making a wide street from Essex Bridge to Dublin Castle, establishing what were officially called the Commissioners for Making Wide and Convenient Ways, Streets and Passages, more commonly called the Wide Street Commissioners. The following year merchants made a petition to parliament for the provision of a convenient place to build an exchange but their pleas was rejected. However, a letter to the *Freeman's Journal* in June 1764 signed 'Poblicolo' ('friend of the people') again mooted the idea of an exchange, now that Dame Street and Parliament Street had been widened. The writer recalled that the recently opened exchange in Bristol had been paid for by the city's corporation and suggested that either Dublin Corporation or the Society of Merchants fund one for Dublin. He

1779

Opening of the first section of the Grand Canal.

Parade of Volunteers in College Green to demand free trade.

1782

Repeal of Poyning's Law of 1494 and the Declaratory Act of 1720.

Viscount Townshend, Lord Lieutenant 1767-72, who laid the foundation stone for the Royal Exchange.

© National Portrait Gallery, London

even proposed that it be called the Royal Exchange in honour of the king. The Committee of Merchants, with the assistance of Charles Lucas, petitioned parliament the following year to have the Wide Street Commission preserve a plot of ground on Cork Hill on which an exchange could be built and parliament agreed to advance £13,500 to buy the site. The Committee was to fund the construction of the new exchange.

In 1768, just as the project was about to begin, the corporation, which, it must be remembered, was populated by members of the guilds, petitioned parliament that the exchange should be vested in a permanent corporate body (the Committee of Merchants did not qualify as it had no legal standing). It suggested itself as the appropriate body and proposed that a committee of aldermen and common councilmen (representatives of the guilds) along with a minority of merchants should have the power of planning, conducting and executing the exchange. Naturally, this was repugnant to the merchants, who presented a counter-petition that it was their 'wish to withdraw themselves to a clean comfortable and convenient building, where business was to be the only object; but they now find that the Corporation of the city of Dublin wants to pursue and haunt them in this retirement, the expected fruit of their own labours.' Parliament had difficulty in vesting the lands in an organisation other than a permanent corporate body, so the merchants, accepting the inevitable, agreed to a compromise: the site would be vested in the Merchants' Guild. Furthermore, parliament, under an act 'for promoting the trade of Ireland by enabling the merchants thereof to erect an exchange in the city of Dublin' set up a statutory trust that would be responsible for the planning and erecting of the building as well as its maintenance. The

THE LOTTERY SCHEME

Lottery schemes for various public and private purposes were well established in Ireland by the 18th century. The Society of Merchants promoted the Exchange Lottery, 1766-9, and most of the fourteen lotteries used the same draw and winning numbers as the government-run lottery in London, although in 1773 the numbers from the Dutch State Lottery were used. Tickets were issued in accordance with the number issued for the lottery to which the Merchants' lottery was grafted, this generally being no higher than 60,000. The Committee decided on the means of operation of the scheme and published invitations to buy in the newspapers. In 1768 it was announced: 'The scheme is conducted by a committee of the merchants of the City of Dublin under whose care the former Exchange schemes were carried into execution and the prises will be punctually paid without any deduction whatsoever ten days after the publication of the numerical book in London at Mr Deey's in Crampton Court where the subscription for tickets will be opened the 9th May next. NB no person be permitted to subscribe for more than 1000 tickets.' The lottery was advertised as being 'very advantageous to the subscribers and adventurers!' Tickets, costing between a guinea and £1/2s/9d, were mostly pre-sold in blocks to the 'adventurers', who put up a 5 per cent deposit, paying the remainder on receipt of their tickets immediately before the draw. They then sold tickets on to individual subscribers. There were discounts for early purchase and block buying. A book of winning numbers arrived from London after the government draw and Deey paid out to the lucky ticket holders.

Profits on the lottery varied, as did the prizes. The bigger lotteries had two first prizes of £5000, while the holders of winning tickets each received £2000 in the smaller draws. The scheme was designed so that a third of the tickets were prizewinners or 'benefit' tickets, the vast majority winning only £1/5s, slightly more than the cost of the ticket. The other tickets were known as 'blanks'. The Committee minutes suggest that the organisers saw the scheme as being for 'such persons as may be comprehended under the title of gentlemen or person of distinction'.

The lottery was run from Christopher Deey's Office in Crampton Court, where Deey kept an iron chest to secure the tickets and money. Lotteries were prone to a suspicion of fraudulent manipulation so it was a priority to assure the public that everything was above board. The Committee instructed Deey that he should be 'acting in the whole with the greatest regard to impartiality' but this did not stop one advertiser in the *Freeman's Journal* in 1766 claiming that the promoters of the Exchange scheme had 'been striving to blindfold the Publick by their puffing Speeches, lying Advertisements, and by Forgery and Fraud', while declaring that the public would not be fooled.

Lottery ticket from the 1778 Exchange lottery draw.

trust was to comprise the Lord Mayor, both high sheriffs, the city treasurer, the two city MPs and the senior warden of the Guild of Merchants, as well as sixteen members of the Committee of Merchants. The sting in the tail was that all the merchants in the trust were to be selected by no fewer than thirty wholesale merchants, freemen and members of the guild. No Catholics were chosen.

Lotteries were a popular source of funding in the 18th century, although prone to fraud or at least manipulation. In 1766 the Committee of Merchants instituted a lottery to raise finance for the building of the new exchange. A portion of the profits in the earlier years was allocated to charitable purposes, primarily the hospitals of Dublin and the Marine Nursery and Hibernian Military schools. Two or three merchants from the Committee were appointed as trustees for each draw to ensure that everything was above board and all moneys were kept in a steel chest in Christopher Deey's office, for which each trustee held a key. The gross profit of the annual lotteries, repeated until 1779, was nearly £87,000, of which £52,619 went towards the construction of the Royal Exchange. A shortfall of £5260 in the overall cost of the building was funded under an act of parliament that levied a charge of a shilling on certain imports at the Custom House. This levy later increased to 1s/6d, with the excess raised contributed to the cost of Commercial Buildings and the Corn Exchange. The lottery fund paid out £15,000 to the various charities between 1767 and 1772 and Christopher Deey did very nicely for himself, pocketing more than £10,000 for his services.

When the accounts of the schemes were finally collated in 1782 the merchants were unhappy because of Deey's charges and discrepancies in the figures. Deey denied any wrongdoing and it was agreed to put the issues to arbitrators, who noted a very inaccurate set of accounts but nevertheless found in favour of Deey. The irregularities were never resolved.

For fourteen years the lottery was the primary focus of the Committee of Merchants. In 1768 they held an architectural competition for the Royal Exchange project and selected a design by London-based Thomas Cooley. The media at the time reported a rumour that among the entrants was King George III 'who amongst other accomplishments possesses the difficult and elegant art of drawing in its greatest perfection'. The foundation stone was laid by Lord Lieutenant Townshend in 1768, followed by entertainments at the Tholsel which cost nearly £300 (including £44 to a Mr Hicky for fruit and sweetmeats). It was paid 'notwithstanding the Committee are of the opinion they are exceedingly extravagant'. The Royal Exchange was completed in 1779 and the Committee of Merchants had a new meeting place. Independently, merchants paid for a statue of Charles Lucas by the

The statue of Charles Lucas by Edward Smyth that the merchants erected in the Royal Exchange in recognition of Lucas's efforts on their behalf.

Charles Lucas (1713-1771)

Charles Lucas was born in County Clare, trained as an apothecary in Dublin and was admitted to the Barbers' and Surgeons' Guild in 1735 (the Apothecaries' Guild had not yet been established). It was his desire to rectify the abuses in his own trade that led him to run for election to Dublin Corporation in 1741, campaigning by issuing numerous pamphlets, a technique he used throughout his political life. While in the corporation he became critical of what he saw as the abuse of power by the aldermanic class over the common council. After Lucas and his allies took an unsuccessful law case in the common council, their enemies had their revenge by vetoing the objectors' re-election in 1747. Lucas then ran for election to parliament but

his strenuous pamphleteering about the ills of that body saw him charged with sedition. He was disfranchised and fled to England and subsequently Paris and Leiden (Holland), where he qualified as a doctor. After he had spent a number of years as a successful practitioner in London, charges against him were dropped and he returned to Dublin to popular acclaim. He was elected to parliament in 1761 and during his decade as an MP he brought forward legislation for more frequent parliamentary elections, as well as helping to obtain public funding for the Royal Exchange. Lucas was a radical and a nationalist and his funeral to St Michan's graveyard attracted attendance from all sectors of society.

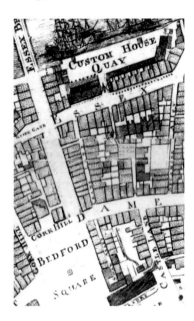

sculptor Edward Smyth to stand in the main rotunda, in appreciation of the efforts he made to obtain the site.

The exchange occupied a prominent position between Dublin Castle and the Custom House, which was then located at Essex Bridge, in the heart of the old city. It was dilapidated, with no room for expansion. The river was prone to silting and a large rock called 'Steadfast Dick' in the riverbed opposite, where the Poddle joined the Liffey near the Custom House (now Wellington Quay), was a nuisance to shipping. The quays, where the merchants' offices and warehouses were located, were not fit for purpose. As Dublin was expanding eastwards in the 18th century, developers wanted a new bridge to be erected upstream to provide access to their sites, while the merchants stood Canute-like against the change. In March 1769 the Committee sent a memorial to the Commissioners of Revenue that the merchants 'have been greatly alarmed with a report which has universally prevailed of an intention to erect a new Custom House on the eastward of the present one' which 'would prove extremely injurious to the trade of this city'. So began twelve years of objections, culminating in failure for the

cause of the merchants. Subsequent to the memorial a deputation from the Committee waited on the Revenue Commissioners and reported to their fellow members that Bellingham Boyle (1709-1771), MP for Bandon and one of the commissioners, entered the room 'and treated your subcommittee in so uncivil and snide a manner that they were nearly a necessity of retiring'. The issue arose again in 1774 and 'a meeting of numerous merchants, traders and manufacturers' assembled in the Tholsel. The Committee proposed that if the Custom House remained in its current site they would remove any stones or impediments in the river at their own expense. They submitted petitions to parliament and to the Lord Lieutenant and enlisted the support of English seaports. They raised subscriptions by advertisement and paid an agent in London to petition against the bill for a new Custom House in the parliament there. Their attempts to thwart this bill were successful and the Committee presented gold snuff boxes engraved with arms (worth 30 guineas) to Robert Allen and Robert Nixon, two London merchants who had taken up their cause. A new bill was put forward the following year but after a petition to the king and Allen and Nixon's intervention, this also failed. In 1777 the Committee submitted a petition to the king and Lord Lieutenant to rebuild the existing Custom House. The merchants' objections extended to other city developments, including a proposal to build a new Four Courts in College Green, on the basis that this too would encourage the erection of a new bridge.

The game changed when John Beresford MP (1738-1805), a competent operator, Wide Street Commissioner and proponent of the enhancement of Dublin's streets by public building in the neoclassical style, was appointed Chief Revenue Commissioner to Ireland in 1780. Beresford received the royal consent and smuggled James Gandon (1743-1823), the architect he

Gandon's Custom House

Building work began on the new Custom House in 1781. Initially the architect, James Gandon, kept himself virtually imprisoned on Beresford's advice because of the strength of the opposition to the project, going on site only with a cane sword. As the building progressed, opposition gradually faded and Gandon moved to Mecklenburgh Street. The building took ten years to finish and was home to the custom and excise department of the port and the country. Until 1896 merchants dealt with officials in the Long Room, located on the first floor. The building also served as home to other state departments.

In May 1921 the IRA attacked and set fire to the building. Five IRA men were killed and three quarters of the attacking force of a hundred and twenty were captured. The building burned for five days, the dome collapsed and it was destroyed internally. Reconstruction was completed in 1929 but much of Gandon's original design and detail were lost, including the Long Room. Between 1984 and 1991 the external stonework was conserved.

James Malton's image of the Custom House. The failure of the Society of Merchants to prevent the construction of the new Custom House downriver from the old building was one of the reasons that its committee proposed the formation of a Chamber of Commerce.

had selected to design the new Custom House, into Dublin in April 1781, keeping him a virtual prisoner while secretly accumulating the site. (Gandon had come second to Thomas Cooley in the competition for the design of the Royal Exchange.) Rumours began to circulate about the construction of a new Custom House. Travers Hartley, a member of the Committee of Merchants, wrote to Beresford to enquire if the rumour was 'ill or well founded', receiving the reply that 'His Majesty [has] an undoubted right to erect a Custom House when and where he may chuse for the collection of his duties.' A further 'numerous and respectable meeting of the merchants traders and other inhabitants' was held in the Tholsel with the Lord Mayor in the chair. Among the objections to the new Custom House included the fact that 'the great convenience which the Merchants and Traders of this city had in view from the erection of that magnificent edifice the Royal Exchange in the neighbourhood of the present Custom House will be thereby lost.' Despite further respectable meetings and petitions the building of the Custom House went ahead. In July 1781 a mob that merchants and property owners had plied with whiskey and gingerbread broke into the site, intent on filling up the foundations, but finding them filled with water on a warm day, frolicked in the pools instead. A rabble made a more serious incursion in August, armed with building tools, after the difficult task of laying the foundations on the swampy ground had been completed, and broke down a section of the boundary wall on the false premise that part of the site belonged to the corporation. Fortunately there was little to destroy. It would appear that at this stage the Committee of Merchants accepted the inevitable, as there is no further mention of the campaign in their minutes. In addition the begrudgers were impressed by Gandon's skill in successfully constructing the foundations in such soft ground. The

Francis Wheatley (1747-1801), 'The Dublin Volunteers on College Green, 4 November 1779', 1779-80.

This muster, which included the Merchants' Volunteer Corps, was reported as featuring cannon with placards declaring 'Free Trade or This!' and helped to persuade the government to grant greater legislative independence to the Irish parliament.

Custom House was finished in 1791 and the unwelcome bridge also came to pass when Carlisle Bridge, designed by James Gandon and named after the then Lord Lieutenant, was completed in 1794.

Aside from these two main issues the Committee dealt with numerous other concerns of the commercial community: helping to 'suppress this dangerous spirit' of solidarity when cooper and baker journeymen combined to seek better wages; seeking a change in law to allow direct imports of spirits (predominantly rum) from the British plantations in the Caribbean without their having to pass through Britain; objecting to restrictions Britain imposed on Irish trade in its own interests; investing in useful projects such as the building of the Grand Canal and a new ring road around Dublin; trying to secure banking and credit systems at a time of unreliable financial structures; prosecuting malefactors for stealing or destroying cargo in Dublin port.

The American War of Independence, which left Ireland without a regular army, led to the formation of a volunteer militia, which numbered 60,000 men by 1782 and which, although loyal to the crown, sympathised with the American colonists' fight for self-determination and supported the demand of Irish parliamentarians for greater legislative independence. The Committee of Merchants supported this agitation, as the British treated Irish trade very unfavourably with regard to taxes and bounties.

General Cornwallis's surrender to American and French forces in Yorktown in 1781 was the end of Britain's hope of winning the war against the American colonists and the following year the Irish parliament received a substantial measure of legislative independence. The development engendered considerable excitement among the Irish ascendancy and merchant classes

'We highly approve of said plan as forming a broad and firm foundation on which may be expected to arise a superstructure of eminent usefulness in the commercial department.'

The final meeting of the Committee of Merchants, 1783

and contributed to the decision of the Committee of Merchants to reconsider its position. Other factors may have been its failure to prevent the construction of the new Custom House, the issue of incorporation raised during the Royal Exchange project and the problems with the lottery accounts. At a meeting in the Exchange under the auspices of the Society of Merchants on 7 February 1783 a paper was produced with a proposition to establish a Chamber of Commerce in Dublin. Twenty-six merchants attended this meeting, of whom eight were members of the Committee and eleven members of the Ouzel Galley Society, while only six belonged to the corporation. All were founding members of the Chamber of Commerce. After twenty-two years, the Committee of Merchants voted itself out of existence.

THE ROYAL EXCHANGE

The intended Royal Exchange will, through the noble spirit and impartial conduct of the Committee of Merchants, in all probability, be such a structure, that when travellers and lovers of Architecture are calling to mind the many magnificent edifices in different parts, they may have reason to remember that on the side of a little hill, in the City of Dublin, stands the Royal Exchange; and to say although it be but small, yet its form is agreeable, light and artfully diversified.

[Letter from 'C' to the *Freeman's Journal*, 10 December 1768]

The competition for the design of the Royal Exchange was the first of its kind in Ireland. It is unclear why the trustees decided to hold one, but it is possible that they hoped by this means to attract a designer of neoclassical style, this being all the rage in London and favoured for Dublin public buildings by the city's Wide Street Commissioners including John Beresford, John Foster and Luke Gardiner. Advertisements appeared in Dublin and London newspapers from July 1768, announcing the competition and offering prizes for the three best proposals received: 100 guineas for first place, 60 guineas for second and 40 guineas for third. The brief was quite specific: in essence a building with two fronts, to the west and north, containing an exchange where merchants could set out their stalls, an assembly room over and two further moderately sized rooms for committees. The basement vaults could be used for other purposes as they would open up to the new Exchange Lane on the east (the remaining, southern side, backed on to Dublin Castle).

'Any gentleman may have an opportunity of viewing [the design competition entries] for the whole month of January, by applying to the Register in Crampton Court, for tickets of admission. The Trustees will think themselves obliged to all persons of taste for their sentiments respecting the merits of the several plans, directed to them at their office in Crampton Court.'

Invitation issued by the trustees of the Royal Exchange, January 1769

The site of the Royal Exchange was originally occupied by Cork House, built about 1600 by the first Earl of Cork, Roger Boyle: Cork Hill was named after him. Its prominent position on the hill, which fell considerably towards Dame Street to the east, and strategic location between Dublin Castle and the old Custom House, made it particularly suitable for the new exchange.

The competition's original closing date was 29 September 1768 but in response to requests by entrants and their supporters, it was extended to 1 January 1769. (It was suggested that some of the Irish architects posted their entries from England, perceiving that this would be to their advantage.) The sixty-one entries were then exhibited in the Exhibition Room of the Society of Artists in William Street. The trustees of the Royal Exchange deliberated in the Exhibition Room on

14 April 1769 and declared the entry of Thomas Cooley (1741-84) the winner. James Gandon was second and Thomas Sandby received third prize. All three winners were English. In addition, three Irish entrants received a prize of a piece of plate, valued at thirty guineas, 'as an encouragement to the architects of this country, and from a due sense of the merits of their several designs'.

Thomas Cooley was somewhat of a surprise selection as he had yet to build in his own name and there is some conjecture that the design was not his own work but that of his employer, architect Robert Mylne. Certainly he did not design again to the standard of the Royal Exchange. His winning drawings are no longer extant but early drafts are in the National Library. When he won the competition, he moved to Dublin and work started immediately on the Exchange site, which

Watercolour of the central rotunda of the Royal Exchange by architect Patrick Byrne,
painted in 1834, before the ownership of the Exchange passed to Dublin Corporation.

needed much effort to prepare the foundations as the ground was relatively soft.

Lord Lieutenant Townshend laid the foundation stone on 2 August 1769, with the city's grandees in attendance. Bells rang out in celebration and Townshend gave the workmen 30 guineas before repairing to the Tholsel for lavish entertainment. It took ten years to complete the building, which was opened for business in 1779, to general admiration of its elegance. It was the first of a number of neoclassical buildings constructed in the city over the next forty years, which have become icons of Georgian Dublin. An account of tradesmen that survives in the Royal Irish Academy lists payments to, among others, John Chambers, carpenter (and timber merchant), Charles Thorpe, plasterer (creator of the decorative plaster in the dome, also alderman and future Lord Mayor), John Semphill, bricklayer, and Simon Vierpyl, stonecutter (and sculptor).

The functions of the Royal Exchange were limited by its charter and it operated as an exchange only between the hours of three and four on Monday, Wednesday and Friday afternoons, business being carried out around the grand central dome on the main floor. Pretty quickly the exchange operated for only two days a week and it never had much commercial use. There was a coffee room over the northern entrance. The trustees had a permanent meeting room on the first floor and employed a 'register' or manager, a keeper of the coffee room and a porter for the building. The Commissioners of Bankruptcy also used the building and the vaults were let to the Revenue Commissioners for bonded storage.

Although the eventual failure of the Exchange as a suitable premises for the commercial activities of Dublin merchants led to the establishment of the Commercial Buildings Company, it remained the first port of call for public meetings. The Committee of Merchants met there until early 1783, when they proposed the formation of a Chamber of Commerce. The new Chamber used

the trustees' room three days a week and when Chamber was reconstituted in April 1805, and again in November 1820, it first convened in the Royal Exchange, then moved to Commercial Buildings. Council minutes show that Chamber considered itself as having a proprietorial interest in the Royal Exchange, as the natural successor to the Committee of Merchants.

In the early decades of the 19th century it became clear that the Exchange had little function, principally because of changes in the banking system after the Act of Union. In addition the method of electing the trustees was no longer fit

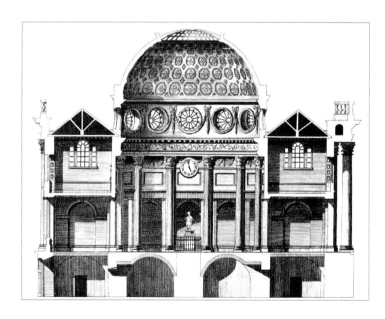

Section through the Royal Exchange, taken from Views of the most remarkable public buildings, monuments, and other edifices in the city of Dublin, *by Robert Pool and John Cash (1780).*
Courtesy of the National Library of Ireland

for purpose and in 1819 the law was changed so that there was no specified quorum of electors. Those chosen were to be 'free of the guild'. (This legal change also allowed Randal MacDonnell, a prominent merchant and former Chamber president, to be the first Catholic trustee.) The trustees, excluding those who were ex-officio, included a large proportion who were Chamber members. Council set up a committee to look

The north portico today.

into the history and future of the building, which presented a report, prepared by the secretary, Charles Haliday, in 1835. The report was of the opinion that the building was best suited to public or governmental purposes. Council submitted a memorial to this effect to the government, asking them to buy the building (for £36,000 it appears) and the proceeds used 'to some purpose beneficial to the trade of Dublin and the Merchants, whose predecessors had erected and upheld the building'. The report was last mentioned in the Council's minutes as being with government for consideration; government, in time-honoured fashion, quietly shelved it.

After the Municipal Corporations Act of 1840 the newly invigorated (and much more democratic) corporation cast a longing eye on the Royal Exchange as a suitable city hall. Council resurrected its report of seven years previously and the Chief Secretary, Lord Eliot, wrote to Chamber raising the prospect of the corporation's interest in the building. There followed from 1846 a series of private bills submitted by the corporation to the House of Commons for additional municipal powers, all of which included a clause seeking the

Thomas Cooley 1741-84

The son of a master mason. Cooley joined the office of architect Robert Mylne as a clerk in 1764. (The position of clerk might be more accurately defined as that of draughtsman.) His salary was £40 per annum, with breakfast and lodgings. He entered a number of drawing competitions in the Royal Society in London, being awarded premiums in 1763, 1764 and 1765, although James Gandon was awarded higher premiums in two of those years.

Cooley, the surprise winner of the competition to design the Royal Exchange, was also the architect of the new Marine School on John Rogerson's Quay and appointed architect to the Four Courts, but had completed only the western block when he died at his home in Anglesea Street at the age of only forty-three. Gandon took over the commission and completed the Four Courts.

The wording (now obscured) on the original foundation stone of the Royal Exchange, as laid by Viscount Townshend in 1768.

In the Ninth year of the Reign

of

His sacred Majesty

GEORGE THE THIRD

King of Great Britain, France and Ireland &c.

and

during the administration

of

GEORGE, Lord Viscount TOWNSHEND

Lord Lieutenant General and Governor-General of Ireland

THE FIRST STONE

of

THE ROYAL EXCHANGE

was laid by his excellency

on the second day of August

ONE THOUSAND, SEVEN HUNDRED and SIXTY-NINE

The building of which which was undertaken

by a SOCIETY of MERCHANTS

of the City of Dublin

Incorporated for that Purpose

in

1768

The wonderful dome of the Royal Exchange's central arcade. It was completely rebuilt in 1926 when it was discovered that the timbers were suffering from dry rot.

Royal Exchange as a new city hall and all of which Chamber vigorously opposed, for various reasons. Council of Chamber was particularly incensed by Clause 125 of the 1847 bill, entitled 'Power to Purchase the Royal Exchange', which, when they looked into it, made 'no reference whatsoever to any power to purchase, or any intention to purchase the Exchange'. The tenuous nature of Chamber's position as guardians of the Royal Exchange ultimately left it in a weak position. When an agreed bill for the reform of Dublin's municipal government was accepted in 1851 a deputation from Council met the Lord Mayor at the Mansion House and reached agreement, a process smoothed, in all likelihood, by the fact

that Benjamin Lee Guinness was Lord Mayor at the time and his father, Arthur Guinness, was Chamber president. The Royal Exchange was transferred to the corporation on 8 October 1851, along with the remaining £1500 in the trust fund.

The corporation immediately set about converting the building for its own use. The ambulatory around the central dome was subdivided into individual rooms but the dome and circular space under remained untouched. New stairs were constructed to the rear. The first meeting of the corporation in its new chamber – the former coffee room – took place on 30 September 1852.

In 1898 the floor to the domed space was replaced, with marble incorporating the city's coat of arms in mosaic in the centre. The building suffered fire damage in 1911 and in 1926 it was found that the timbers to the copper dome were rotting so the dome had to be rebuilt.

In 1995 the corporation moved to its new offices in Wood Quay. Restoration of City Hall was carried out, 1998-2000, with the removal of the internal partitions and the 1852 staircase, returning the hall and ambulatory to their original glory. A museum of Dublin's civic history opened in the converted vaults, while Dublin City Council still meets in the municipal chamber on the first Monday of each month.

City Hall remains one of the more elegant buildings in Dublin today. Nevertheless, there is something unsatisfying about the design because the northern portico, while central to the building itself, is offset to the central axis of Parliament Street which it addresses and partially hidden by the buildings on the right side of the street when viewed from Capel Street Bridge.

View of City Hall, the former Royal Exchange, up Parliament Street. The site was chosen for this relationship but the façade is slightly off-centre to the street.

IV

TWO EARLY STARTS, 1783-1819

We have the mortification to find our trade to that Kingdom in respect to the admission of our manufactures still labouring under restraints and difficulties nearly amounting to a prohibition...The weight of the subject and its importance to the country (which has been taken so peculiarly under your Excellency's patronage) we are convinced render it unnecessary for us to implore your Excellency's attention to this business, which we cannot regard but with considerable anxiety.

Address to the Lord Lieutenant, the Earl Temple, April 1783

After a meeting at the Royal Exchange on 10 February 1783, a detailed plan for the formation of a chamber of commerce for Dublin was published. Any merchant or trader in the city was free to join on payment of a guinea. When there were a hundred subscribers a meeting would be called at which a president, two vice-presidents and a treasurer would be elected. As it happened two hundred and eighteen names are included in the published list of original subscribers and by the end of the first year the new body had a membership of just under three hundred. After a ballot a secretary, William Shannon, was appointed on an annual salary of £30. Shannon was a notary public whose office was in 5 Dame Street. On 18 March 1783 the subscribers met and elected forty-one members to act as their Council for the following year. Travers Hartley was elected the first president at a meeting four days later.

The first Council minute book of Dublin Chamber of Commerce, containing minutes from the first and second Chambers, 1783-1807.

timeline

1783
Establishment of the Bank of
Ireland.

1786
Laying of foundation stone of
Four Courts.

1788
Incorporation of Royal Canal.

1791
Completion of new Custom
House and construction of
Carlisle (now O'Connell) Bridge
begins.

1792
Founding of United Irishmen.

1793
Catholic Relief Act allows
Catholics to practise law.

1794
Opening of Carlisle Bridge.

1798
Rebellion in east Leinster and
Ulster.

The choice of officers was ecumenical: Hartley was a Presbyterian, prominent in the Committee of Merchants, member of the Ouzel Galley Society, early dissenter member of the Merchants' Guild, and shortly to be elected MP for Dublin. Anthony McDermott, a Catholic, and Daniel Marston, a member of the Church of Ireland, were chosen as vice-presidents, while Joshua Pim, a Quaker, was elected treasurer. Chamber was allowed to use the trustees' room in the Royal Exchange three days a week.

Council minutes from this first chamber have survived and give us an insight into its preoccupations and how it operated. With the enthusiasm of novelty, Council met every week and came quickly to confront issues affecting the mercantile world, including the much hoped-for free trade on equal terms with England. The first test concerned trade with Portugal. In 1703 England had signed the Treaty of Methuen with the Portuguese (named for John Methuen, the English envoy to Portugal, who negotiated it), by the terms of which Portuguese wines might be imported to England with the same duties as French wines and British woollen goods might be exported to Portugal duty free. Trade embargoes in place due to the American War of Independence were lifted in 1783 but Portugal refused to accept that Irish woollen goods were covered by the Treaty of Methuen (part of the Portuguese attempt to renegotiate its terms). Chamber sent Council's first memorial on the subject to the Lord Lieutenant in 1783 but the situation did not change until 1787 when the Portuguese suddenly dropped their levies and Irish woollen goods could be freely exported to Portugal.

Concessions such as the lifting of embargoes could not hide the inequity with which Britain dealt with Ireland in terms of trade. British goods could be freely imported in all Irish ports while Irish trade to Britain was frequently barred. Ireland was not allowed to import goods directly from the colonies or from Britain's trading partners but had to receive them through Britain, naturally adding to the cost. A petition to parliament sought equal duties between the two countries while insisting that the merchants 'feel as well as possess for their sister kingdom the most cordial affection'. Tobacco exports from Ireland to Britain were also prohibited, which elicited a further petition to parliament, presented by Travers Hartley. The Irish House of Commons refused to accept this petition because the petitioners had no statutory standing, a difficulty the Committee of Merchants had also faced. Ultimately this would prove to be the undoing of the early Chamber.

In an attempt to adjust the commercial relationship between the two countries the Prime Minister, William Pitt, introduced eleven 'Commercial Propositions' to both parliaments, later extended to twenty to satisfy initial English objections. The Chief Secretary, Thomas Orde, brought the case to the Irish parliament. The proposal met resistance in England, and Chamber, upon consideration and after various deputations, felt that it would be inequitable to have free trade where one country's industry was well developed and the other was in its infancy. The issue was the subject of thirty-five meetings of Council between June and August 1785. The propositions were unsuccessful in the Irish parliament and were quietly forgotten.

The export of corn had been free of tariffs since 1766, when England became a corn importer and needed the corn Ireland could supply. The Irish parliament had introduced bounties for transportation of corn from the country to Dublin in 1758, which led to an increase in tillage and mill construction throughout the country. In 1784 the Chancellor of the

1798
French force under General Humbert lands in Killala.

1799
Opening of Commercial Buildings.

1800
Act of Union abolishes the Irish parliament.

1803
Robert Emmet's rising.

1808
The Bank of Ireland moves to the empty parliament building in College Green.

1815
Battle of Waterloo and final defeat of Napoleon.

The Dublin (later Royal Dublin) Society buys Leinster House.

1816
Building of Halfpenny Bridge (officially Wellington Bridge, but more commonly known as 'the Metal Bridge').

Exchequer, John Foster, introduced a new Corn Law in the Irish parliament with bounties for exportation of corn but Dublin was excluded from this arrangement, receiving only the smaller bounties of 1758. Chamber campaigned for similar bounties for exports from Dublin as for other ports.

Chamber members raised difficulties regarding apparently random decisions of custom officials and arbitrary import fees and Council queried them with the Revenue Commissioners. It was resolved in 1784 'that the extractions of many of the Custom House Officers in the Port of Dublin under the title of fees are become of late so enormous and oppressive that they ought to be resisted by every fair trader.' Council was also dissatisfied with the performance of the Ballast Office, which was under the control of the corporation and had responsibility for the port of Dublin, as it had become ineffective and expensive. Furthermore, parliament was questioning its financial management, especially its spending on constructing the South Wall, for which work had been ongoing for a number of years, with no end in sight. In 1785 Council resolved that control of the port should be taken out of the hands of the Ballast Office and 'that the most proper persons to entrust it to, would be those particularly interested in the trade and shipping of Dublin'. John Beresford, who had displeased the merchants by building the new Custom House, regained their support when he proposed a bill to reform the Ballast Office and, despite the reservations of members on some issues, the Corporation for Preserving and Improving the Port of Dublin, or Ballast Board as it was known, came into being. It transferred control of the port from the corporation to a board that Beresford initially established but that would be self-perpetuating. Eight members of Council were nominated to the new board but it was an institution with which Chamber would have many disputes in the future.

Results of the first election to Council on 18 March 1783 from the original Council minute book. The names are a broad representation of business at that time.

List of the Council of the Chamber of Commerce
18th March 1783

#	Name	Votes	#	Name	Votes
1	Travers Hartley	153	22	Hugh Hamill Junr.	99
2	Alexander Jaffray	152	23	James Hartley	96
3	Joshua Pim	148	24	Alderman George Sutton	91
4	Robert Black	136	25	William Alexander	87
5	Daniel Marston	132	26	Patrick Pease	87
6	Robert Magee	131	27	Samuel Dick	86
7	William Cope	127	28	John Allen	83
8	Abraham Wilkinson	127	29	Patrick Bride	80
9	William Colvill	126	30	George Maquay	80
10	George Godfrey Hoffman	123	31	Hugh Crothers	79
11	John Binns	122	32	Frederick Geale	79
12	Valentine O'Connor	120	33	Robert Brooke	77
13	Dennis Thomas O'Brien	115	34	Amos Strettell	77
14	Alexander Armstrong	113	35	Francis Cahill	76
15	Michael Cosgrave	109	36	Arthur Bryan	75
16	Edward Byrne	108	37	Francis McDermott	74
17	Leland Crosthwaite	102	38	Edward Forbes	73
18	John Patrick	102	39	Jeremiah D'Olier	72
19	Jeremiah Vickers	101	40	John Comerford	70
20	Anthony McDermott	100	41	Benjamin Wills	69
21	John Darragh	99			

Travers Hartley (1723-96)

Travers Hartley traded out of 89 Bride Street as Travers & Son and was in business since 1745, initially as a linen merchant. He was admitted to the Merchants' Guild by service in Michaelmas 1745, one of the first Presbyterians to be so enrolled. Captain of the Ouzel Galley Society and a member of the Committee of Merchants, Hartley, its highest profile member, was chosen as president of the 1783 Chamber of Commerce, a position he held until he died.

In 1782 Hartley ran against Alderman Nathaniel Warren, the establishment candidate, in a by-election for parliament. The election is remembered for the collapse of the first floor of the Music Hall in Fishamble Street during a debate between the two candidates, causing serious injuries but no fatalities. Hartley won by 1472 votes to 1202 and held his seat in the general election the next year. His obituary described him as 'a dissenter, a merchant of eminence in respect of opulence, knowledge and integrity'.

Travers Hartley

By 1787 Chamber membership was falling off. The minutes have no mention of elections for Council after 1785. In December 1787 a special meeting was called to 'take into serious consideration the present state of this Council'. While Council continued to meet for the first three months of 1788, the meeting on 29 March was to be the last recorded for that year. At this meeting Council issued a statement approving of the actions of the British parliament in moving to abolish the slave trade. The Council minute book includes only one more meeting, called for February 1791 to form a committee to petition parliament in relation to duties on rum. It appears that there were some further meetings but they were not entered into the book. *Watson's Directory* continues to list the names of Council members with a few variations until 1795. Travers Hartley died in 1796.

It appears that the first Chamber's failure to obtain a royal charter or statutory recognition left it in a weakened position relative to the Merchants' Guild and that its membership declined when these limitations became apparent. It had been established in the optimistic climate of partial legislative independence but the 1780s also saw the beginning of a severe economic depression. The so-called 'patriot' parliament proved unable to fulfil the radical hopes that created it and the 1790s were unstable politically. In 1795 the Irish parliament

Three prominent individuals with whom the early Chamber was in correspondence:

Right: *Thomas Orde (1740-1807), Tory MP for Harwich, who was Chief Secretary in William Pitt's government 1784-7. Orde was unflatteringly described by a contemporary as 'a cold, cautious, slow and sententious man, tolerably well-informed, but not at all talented, with a mind neither powerful nor feeble'. He was charged with bringing Pitt's plan for free trade between the two islands to fruition in Ireland but failed to achieve this.*

Below left: *George Nugent-Temple-Grenville (1753-1813), Earl Temple, Lord Lieutenant 1782-3, wearing the regalia of the Order of St Patrick. Temple was in receipt of the Chamber's first address, on trade with Portugal.*

Below right: *John Beresford (1738-1805), MP, Revenue Commissioner and supporter of the British government. Beresford pushed through the building of the new Custom House and, supported by Council, was the prime mover in replacing the Ballast Office with the Corporation for Preserving and Improving the Port of Dublin, commonly known as the Ballast Board.*

passed a further relief act, allowing Catholics to enter the legal profession, but failed to grant full emancipation. The Catholic Committee, which had campaigned for emancipation and included many of the Catholic members of Chamber, wound itself up.

In 1791 the United Irishmen were founded in the radicalisation born of the American and French revolutions. (James) Napper Tandy and Oliver Bond, two leading United Irishmen, were members of the first Chamber. (Chambers of Commerce do not naturally attract revolutionaries and the membership of these men is indicative of this Chamber's reformist nature.) Bond was executed and Tandy exiled in 1798. The rebellions that broke out in several parts of the country and the French landings of that year were the death knell of the Dublin parliament, as the government in London believed that the ineffectiveness of that parliament in responding to sedition had contributed to the uprising. The prime minister, William Pitt, had expressed the opinion that free trade would occur only with parliamentary union of the two countries and, for many Catholics, such a union also seemed to hold out the best prospect of emancipation. Free trade and emancipation were two of the promises made in the government's campaign to persuade the Irish parliament to accept the Act of Union (but not kept). After the Union, Ireland became more of a colony than part of the United Kingdom. Soon the aristocracy left Dublin for London and much of the city's Georgian development was abandoned to the members of the professional and mercantile classes who remained behind.

In was in these early days of the new dispensation and the new century that an attempt was made to reinvigorate Dublin Chamber of Commerce. According to a pamphlet published in 1805, the new body was intent on 'maintaining respectful communication' with His Majesty's ministers, members of parliament, commercial institutions and revenue officials. Its intention was to superintend commercial and manufacturing interests of the city and recommend improvements. The first minutes, dated 27 May 1805, note only the names of the Council of twenty-one that had been elected. Ninety-two members voted and Randal MacDonnell, a Catholic merchant with extensive interests in Spain, was first on the ballot, while Arthur Guinness was second. The original minute book of the first Chamber of 1783 continued to be used and this entry immediately follows that of 25 February 1791. One merchant, Alexander Jaffray, junior of the firm of Jaffray, Fayle & Hautenville, had served on the original Council, while three others were founding members of the first Chamber.

List of Council members of the revived Chamber elected on 27 May 1805, as noted in the Council minute book.

This Chamber funded itself by a two-guinea admission fee and ongoing voluntary contributions of one shilling from imports and exports at the Custom House. Joseph Miller, an attorney of 31 Westmoreland Street, was employed as secretary, with a salary of £100. Chamber also paid for the services of a law agent. In June a set of rules and regulations, signed by Arthur Guinness, were approved. Whether or not they are indicative of Guinness's own mindset they seem excessively involved, particularly in regard to attendance at Council meetings and fines for non-attendance, the obligations of the chairman and qualifications for honorary membership.

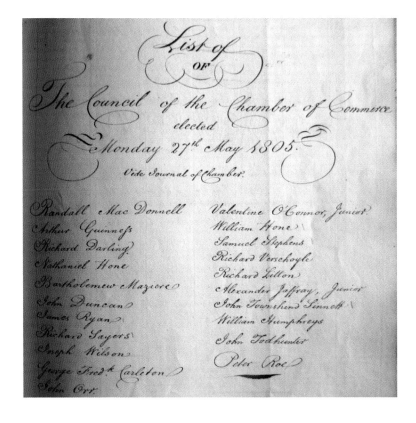

THIRTEEN MERCHANTS, 1805

At a meeting at the Royal Exchange on 16 April 1805 thirteen merchants presented a proposal for reforming a Chamber of Commerce in Dublin. They would then 'retire from the charge we have assumed, trusting that our brethren will acquit us of any arrogant pretensions'. Carleton, Hone, MacDonnell, Mazière and Wilson, an ecumenical group, all went on to be chairmen of the new Chamber and half the individuals named were on the board of the Commercial Buildings Company. All but Hugh O'Connor were elected to Council.

This Chamber's original manifesto was published in *Saunder's Newsletter* on 10 April 1805: 'To the Wholesale Merchants and Manufacturers of the City of Dublin. We, the undersigned members of your body, have the honour to represent you, with the acquiescence of a considerable number of our brethren, we have been induced by disinterested motives of regard and solicitude for the public advantage, voluntarily to associate and apply ourselves diligently for a considerable time, in maintaining an intercourse with some of His Majesty's ministers, and in corresponding with the representatives in Parliament for the City of Dublin, and with commercial institutions and individuals at the outports of Ireland, respecting the regulation of several affairs interesting to that commercial prosperity which is our common concernment.'

Name	Business	Address	Denomination
George F. Carleton (1760-1831)	Merchant	12 Eustace Street	Church of Ireland
Richard Darling (?-1822)	Merchant	132 Townsend Street	Church of Ireland
Nathaniel Hone (1760-1819)	Merchant	79 Fleet Street	Church of Ireland
Richard Litton (?-1830)	Merchant	21 Lower Ormond Quay	Presbyterian
Randal MacDonnell (1762-1821)	Merchant	Allen's Court, Mullinahack	Catholic
Bartholomew Mazière (1753-1823)	Merchant	6 St Mary's Abbey	Presbyterian
James McCall (?-?)	Merchant	16 Bachelor's Walk	Presbyterian
Valentine O'Connor Junior (1773-1829)	Merchant	37 Queen Street	Catholic
Hugh O'Connor, brother of Valentine (1771-1839)	Merchant	London	Catholic
James Ryan (?-?)	Merchant	77 Marlborough Street	Catholic
John Todhunter (1772-1844)	Corn merchant	85 Rogerson's Quay	Quaker
Richard Verschoyle (1751-1827)	Land agent	Mount Merrion	Church of Ireland
Joseph Wilson (?-1809)	Merchant	10 Ormond Quay	Presbyterian

A deputation from Council met John Foster, Chancellor of the Exchequer, in December 1805 to discuss a list of issues regarding trade and regulation that were the priority of the revived Chamber. The primary focus was the multiplicity of charges levied on imports and exports in Dublin port, as an array of officials, some of them wonderfully titled, had to be paid to smooth the passage of trade through Customs and Revenue: these included surveyors, land waiters (who assessed imports for taxation purposes), storekeepers, tasters of wine, jerquers (who searched ships for unentered goods), tide waiters, gaugers and examiners of permits. Clearly such a system was open to abuse.

An early Council meeting acquired a copy of the Act of Charles II that regulated the fees of the officers of customs and wrote to several officials asking them to explain their charges. The first to be addressed were Charles Trench, Surveyor and Controller of Stores, who had an impressive salary of £1620 per annum (at this point the secretary of Chamber received £100 per

annum) and his deputy, John Fitzpatrick (a more humble £371 per annum), followed by John Monck Mason, the Landwaiter of Exports (£873), William Fenwick, Surveyor of the Custom House (£583) and John O'Beirne, first clerk in the Commissioner's Cheque Book (£676), Jerome Smith, a clerk in the Examiner of Customs Office (£120), Thomas Burgh, Commissioner of Excise (£1000) and the Honourable Francis Hely Hutchinson, the Collector of Customs (£1809). Many of these posts were little more than sinecures. Council paid a clerk in Robert Marshall's office in the Custom House to collate a digest of fees, charges and services provided and eventually Chamber succeeded in getting the Revenue Commissioners to agree to levy a single port charge out of which the various officials would be remunerated. The new scheme, although universally popular among the merchants initially, later proved unsatisfactory as it removed the opportunity for them to grease the wheels with individual officers.

In September 1805 Chamber negotiated the lease of two apartments on the top floor of Commercial Buildings and furnished them as offices. William Badge, porter to Commercial Buildings, was paid to provide fires. Some of the items raised at subsequent Council meetings appear rather trivial to modern eyes, such as delays in the delivery of letters and the integrity of butter tasters. At this time the West Indian trade, which involved provisioning His Majesty's Caribbean colonies, was the mainstay of many Dublin merchants. The British West Indies attempted to persuade Chamber to assist them in overturning the British ban on importations from America, an ally of France, but Council approved of the ban as it was beneficial to Irish exports. The Napoleonic Wars of the early 19th century exposed trading ships to attack and convoys had to be arranged to alleviate the problem.

Although membership lists are mentioned in the minutes of this period, and, as early as 1807, it was apparent that membership numbers had fallen and receipts were insufficient to fund Chamber, none of these lists has survived. The official minute book is a fair copy prepared from rough minutes. P.L. Prendeville and L.M. Cullen, the authors of previous Chamber histories, both mention a rough copy of minutes among Chamber files, in very bad repair, entitled 'The Chamber of Commerce, Blotter No. 1'. This rough book, now lost, contained minutes for meetings from 2 May 1805 to 29 December 1812, at the latter of which Robert Orr presided. Arthur Guinness's convoluted rules allowed for chairmen (rather than presidents) to be chosen for a three-month rotation. Subsequent Chambers considered these chairmen to have been presidents and the list of presidents includes seven for these years – Joseph Wilson, Nathaniel Hone and John Duncan for 1805; Randal MacDonnell, Bartholomew Mazière and William Hone for 1806 and George Carleton for 1807. However, the existing minutes indicate

'The voluntary association of the Merchants, Manufacturers and Traders of Dublin, under certain Articles of Agreement, for the purposes of promoting the Convenience of Commercial Dealing in the City, and to watch over the general interests of Irish Trade.'

Description of Dublin Chamber in *Watson's Directory*, 1807

that Wilson served for only a week before he resigned and William Hone does not appear to have been appointed at all. The one public indication of activity after 1807 is a letter from Chamber to the Board of Treasury in March 1808 in relation to fees to Custom House officers.

It has been suggested that the second Chamber had a political agenda which made it difficult for it to survive. The two early Chambers included Catholics, a policy at variance with that of the corporation, parliament and guilds, all of which were probably suspicious of Chamber on this account, especially as Catholic members strongly supported associations to achieve emancipation. Lessons learnt in these early Chambers and the weakened position of the Merchants' Guild made the third and final attempt to establish Dublin Chamber of Commerce more successful.

TWO SECRETARIES

William Shannon: the First Chamber

According to an advertisement in *Saunder's Newsletter* it was 'resolved that it shall be the duty of the Secretary to attend every meeting of the Chamber or the Council or any committee of either to keep fair register of their proceedings, to summon meetings when duly required, to receive such letters or memorials as may be delivered to him and write such letters or answers as he may be instructed to do, to collect the annual subscriptions and account for them with the treasurer and in general to transact all such business as shall be committed to him by the Chamber or the Council.' William Shannon, a notary public, was selected as secretary from among eight candidates. His office was in 3 Exchange Street, from where he also sold state lottery tickets in 1781.

Joseph Miller: the Second Chamber

The son of a Dublin merchant, Joseph Miller qualified as an attorney in 1791 and was appointed law agent to the Board of Bankruptcy Commissioners – with offices in the Royal Exchange – in 1793. From 1799 he spent two years on trading voyages to the Mediterranean and the Levant, later travelling to the US. He returned to Dublin in 1804 and was appointed secretary and law agent to the second chamber, without competition, on 13 June 1805. Miller was also law agent to the Commercial Buildings Company and secretary to the Association of Distillers in 69 Grafton Street. He lived in 4 Dawson Street and had offices in 13 Westmoreland Street.

COMMERCIAL BUILDINGS

The exterior of the edifice is plain but chaste and elegant. It is built of mountain granite. It stands simple and grand in the spacious area, on one side of which it is placed. It consists of three storeys surmounted by a cornice; the bottom is in rustic; in the centre of which is the door-case supported by Ionic pillars; the middle storey consists of seven windows, surmounted with alternative angular and circular pediments.

Warburton, Whitelaw and Walsh,
A History of Dublin from Earliest Accounts, 1817

For many years a landmark on Dublin's Dame Street, Commercial Buildings are, alas, no longer extant, although a replica of their front elevation, turned through 90 degrees, was erected as part of the Central Bank scheme designed by Stephenson Gibney. The doorcase mentioned above is the sole surviving item of the original façade.

The Royal Exchange had one function only – dealing in bills of exchange – and very limited hours and days of operation, in accordance with its charter. The main business of merchants – displaying samples of their merchandise and buying and selling – had to be carried on in unsuitable and cramped premises in Crampton Court, off Dame Street. The merchants agreed to erect a 'more commodious building' to serve their purposes and four hundred shares of £50 each were sold in what was to become the Commercial Buildings Company. The shortfall in funding, amounting

The seal of the Commercial Buildings Company, incorporating a picture of the building, the Ouzel Galley, Equity, a trident and an anchor.

to £13,000, was loaned by the government, and repaid from the port charges originally raised to top up funding for building the Royal Exchange. The architect Edward Parke was engaged, without a competition, to design the building. Parke was favoured by the patronage of John Foster, the very influential speaker of the Irish parliament, and his best-known surviving building, from 1808, is the original Royal College of Surgeons on St Stephen's Green.

At the end of the 18th century, after the Custom House moved downriver and Carlisle Bridge was erected, the commercial centre of the city relocated to Dame Street and its adjoining streets. The Wide Street Commissioners, wishing to broaden Dame Street, had acquired a block enclosed by Anglesea, Fownes, Cope and Dame Streets and set back the building line to Dame Street. The block included a narrow lane, part of Crown Alley, and the Commercial Buildings Company took a lease of a plot in the middle of it, incorporating Crown Alley and fronting on to both Dame Street and Cope Street. Parke's design was for four blocks around a central courtyard, which would allow natural light within the block, and a through-passage maintaining the old route of Crown Alley.

The foundation stone was laid on site in July 1796, the Commercial Buildings Company was incorporated by Royal Charter on 1 January 1798 and the building was opened in 1799. A commemorative stone with the image of a sailing ship, supposedly representing the *Ouzel Galley* and bearing the date 1799, was installed over the door from the courtyard to Dame Street and survives in a brick panel beside the reconstructed façade. The building was three storeys high over a basement, stone-faced to Dame Street, elegant but somewhat austere, which was not helped by the blackening of the stonework that resulted from pollution. From the start the building was perceived as being multifunctional. The main entrance, from Dame Street, was through a twenty-foot-high plastered vaulted vestibule with an inner hall containing an elegant staircase to the first floor. Initially there was a coffee room on the left which was run in conjunction with a hotel on the upper floors 'for the accommodation of foreign merchants or for any respectable person who preferred this part of town as a temporary residence'. The Marine Insurance Company office was to the right.

Passing through the front building, one arrived in the courtyard, with a block on each side containing three brokerage firms, two in one block and one in the other, with a stockbroker taking the remaining half-block. The brokerages opened for business between 2pm and 4pm: they contained the desks of various retailers and there was a table for samples on the upper floor. In *St Catherine's Bells*, Walter Meyler noted that during the day the businessmen, 'when not engaged, assembled around the fires in offices, or sauntering in the courtyard when fine, confidential whispers passed as to the solvency of buyers, and ominous looks and hints were evinced on an approaching smash.' The courtyard was enclosed by a building to the north, through which a second, smaller arch led to Cope Street.

The courtyard buildings were faced in brick and divided into blocks, A-G, each with its own staircase.

James Malton's image of Commercial Buildings, shortly after they were opened in 1799.

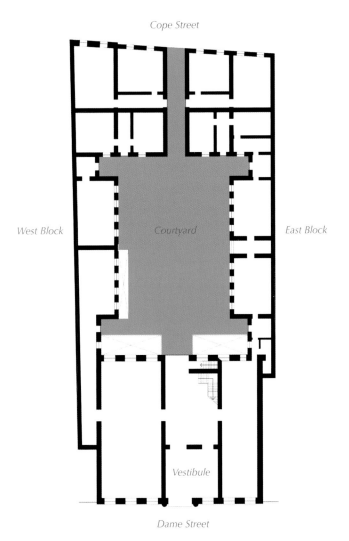

The ground-floor plan of Commercial Buildings. The east and west blocks were accessed through the courtyard. Initially Chamber's rooms were at the Cope Street end, later in the Dame Street block and finally on the upper floors of the west block.

Cope Street

West Block

Courtyard

East Block

Vestibule

Dame Street

The Commercial Buildings Company employed a porter in the entrance hall and a clerk, styled a register or secretary, to manage the building. The porter of old held a staff with a brass model of a ship on the top and the buttons on his livery had the image of a ship. The company kept an office in the building and the porter lived on the premises, in an apartment in Cope Street.

From the start there was a very close relationship between Chamber and the Commercial Buildings Company, although the complex was built during a period of hiatus for Chamber: as soon as Chamber reformed, in 1805, it took rooms there. The 1820 Chamber also made Commercial Buildings its home and in 1822 ten of the sixteen board members of Commercial Buildings were on the Council of Chamber. (This closeness dissipated somewhat towards the end of the 19th century as the shareholdings in Commercial Buildings moved on from the original families.) The Commercial Buildings Company register (secretary) was also register to Chamber, a situation that continued for most of the 19th century.

Chamber soon relinquished the first rooms it leased for £50 per annum in favour of better accommodation. In 1823 it agreed to take rooms on the west side of the courtyard instead of those on Cope Street. Chamber used these offices until it left the building for 7 Clare Street nearly a century and a half later. Sanitation was a cause for complaint in the early decades and the dual issues of removal of effluvia and provision of adequate ventilation were tackled several times before what was apparently a satisfactory resolution in 1868. In 1828 Chamber took over the old coffee room in the Dame Street building and in 1867, when the Freemasons moved to their new premises in Molesworth Street, it leased the latter organisation's rooms over the coffee room to Dame Street and spent nearly £1000 on improvements.

By the time of the renewal of its lease in 1917 Chamber had scaled back its premises to comprise only the left room on the ground floor, front of the building, and the upper two floors of the western block to the courtyard. In the renewal of 1937 Chamber surrendered the large room to Dame Street and subsequently it occupied only the premises in the courtyard.

Drawing by Fergus O'Ryan (1911-89) of the courtyard exit to Dame Street with the carving of the Ouzel Galley *over the doorway. The president, Michael P. Rowan, used the print for Chamber's 1951 Christmas card.*

From 1821 the Ouzel Galley Society leased accommodation for holding arbitrations in Commercial Buildings. It moved in 1831 to a larger boardroom in the same building on the western side of the courtyard. According to George Little, author of the Old Dublin Society book on the galley, a brass plaque, bearing the inscription 'The Ouzel Galley' remained on the door until the 20th century. From 1852, no longer in need of so much space due to a fall in arbitrations, the Society sublet space from Chamber, which contributed to the close association of the two bodies.

To complete this account of Commercial Buildings it is necessary to write about their sad demise. The original shareholders of the Commercial Buildings Company elected the board from among their number. Over the years some shares were accumulated when offered for sale but the share value increased little. In 1938 the Commercial Buildings Company applied to the courts to dissolve its founding charter 'for purposes of bringing the company's constitution into line with modern requirements, as it had been found that the provisions in the charter were out of date in many respects'. The four hundred original shares at £50 each were converted into 20,000 £1 shares in a new company called Commercial Buildings (Dublin) Ltd. This change facilitated the redevelopment of the building. The company made a modest profit of £1315 in 1961 and paid a dividend of 7 per cent but the £1 shares were trading at no more than 30 shillings each, while the building was still in need of modernisation

– although in the 1950s some refurbishment had been carried out and a lift installed (a peculiar device accessed up seven steps!).

In the 1960s a commercial development boom took place in Dublin, much of it of poor design standard and insensitive to its context. Early in 1962 there was a sudden demand for Commercial Buildings (Dublin) Ltd shares, which increased in price by ten shillings to £2, and in June of that year shareholders accepted an offer of £3 per share from the anonymous Merrie Inns Ltd, valuing the company at £60,000. The declared intention of the new owners was to demolish the building and they were prepared to buy out leases to accelerate the vacating of the premises. Some of the tenants, notably the Ouzel Galley Lounge, were adamant that they would stay put but the premises were eventually emptied and demolition began in 1971. The Central Bank had acquired Commercial Buildings and adjoining properties to the west as far as Fownes Street for its new headquarters.

It appears that the building had been listed but in that era of even weaker conservation regulation than nowadays, in was accepted that the façade

The reconstruction of Commercial Buildings in the Central Bank plaza at right angles to Dame Street. The stonework of the main doorcase appears to be the only remaining piece of the original elevation.

was all that needed to be retained. Stephenson Gibney, architects for the new Central Bank, proposed carefully removing the existing façade, numbering the blocks and re-erecting the façade at right angles to Dame Street. The ashlar blocks were duly numbered and removed but, it was claimed, the numbers washed off in the rain and, excepting the main doorcase, what we see is a relatively faithful replica of the original façade in new granite. Supposedly the original stones remain in a pile in Sandyford. Interestingly, the design for the Central Bank maintained access through the site in recognition of the old Crown Alley, which had been absorbed into the redevelopment.

Headed notepaper of the Commercial Buildings Company, 1964, the year the buildings were sold. G. Dudley Woodworth, father of Irish Times *journalist, Paddy Woodworth, was secretary to the company.*

V

THE RECONSTITUTED CHAMBER, 1820-55

In pursuance of the Laws of Chamber, you have been convened to receive from your Council, a compendious statement of those proceedings, by which, during the period of their office, they have endeavoured to execute the trust committed to their discretion, and promote the objects for which you are associated.

Opening statement of the first annual report

By 1820 it was clear that the Act of Union had had a negative effect on the commercial life of Dublin. Although the Lord Lieutenant and his administration remained in the city, mitigating somewhat the loss of the local parliament, the parliamentarians and a large proportion of the landed gentry had moved to London. As a result the standing of the city's merchants increased. The Act of Union had allowed protective tariffs to continue until 1808 but when they were reduced the smaller Irish market was opened to English imports. The economy, which had received a boost during the Napoleonic Wars, entered a period of decline when these ended in 1815. By the time Chamber was revived in 1820 the indigenous weaving industry in the Liberties had collapsed in the face of English competition. Parliament had contributed to Dublin's physical development in the 18th century, with public buildings like the Four Courts and the Custom House,

Chamber stamp from the 1840s. Before the arrival of letterheads the stamp was the only corporate logo.

timeline

1821
George IV visits Ireland.

1823
Custom & Excise Act consolidates Board of Customs of Ireland and Britain.

1824
Removal of duties on goods traded between Great Britain and Ireland.

1825
Introduction of gas street lighting in Dublin.

1826
Amalgamation of Irish and British currencies and standardising of weights.

1829
Passing of Catholic Relief Act. Irish Parliamentary Election Act raises the valuation for voters from forty shillings (£2) to £10.

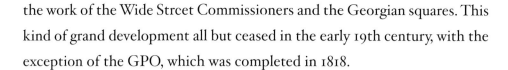

the work of the Wide Street Commissioners and the Georgian squares. This kind of grand development all but ceased in the early 19th century, with the exception of the GPO, which was completed in 1818.

In 1796 the Grand Canal extension to Ringsend Docks had opened: along with the Royal Canal, it effectively delineated the boundary of the city. The population of Dublin in 1821 was 185,881. We now think of Dublin as being divided into north and south by the River Liffey but at this time the division was between east and west. The western half of the city was the main commercial area and contained the poorer dwellings, while better-off people lived in the residential eastern half.

Although the Chambers of 1783 and 1805 had failed, Dublin merchants still needed a representative body, free from politics and sectarianism. In 1820 the economic downturn and Dublin's weakened political position under the Union were the main drivers for the creation of the third Chamber. At a meeting of merchants in 1818, Joseph Hone (1775-1857), a wholesale merchant in Commercial Buildings, noted that the most recent Chamber 'which then existed, embraced everything respectable and enlightened among the merchants of Dublin' and commented on 'the disadvantages which the trade of this city suffers at present, from the want of a similar institution, and expressed a hope that a project for the formation of a Dublin Chamber of Commerce, might emanate from the present meeting.'

Hone was not among the eight merchants who met on 5 October 1820 and resolved 'to prepare a plan for the formation of the Chamber of Commerce in the City of Dublin'. A public meeting convened in Commercial Buildings a week later, under the chairmanship of Randal MacDonnell, and a committee met several times over the next month to formulate the rules of the new Chamber. Subscription books in Commercial Buildings, the Royal Exchange and the Corn Exchange invited membership applications, with the inducement that members joining before 1 January 1821 would not be subject to a ballot. It was agreed that there would be an admission fee of one guinea and an annual subscription of the same sum. General meetings held at the Royal Exchange, again with Randal MacDonnell in the chair, approved the rules and on 16 November 1820 Joshua Pim was elected president. The president, four vice-presidents and twenty-one ordinary members formed the Council of Chamber. Pim, a Quaker wool merchant, had been honorary treasurer of the first Chamber in 1783.

An anonymous letter to the *Freeman's Journal* commented that the formation of a Chamber of Commerce at this time was 'locking the stable door when the steed is stolen' in the light of the failure of the Act of Union to develop Irish commerce as promised. Dublin's position as second city of the United Kingdom was being eroded. Liverpool, Birmingham, Manchester, Glasgow and eventually Belfast would overtake it in size. The writer also emphasised that Chamber should be for merchants, manufacturers and traders and not confined to importers and exporters.

The new Chamber leased the coffee room in Commercial Buildings at a rent of £50 per annum and converted it into a subscription room. It employed Thomas Jameson, secretary to the Commercial Buildings Company, as register for an annual salary of £60. From the beginning Chamber had an aura of a gentleman's club, open seven days a week. The daily newspapers were available and a library of parliamentary papers developed over time. In 1823 it moved to larger premises on the west side of Commercial Buildings,

1832

Cholera epidemic in Dublin and countrywide.

1833

Appointment of Commission of Enquiry into Municipal Corporations.

Big fire in Custom House store.

1834

Opening of the country's first railway, Dublin to Kingstown.

1836

Establishment of Dublin Metropolitan Police (DMP).

1839

The 'Big Wind' (night 6-7 January) and flooding of the River Liffey.

1840

Municipal Reform Act re-constitutes Dublin Corporation.

1844

Opening of Dublin-Drogheda railway.

which included a meeting room, coffee room, reading room and water closet. Gas lighting arrived the following year.

One of the earliest initiatives of the reconstituted Chamber was to raise the issue of abuses in the Custom House porterage. Quay and store porters handled imported goods in the Custom House: their charges were loosely regulated and a source of irritation to the merchants. The Commissioners of Customs agreed that Chamber would assume the running of the porterage and it took into its employ William Hughes, the superintendent of porters, and J.G. Jones, the receiver of porterage charges. After some initial success in managing and reducing charges, Chamber's annual report noted: 'Some impediments have arisen from the insubordination and irregularities of the working porters.' It proved difficult for Chamber to collect porterage payments because of its lack of recognised status. By 1827, after a number of years when porterage income did not meet expenditure, Chamber had returned management of the quay porterage to the Custom House.

Financially the 1820 Chamber began on a positive footing. In 1822 Peter Brophy (1775-1857), a wine merchant of Abbey Street and a Council member, challenged another set of port charges levied by Lord Henry Seymour Conway, the wonderfully titled Patentee Craner and Wharfinger. The Court of the Queen's Bench found that these charges were illegal and in settlement of all possible future claims by the merchants, HM Treasury agreed to pay Chamber £10,000. Ironically, the Merchants' Guild, although it would not accept Brophy as a member because he was a Catholic, made an unsuccessful attempt to claim the compensation. In celebration of its triumph Chamber hosted a 'splendid dinner' at Morrisson's Hotel, with Peter Brophy presiding. Seventy prominent merchants attended, as well as Chamber's legal team, which included Daniel O'Connell. Peter Brophy received £1000 for his efforts and, after paying costs, Chamber purchased 3300 Bank of Ireland shares for £8222, which gave it a financial cushion. A century later Chamber still owned £3000 worth of shares.

The year after Brophy's successful action Chamber set up a committee to look into the numerous other charges on ships arriving in Dublin, including slippage and anchorage, the Lord Mayor's fee, the recorder's fee, the water bailiff's fee, the sheriff's fee and Edward Hampton's fee, some of these of doubtful legality and dating back to the time of the guilds and the city assembly's management of the port. But this committee's efforts did not have the same success as Brophy's action.

From the beginning Chamber declared that it did not takes sides in politics but when a faction of the Orange Order (founded 1795) disrupted a performance in the Theatre Royal on 14 December 1822 it did express 'indignation at the late disgraceful occurrences' and 'abhorrence of its perpetrators'. The Lord Lieutenant and Lord Mayor, who were among the audience, were the focus of the Orange protest because of their decision that the order should not be allowed to carry out its annual decoration of King William's statue on College Green – a cause of repeated sectarian disturbances in the city.

Although Chamber elected a president and four vice-presidents as well as a Council, it was the honorary secretary who in reality drove most of the policy. Robert Roe (1788-1836), the first honorary secretary of the revived body, held the post for thirteen years. In 1824 Chamber resolved that an assistant secretary should be employed in addition to the register and

1852
Electrical telegraph service begins between Holyhead and Dublin.

1853
Queen Victoria visits industrial exhibition in Dublin.

Extension of income tax to Ireland.

1854
Outbreak of Crimean War.

1855
Opening of final section of Belfast-Dublin railway line.

The Chamber ballot for membership involved the electors placing either a white or black pebble in a box with the applicant's name. If a certain percentage of pebbles was black, the applicant was refused admission.

This method of election was popular with gentlemen's clubs but probably unsuitable for a business organisation. Peter Brophy, a Council stalwart, and Daniel O'Connell had both been blackballed when they applied to join the Royal Dublin Society in 1811.

There seems to have been no particular sectarian or political reason for the early rejections but this was not the case for the thirty-six applicants blackballed 1868-94, some of them twice. Amongst them were nationalist MPs William Field and Tim Harrington and councillors Daniel Tallon and Joseph Hutchinson, who was also high sheriff. Councillor Henry Brown raised the issue at the 1896 AGM, alleging that 90 per cent of Chamber members held the Tory view, and the blackballing ended.

almost the entire Council met to appoint Lundy Edward Foot (1791-1863), an attorney and the son of a well-known snuff manufacturer with premises in Parliament Street.

Chamber held the ballot for the election of members every quarter, with those present placing either a black or a white bean in each applicant's designated box. A black bean meant rejection (hence the term 'blackballed') and initially one black bean in four meant that the applicant in question failed to be elected. There were no rejections during the first two years but, after a spate of refusals in 1823-4, the rules were changed to require half the balls to be black. Most of the applicants who were rejected initially were subsequently elected.

Council also engaged what they called a pier-head officer in Dublin port (and later Dún Laoghaire/Kingstown pier) to send daily lists to Chamber of ships arriving and departing the port and their cargo. This officer and his messengers cost £100 per annum. Chamber sold this information on to interested businesses and insurance companies such as Lloyds.

From the inception of this third Chamber its four primary interests can be inferred from Council minutes – Dublin Corporation; Dublin port and its management and fees; communication; and HM Customs and Excise. Many of these issues involved dealings with the parliament in Westminster. In the 19th century individual MPs or outside bodies often presented bills in the Houses of Commons and Lords – a system very different from the government-driven legislative programmes with which we are now familiar. Bills were very precise in specifying levies and dues, so bodies like Dublin Corporation and the Ballast Board had to present new bills if they wished to raise fees. Chamber generally opposed increased fees so in its turn it had to petition against the bills, retaining an agent in London as well as a lawyer in Dublin. To give gravitas and status to its petitions Chamber decided in 1823 to apply for a charter but although it spent nearly £1000 on this exercise over the next few years it came to consider the charter unnecessary and not worth the expense. It has been shown that during these years the Irish chambers, particularly Dublin, presented parliamentary petitions more often than their British counterparts: each one cost several thousand pounds, with no guarantee of success.

By the first half of the 19th century, Dublin Corporation had become somewhat anachronistic. It still had two houses, a commons comprising ninety-six representatives of the Dublin guilds and an upper house consisting of the Lord Mayor, aldermen, sheriffs and sheriff's peers (former

Drawing of the Custom House from George Newenham Wright's An Historical Guide to the City of Dublin *(1825).*

Many members at this time were importing wholesale merchants whose trade passed through the Custom House and it was the source of many of Chamber's grievances.

Courtesy of the National Library of Ireland

sheriffs). Only aldermen could be elected Lord Mayor. But the most archaic and undemocratic aspect of the corporation was that members of the guilds and freemen made up its entire electorate. Despite the Catholic Relief Act of 1793 which allowed Catholics to vote, very few Catholics were admitted as members of the guilds. After Catholic Emancipation in 1829 the government established an investigation into irregularities in local government. The Report of the Commissioners on Municipal Corporations in 1835 led to the Municipal Corporations Act of 1840 which created a single-chamber corporation and expanded its electorate to include all 40-shilling freeholders. Significantly, the report noted that no corporation member was also a member of Council of the Chamber of Commerce.

Unlike Dublin Corporation, the self-perpetuating Ballast Board that replaced the old Ballast Office in 1786 included Catholics, not on its first

Eight merchants

The following merchants signed the request to form a Chamber of Commerce on 5 October 1820: four Church of Ireland, two Catholics, one Quaker and one Presbyterian. All but John Rainsford and Jonathan Williamson were subsequently elected Council members. Only George Drevar was a member of the Ouzel Galley Society (he had been a member since 1811).

Name	Business	Business Address
Edward Croker (d. 1839)	Wine merchant	7 North Great George's Street
George Drevar (d. 1829)	Drevar & Sons import merchant	83 Abbey Street
Thomas MacDonnell (d. 1826)	Randal MacDonnell and Sons	Allen's Court
Joseph Robinson Pim (d. 1858)	Merchant and shipowner	
Peter Brophy (d. 1857)	Wine merchant	12 Lower Ormond Quay
John Barber (d. 1828)	Notary public	85 Dame Street
John Rainsford (d. 1825)	Merchant	116 Abbey Street
Jonathan Williamson (d. 1831)	Director Marine Insurance Company	Commercial Buildings

THE BALLAST BOARD

The Lord Mayor and corporation traditionally managed Dublin port: the upkeep and construction of quay walls; dredging of the river; and the provision of ballast for ships with insufficient cargo to allow them to set sail. In 1707, an act was passed 'for Clensing the Port, Harbour and River of Dublin and for Erecting a Ballast Office in the said City' and a committee appointed to manage the Ballast Office, as it was called. By 1782 the committee was subject to inspection of its finances, particularly in regard to an overrun of expenditure on work to the South Wall, and the delay in completing it.

A bill promoted by the Revenue Commissioner, John Beresford MP, and supported by the merchants, was moved in parliament in 1786, transferring control of the Ballast Office from the Lord Mayor to a selected board. The Corporation for Preserving and Improving the Port of Dublin, which became known as the Ballast Board, came into existence on 8 May 1786, including the Lord Mayor, high sheriffs and three aldermen along with seventeen others, including eight Council members of Dublin Chamber. New offices for the board were built on the corner of Westmoreland Street and Aston Quay. In 1810 responsibility for all lighthouses was vested in the Ballast Board and a statute of 1811 gave it responsibility for existing quay walls and Liffey bridges; from 1825 Kingstown harbour came under its remit.

The method of selection of Ballast Board members was the kernel of Dublin Chamber's objections to it in the 1860s, leading to a further change to the board. Shipping had developed considerably since the introduction of steam and ship-owners who were members of Chamber objected to the decisions of the Ballast Board that involved charges on their businesses while they had no representation on the Board. In 1867 an act transferred responsibility for lighthouses to a new Commissioner of Irish Lights and the Ballast Board was again reconstituted as the Dublin Port and Dock Board in 1899, when Sir Richard Martin, former Chamber president and a board member since 1867, was appointed chairman. Traders elected twelve board members to the new board of twenty-eight; nine were from among shipowners, the corporation had six others and the Lord Mayor was ex-officio.

Ballast Board logo.
Courtesy of Dublin Port Company

Arthur Guinness joined the second Chamber in 1805 and was president from 1825 until his death in 1855.

but on subsequent boards. The board was charged with the development and maintenance of the port and its quays and walls and dredging the river as necessary. It also had responsibility for bridges. Chamber frequently complained about the way the board carried out its responsibilities in these areas, as well as its fees.

When the revived chamber was founded in 1820 communication with London was by sailing ship and carriage but that same year the first steamships began to ply between Dublin and Liverpool – shortening the crossing from, at worst, several days to under eight hours – and in 1824 the City of Dublin Steampacket Company was founded. Chamber was quick to advocate that the Post Office contract steamships for carrying mail. Commercial rail travel began in England in the 1820s and Chamber encouraged the development of a railway between Dublin and Kingstown (Dún Laoghaire was called Kingstown after George IV departed from there at the end of his 1821 visit) that was first proposed in 1825 for the more rapid carriage of post and goods.

The two major canal lines had been completed no more than three decades earlier and their proprietors were not slow to realise that the arrival of railways would be detrimental to their business. In 1827 they introduced to parliament an unsuccessful bill for a ship canal between Dublin and Kingstown, to challenge the proposal for a railway on the same route. Chamber did not support the bill as the proposal did not appear 'in the opinion of the council to confer any benefit upon the trade of Ireland in general or that of Dublin in particular' and the campaign did no more than delay the inevitable.

HM Customs and Excise was a continual source of aggravation to the commercial community of Dublin not just because of the impositions but because delays in clearing through the Custom House and management of the Custom House docks and quay caused constant difficulties, costs and delays. Council's recourse was generally by memorandum to the Lord Lieutenant or the Board of Treasury but these representations were often unsuccessful.

Chamber president Joshua Pim died in office in 1822 and was replaced by Leland Crosthwait, a Presbyterian merchant with milling interests. He also died in office, in 1825, and Arthur Guinness, son of the founder of the brewing company, replaced him. He had been a Council member of the second chamber but failed to get election to Council of the 1820 (third) Chamber until 1822. Although he favoured Catholic Emancipation he was conservative and pro-union and, unlike his predecessors as president, made attempts to politicise Chamber. In the election to succeed Pim as president Guinness ran against Leland Crosthwait but received only two votes, the same number he received when he ran again in 1826. He was, however, elected a vice-president in that year and finally elected president when Crosthwait died. During his long presidency Guinness was much more rarely in attendance than his predecessors, Pim and Crosthwait, but Council became dominated by his supporters, with fewer liberal members.

Chamber rejected an early attempt by Arthur Guinness and his faction to have the organisation endorse a parliamentary candidate of conservative

Arthur Guinness (1768-1855)

The second son of Arthur Guinness, founder of the eponymous brewery, Arthur II was the foremost businessman of his day. He was described as 'shrewd, forthright and immensely able'. With his two brothers Benjamin (1777-1826) and William Lunell (1779-1842) he inherited the brewery on his father's death in 1803. As principal partner he developed the business greatly, particularly during the Napoleonic Wars.

Brewing, like all trade, greatly declined after the Battle of Waterloo but by then Guinness had turned his attention to other interests, particularly banking and politics. He was a member of the board of the Bank of Ireland from 1804 and, although he never ran for political office, he liked to use his influence in political matters. A supporter of Catholic Emancipation, he fell out with Daniel O'Connell later over his campaign to repeal the Union. The brewing business reached its nadir in 1823 but diversification into the exporting of extra stout revived the company's fortunes, leaving it is a healthy position when Arthur Guinness retired in 1839.

views. This occurred in April 1826 at a general meeting chaired by Arthur Guinness's brother William Lunell (who, incidentally, was not to be elected a member of Chamber until the following June). The popular opinion was that Chamber should maintain strict neutrality rather than allow political division to distract it from its proper commercial concerns but Council couldn't resist when a member, Robert Orr, advanced the apparently innocuous resolution that Chamber should support George Ogle Moore, a candidate in the general election of 1830. A deputation headed by Arthur Guinness presented the resolution to Moore, who immediately had it published in the Dublin newspapers. Moore had been very attentive to Chamber's business in parliament but he was the nephew of George Ogle, an infamous militia leader in Wexford during the 1798 Rebellion, and very much opposed to Catholic Emancipation. The publication of the letter immediately raised a requisition among Chamber members that Henry Grattan Junior, the pro-emancipation candidate, should receive the same endorsement. At the subsequent general meeting, Council had to concede that its actions had not been politically neutral and wrote an endorsement for both candidates. Thereafter, until the formation of the Irish Free State, Chamber avoided political endorsements at election time.

Arthur Guinness had encouraged the membership of conservative, like-minded merchants but a few years after he became president the growth in membership ceased and did not resume until after he died. Although Guinness controlled Council, Chamber's rules and bye-laws ensured that it remained relevant to all its members by focusing on the mechanics of doing business. Guinness had not been president for long when his input into Chamber became less significant, perhaps as a result of his having been unsuccessful in the George Moore controversy, with the result that the role of honorary secretary increased in importance. Robert Roe attempted to leave the position for 'business reasons' in 1824 but was persuaded to remain despite being at odds, as a liberal, with the conservative-dominated Council.

Chamber took two early cases against Dublin Corporation that were successful to different degrees. The first, which came to court in 1826, was in relation to the corporation's imposition of dues for slippage and anchorage on all ships arriving in the port. Chamber opened a subscription list to fund the case, which it won (Daniel O'Connell was among the barristers appearing for it) but it cost £2100, requiring the sale of some of Chamber's bank shares.

The second case was against the coal meters, who measured the coal delivered to the Dublin port in cauldrons, as opposed to weighing it. Until 1794 they were paid 2 pence a ton but this was gradually increased, reaching 6 pence a ton in 1802. The positions of coal meters, of which there were eighty in 1825, were in the gift of the Merchants' Guild and the fee paid for these appointments, £25 each per annum, provided a large proportion of the income of the declining guild.

Chamber was reluctant to go to court because of the high cost of the previous case but by 1830 all attempts to resolve the issue by petition and deputations had failed. Dublin Corporation, realising the strength of Chamber opposition to this unjust imposition, took a case in the name of a coal meter

The decorative tombstone of William Taylor in Mount Jerome Cemetery, Dublin. Taylor was one of the eighty or so coal meters to whom Chamber so strongly objected.

Taylor died in 1843, eighteen years after Chamber succeeded in having coal meters abolished, but had received a pension to compensate for the loss of his position.

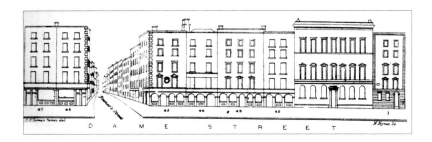

Dame Street from Shaw's Dublin Directory *of 1850. Chamber's rooms were in Commercial Buildings (second from the right) overlooking Dame Street.*

named John Whelan against a ship's captain, John Cairns, in the Court of Conscience, an archaic municipal court in the control of the corporation, with the Lord Mayor in the chair. Not surprisingly, this court found in favour of the meter. An enraged Chamber responded by bringing a successful case to the Recorder's Court to overturn the Court of Conscience. It found that an act of 1824 regulating weights and measures required coal to be sold by weight rather than measure, which meant that the role of coal meter had no purpose. But the Chamber victory was somewhat Pyrrhic: although parliament abolished the position of Dublin coal meter, a levy of 4 pence per ton was applied to coal to pay for the superannuation of the meters. For many years Chamber asked Treasury that this levy be reduced because the number of meters receiving the superannuation decreased as the holders of the position died.

In 1827 an opportunity arose for Chamber to relocate to better and more prominent rooms to the front of Commercial Buildings. The annual rent was £200 and the subscription increased to £1/10s a year to pay for this.

By this time many other cities in the United Kingdom had established chambers of commerce. Dublin developed relationships with these chambers although there was as yet no formal umbrella organisation. Liverpool Chamber was in the lead in raising objections to the monopoly held by the East India Company, not only in trade but in its contact with the Indian subcontinent. It wrote to Dublin Chamber seeking its support. The industrial revolution encouraged a laissez-faire outlook (an opposition to regulation) among business people in their search for markets and the East India Company's charter was an impediment to the free market. A Reverend James William Massie held a meeting in Dublin, with Arthur Guinness in the chair, to encourage free intercourse with India, chiefly in regard to the 'moral and religious advancement of the natives'. Chamber supported Liverpool and in 1833 the Government of India Act removed many of the East India Company's remaining monopolies, although granting it another twenty years' domination in India.

Council gave concerted attention to the management of the Custom House docks in Dublin, as the import and export of goods were of crucial importance to many of its business members. In 1824 the Treasury leased the buildings and quay to the Scovell brothers from London. The original letting was of no interest to Chamber but when the Scovells demanded that all importers on the docks had to use – and importers pay for – their services whether or not duty was payable on the imports, this raised the merchants' ire.

Before the lease was due for renewal seven years later Chamber made petitions to Treasury and the Lord Lieutenant objecting to the Scovells' management but to no avail – the Scovells received their renewal. Council gave evidence that the lease was an effective monopoly and proposed that the premises be divided into two. To supply grist to Chamber's mill, management's incompetence in allowing the fire doors to be left open combined with the insecure storage of inflammable material was the

The newly-opened Dublin-Kingstown railway had to provide Lord Cloncurry with an elaborate bridge from his house to the shore.

Cloncurry was a director and major shareholder in the Grand Canal Company which unsuccessfully tried to stifle the new railway by proposing a canal from Dublin to Kingstown. The railway had to cross his land and he had his revenge by extracting the maximum fee in negotiations with the railway company.

catalyst for the Custom House store being burned down on 9 August 1832. Many goods belonging to the merchants were destroyed and Chamber raised a fund, itself contributing £250, to help merchants who were at a loss. Chamber also objected to another renewal of the lease and a plan was enacted to divide the Custom House stores in two parts, with the Ballast Board taking responsibilty for one part, the Scovells for the other.

In 1834 Robert Roe retired after thirteen years as honorary secretary and the antiquarian and merchant, Charles Haliday (1789-1866), who took his place, was equally efficient and diligent. The assistant secretary, Lundy Edward Foot, left the employ of Chamber in 1836 after the murder of his father in New Ross and was not replaced for eight years.

In 1831 Chamber supported the Dublin and Kingstown Railway Bill rather than the canal. Among the original directors of the Dublin and Kingstown Railway Company were Robert Roe, as well as several other Council members. Lord Cloncurry, director of the Grand Canal Company and sponsor of the scheme to extend the canal to Galway, got some revenge when he obliged the railway to pay him £3000 to be allowed to cross his land. The line, built by William Dargan, was opened to the public in December 1834. Kingstown was the inward port of all mail from 1833 and the ongoing development of the railway system in England meant that getting post to and from London more quickly, even in one day, was coming closer to reality. As early as 1835 the best rail route to Wales was being investigated, with Holyhead, the traditional port for Ireland, being one option. Chamber supported the initiative strongly, without expressing an opinion on the most suitable port, and was regularly in touch with the Postmaster General about improved efficiencies in the postal system.

During these first decades of the reconstituted Chamber the management of Dublin port was a recurring preoccupation. It must be remembered that many members of the board of the Ballast Board were also members of Chamber. The proposal to erect a bridge closer to the Custom House – now Butt Bridge – was a cause of concern for those with businesses near Carlisle (O'Connell) Bridge and also for merchants who would suffer the loss of quay wall for anchorage. The Ballast Board suggested the provision of additional quay frontage but, in any case, the bridge was not built for another forty years. In 1829 Chamber first lamented the loss of employment in ship maintenance to the ports of Liverpool and Glasgow and requested a graving dock to allow for repairs to large seagoing vessels. After many years of petitions to the Ballast Board, the Lord Lieutenant and Treasury, the Ballast Board approved the construction of a new graving dock to the design of George Halpin in 1852 and William Dargan's contracting company began construction work the following year. It was completed in 1860.

Chamber also pursued the issue of unjust levies and imposition on ships. One of the most far-fetched was the right of Ramsgate in south-east England to levy all ships that passed its harbour, not just those that docked there. (This levy, imposed by a bill in the late 18th century, was collected in Dublin's Custom House.) There was a similar issue with Skerries Rock Lighthouse (near Anglesey), which was entitled to levy shipping in Dublin port under an old law, whether or not the vessel used it. After many representations both imposts were removed. Not so easily resolved was the two-shilling charge on all Dublin shipping imposed by an act of 1823 to pay for the construction of Kingstown Harbour. Chamber first opposed this charge in 1851, feeling that it was no longer needed, noting also that such a charge, for an adjoining

James Gandon's Long Room in the Custom House, where the merchants paid the customs and excise on imports and later other harbour dues. It was destroyed in 1922 and never rebuilt.

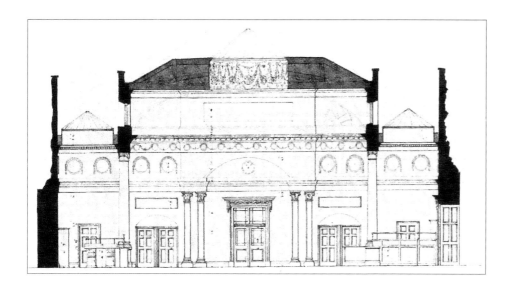

port, was not levied on any other port in the United Kingdom. There were letters, petitions, deputations to London, the Lord Lieutenant and the Treasury, both by Chamber and by the two Dublin MPs – and flattery in a letter to William Gladstone, then Chancellor of the Exchequer, when 'Council ventured to express a hope that a Minister so enlightened, and so conversant with the interests of trade, would not permit an injustice so irritating and so indefensible to be continued.' But years later the issue was still live and the Privy Council informed Chamber that the charge would not be abolished.

Samuel Price Edwards (1799-1877), the Collector of Customs, removed another irritant in 1853, when he agreed that custom and Ballast Board fees could be collected together in the Custom House Long Room, rather than ships having to stop twice to pay separate fees. Council presented a testimonial to Price Edwards in appreciation of his efforts when he moved to the port of Liverpool two years later.

The Municipal Corporations Act of 1840 tackled the intrinsically un-democratic nature of Dublin Corporation. The municipal electorate was increased to include all 40-shilling property owners within the city boundaries and Daniel O'Connell was elected the first Catholic Lord Mayor since the 17th century. (This, like most political developments, received no mention at the Council meetings.) The act did not change the functions or operations of the corporation: many local administration functions were still carried out by the Wide Street Commissioners, the Paving Board and the Grand Jury, and all these bodies retained the same membership as before. The corporation made attempts to change its modus operandi through a

EXPRESS NEWSPAPER OFFICE.

Johnston's Express.

JOHNSTON & CO.
Newspaper and Advertising Agents,
EDEN-QUAY, DUBLIN.

Johnston & Co provided the Chamber with its extensive collection of daily newspapers. Prior to the arrival of the telegraph to Ireland, Johnstons also supplied daily intelligence that arrived by telegraph in Liverpool, thence by steampacket to Dublin.

William Henry (W.H.) Smith took over the business of Johnston & Co in 1850 and installed Charles Eason from Yeovil as manager, later selling the business to Eason.

Walter Thomas Meyler (1814-74)

Meyler was born in St Catherine's parish, Dublin. He served apprenticeships with several concerns in Dublin and London and travelled in North America for a year before setting up in business as a corn and wine merchant on the corner of Fownes Street and Cecilia Street in 1839. He had a desk at a brokerage in Commercial Buildings and his business was initially successful but a fire in his warehouse resulted in his bankruptcy and incarceration in the Four Courts Marshalsea. He was a member of Dublin Chamber 1835-65.

Meyler was a Young Irelander and after the 1848 Young Ireland rebellion he was arrested and imprisoned in Newgate. He was a member of the RDS and in 1868, while again in the Marshalsea, wrote an autobiography, *St Catherine's Bells,* which gives an interesting insight into Dublin business of his era. After another spell in prison, he went to America, where his son was living, and died in Amesbury, Massachusetts. His death certificate, sadly, gives his occupation as 'labourer'.

series of Dublin Improvement Acts brought to parliament but Chamber aggressively opposed them. The Dublin Improvement committee, set up in Commercial Buildings, coordinated opposition by Chamber and other commercial bodies to the proposed improvement bills. Chamber agreed that the management of the city needed to be improved and streamlined but pushed for a corporation more representative of those who paid for it than of citizens in general. Council was particular opposed to the corporation's attempts to acquire the Royal Exchange as its city hall. The whole exercise in opposing the corporation was very expensive and time-consuming, draining a considerable amount of Chamber's resources. By the end of the 1840s agreement was reached and the Dublin Improvement Act of 1849 and associated bills were passed, amalgamating various charges and levies, including the powers of the Wide Street Commissioners, into the new corporation. In a gesture of goodwill Chamber relinquished its interest in the Royal Exchange and accepted the corporation's wish to use it as City Hall. Several members of Chamber Council were elected to the corporation: by 1858 ten of the sixty councillors were on the Council of Dublin Chamber.

The Annual Report for 1846 states that 'in the month of July the attention of the Council was directed to the appearance of failure in the potato crop throughout Ireland.' It was the second year of the Great Famine. Council recorded that the government had imported Indian corn for sale below cost in the previous year and had written to the Lords of the Treasury asking them to repeat the importation for the current year. Prior to the annual meeting in 1847, a radical and progressive member, Walter T. Meyler, wrote an open letter to Chamber, published in the *Freeman's Journal*, with a number of proposals for the general meeting including one that Chamber's reserve of £544 be donated to the General Relief Committee. Meyler also raised objections to the stasis of Council – its members had not changed in ten years save for death or insolvency – and the high rent charged by the Commercial Buildings Company, noting that a number of members of that company were also members of Council. Finally he suggested that money saved by getting a reduction in rent could be used for the 'purpose of establishing a respectable library, in lieu of the abortion we have at present'. Council minutes make no mention of Meyler's letter or proposals.

When Queen Victoria and Prince Albert visited Ireland in 1849, after much excitement, discussion and planning, a Chamber delegation led by the president, Arthur Guinness, presented an illuminated address. The queen later wrote that 'the entrance at seven o'clock into Kingstown Harbour was splendid; we came in with ten steamers, and the whole harbour, wharf, and every surrounding place was covered with thousands and thousands of

'We desire to record our grateful admiration of the magnificent benevolence which under the auspices of your majesty rendered the abundance of our sister island tributary to the relief of our suffering millions.'

Chamber address to Queen Victoria

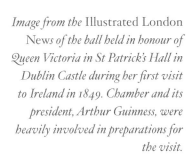

Image from the Illustrated London News *of the ball held in honour of Queen Victoria in St Patrick's Hall in Dublin Castle during her first visit to Ireland in 1849. Chamber and its president, Arthur Guinness, were heavily involved in preparations for the visit.*

Courtesy of the National Library of Ireland

people, who received us with the greatest enthusiasm,' but also, 'You see more ragged and wretched people here than I ever saw anywhere else.' The famine had left its mark.

After the Queen's visit the government proposed that the position of Lord Lieutenant be abolished. This was the last remnant of Irish independence of the English parliament as the Irish Office was run from London and its Chief Secretary spent most of his time there. Chamber lobbied extensively against the proposal, sending a deputation to London to meet the prime minister, Lord John Russell, who, the deputation noted, 'was the head of a school of politicians who always admitted the undeniable fact that Ireland had been the victim of misrule which had destroyed the energy and enterprise of her people, while England on the contrary had been nurtured by good government.' Russell promised to reconsider the issue and the proposal was scrapped shortly afterwards.

The Magnetic Telegraph Company

The Electric Telegraph Company, established in London in 1845, grew rapidly throughout England and Scotland. In Ireland Johnston & Company, newsagents and agents for the Electric Telegraph Company, received telegraphic intelligence by mail boat from Liverpool and, from 1848, supplied it to Chamber for a fee of £50 per annum.

In 1852 the (English and Irish) Magnetic Telegraph Company was established by charter, with an office in College Green, opposite Chamber, and the following year it laid cables across the Irish Sea via Scotland and lines along the railways in Ireland. From 1854 Chamber received its commercial intelligence directly from this company at a cost of £250 per annum. In 1857 the English & Irish merged with the British Telegraph and the company was renamed the British & Irish Magnetic Telegraph Company.

The Electric Telegraph Company, by then called the Electric & International Telegraph Company, finally entered the Irish market and in 1857 unsuccessfully solicited for Chamber's business. In 1870 the telegraph system became a state monopoly, although the information for which subscribers paid was still supplied by other companies, such as the Press Association, through the Post Office telegraph lines.

HONORARY SECRETARIES

Gradually the management and direction of Chamber were placed on the shoulders of the honorary secretaries and the first three appear to have been men of exemplary ability and industry. The first, Robert Roe (1788-1836), lived in 'Sans Souci', Monkstown and Fitzwilliam Square. He was a wine and commission merchant with Robert and Henry Roe of Temple Bar and 1 Crampton Row and a founding shareholder of the City of Dublin Steampacket Company. He was also on the board of the Bank of Ireland and a member of the Ouzel Galley Society from 1821. He was described as an 'indefatigable and intelligent Secretary' and served for thirteen years.

Charles Haliday (1789-1866) replaced Roe in 1834. His brother William had worked with his father-in-law, Finlay Alder, a timber and bark merchant on Arran Quay. When William died in 1812 Charles replaced him in the concern. He was a successful businessman, a JP and consul for Greece, a member of the Ballast Board from 1833 and the board of the Bank of Ireland from 1838. A voracious collector of books and particularly pamphlets of Irish interest, Haliday offered his resignation as secretary in 1848, after sixteen years, 'desirous of more leisure for other occupations, than the duties of that office permit me to enjoy'. One of his great interests was Viking Dublin and his book on the subject was published posthumously. He served as a vice-president of Chamber until his death. On his death his widow presented his collection of 35,000 pamphlets to the Royal Irish Academy, of which he was a member.

By permission of the Royal Irish Academy © RIA

Francis Augustine Codd (1808-67) replaced Haliday in 1848 and served as honorary secretary for nineteen years until his death. He was a Catholic and a partner with Edward Croker in Codd and Croker, corn and malt merchants of 52 Townsend Street and later 7 Fleet Street. He was on the boards of both the Commercial Buildings Company and the Corn Exchange Building Company and a Councillor for Royal Exchange Ward until 1860. He was described by a contemporary as 'a clever man on commercial and general subjects, spoke well and effectively' however 'his manner was exceedingly brusque, his temper not the most amiable, and his personal encounters in debate assumed a good deal of the gladiatorial style.'

The extended rail network improved postal communication within Ireland and when the new railway from Chester to Holyhead was finally completed with the construction of the Britannia Bridge over the Menai Straits in 1850, Chamber wrote to the Postmaster General seeking better postal communication with London. Unfortunately four bodies were involved in providing the service – the London & North Western Railway Company, the Chester & Holyhead Railway Company, the City of Dublin Steampacket Company and the Postmaster General – and it took years of negotiation to reach agreement with them all. In 1854 Chamber took a step into the world of early telecommunications when it agreed to pay the Magnetic Telegraph Company £250 annually for stock exchange, corn market and political and parliamentary news on a daily basis.

Arthur Guinness served as president until his death in 1855. He had suffered ill-health in his later years and several mentions in the minutes note his inability to attend due to infirmity. Other vice-presidents of this period, such as William P. Lunell and James Chambers – who held the office for twenty-two years – were also poor attendees. Interestingly, eight of the ten Chamber vice-presidents served with Arthur Guinness on the board of the Bank of Ireland and another, James Digges La Touche, had his own bank. Falling membership was the consequence of inactive leadership towards the end of the Guinness presidency and some Council meetings were postponed as they could not provide a quorum of four.

VI

CONSOLIDATION, 1856-81

*The short but brilliant course of prosperity, unsurpassed in rapidity and extent,
which marked the latter period of our history, has unhappily been arrested by
a succession of unfavourable harvests, which impoverished and depressed some
of the most valuable classes of our community, and assisted those allurements
which attracted emigration from every quarter of Europe.*

Chamber address to Lord Woodhouse
on his appointment as Lord Lieutenant, 1864

Arthur Guinness died in June 1855 and, perhaps out of deference, no AGM
was held in 1856. Thomas Crosthwait, one of the four vice-presidents, son of
Leland Crosthwait, who had preceded Guinness as president, was elected his
successor in 1857. Unlike Guinness he was regular in attendance at Council
meetings and for the previous decade had chaired many of the meetings as
vice-president.

*The first Dublin Chamber logo. The
erroneous foundation date of 1785
persisted until the 1920s.*

With each change of government a new Lord Lieutenant was appointed to
Dublin Castle. Generally the Lord Lieutenant remained for the duration of
the government but many Victorian administrations were brief. After Queen
Victoria's visit in 1849 it became the practice of the Council to present
an illuminated address of welcome to each incoming Lord Lieutenant. As
well as the usual fulsome expression of loyalty to the crown, Chamber used

timeline

the address as an opportunity to give its views on the state of commerce in Ireland and its aspirations for the period of the Lord Lieutenant's rule. An exception was Charles Howard, 7th Duke of Carlisle, who received no address on his second appointment as Lord Lieutenant in 1859. Howard, as Viscount Morpeth, had been a popular Chief Secretary, 1835-41, but his Whig politics were not popular with the Chamber.

In 1855 Lord Mounteagle, chairman of the Royal Commission on Decimal Coinage, wrote to Council about decimalisation. Council had some concerns about loss of value, particularly in relation to the small denominations, but did not reject the idea. French engineer Ferdinand de Lesseps spoke (in French) at the Council meeting in May 1857 about his proposed canal in the Isthmus of Suez. Lord Palmerston and the British government had rejected the scheme but Chamber was in favour of it as being good for commerce, assuming moderate rates of charges and impartiality of management.

William Neilson, solicitor to Chamber for the previous fifteen years, died in 1856 and David and Thomas Fitzgerald were appointed in his place, beginning the association with D. and T. Fitzgerald that would last for more than a century. In 1859 Chamber spent £62 covering the floor of the reading room with a new material, 'kamptulican', which replaced old reed mats. Kamptulican, which deadened noise, was made from powdered cork and natural rubber, decorated with a pattern and finished with linseed oil varnish. Plate glass was fitted to the windows, the expense of which necessitated Chamber taking out insurance for the first time.

In this period Chamber had particular concerns about transport. The Grand Canal Company had suffered serious losses since the arrival of the railway and was unable to repair its network, so it was proposed to sell the company to the Great Southern & Western and Midland Great Western Railway companies. Chamber, which had members representing the various interests, was inherently against all monopolies, but was obliged 'to consider this as one of those cases in which the abstract principle must yield to practical expediency' and decided not to oppose the bill authorising the amalgamation. The bill was eventually dropped as the committee dealing with it in the House of Lords considered that its promoters had failed to consider the public interest. The Grand Canal Company remained independent until the Transport Act of 1950, when it passed to CIÉ.

In general the Council avoided making any comments about politics or getting involved in world issues. The Crimean War of 1853-6 passed without a mention in the minutes. The American Civil War of 1861-5 did merit comment because of its effect on the economy of the United Kingdom, especially as a result of the so-called cotton famine in the Lancashire mills. The report for 1862 noted that the mercantile community's attention had 'been almost monopolised by the tragic events which have arrested the prosperity of America'.

The 1840 Municipal Corporations Act defined the extent of Dublin borough as being within the canals. Since the Act of Union many of the better-off citizens had left the fine Georgian buildings in the city for new houses constructed in a ribbon development outside the canals, primarily along the coast. Besides, there was little development space remaining within the city boundaries. The development of Kingstown after the construction of the harbour and the arrival of the railway accelerated the departure of the affluent classes from the city. Their old residences were converted into

1868
Completion of Vartry Waterworks and the end of canal water supply to Dublin.

1869
Disestablishment of the Church of Ireland.

1871
Dublin Corporation pledges itself to the Home Rule movement.

1872
First tramway begins operation in Dublin, from College Green to Rathmines and Rathgar.

Ballot Act introduces the secret ballot.

1874
Return of sixty Home Rule candidates in general election. Home Rule Party formed with Isaac Butt as chairman.

1877
Prime Minister, William Gladstone, visits Dublin and receives the freedom of the city.

1880

Royal University receives its
charter.

Use of boycott in County Mayo.

First telephone in Ireland.

1881

First land act allows tenants to
purchase farms.

1886

Defeat of first Home Rule Bill in
House of Commons.

tenements and their valuation dropped but the rates were increased to provide services. The residents outside the city saw the financial benefit of not being part of the borough rateable area and lobbied to create their own administrations. Kingstown was the first district council set up in 1838, followed by Rathmines in 1847, Blackrock in 1860 and Pembroke in 1863. When Chamber attempted to amend the Special Juries Act in 1862 it was reacting to this reality as so few eligible citizens remained to act as jurors and businessmen spent so much time on jury duty that it interfered with their work. Chamber proposed to lower the property requirement and its solicitor suggested that the pool of jurors could include the whole county of Dublin as 'this would render liable to serve as jurors a large class of well-qualified persons resident in Rathmines, Rathgar, Dundrum, Booterstown, Blackrock, Kingstown etc.' This was a live issue for a number of years.

From a low point at the end of the Guinness presidency, membership of Chamber increased, particularly after John Bagot's election as honorary secretary in May 1867, when numbers exceeded a thousand, nearly double those at the end of the Guinness presidency. John Bagot was a particularly efficient secretary. The nature of business in Dublin continued to change, as did the profile of Chamber's membership. At the beginning of the reconstituted Chamber many members were described simply as 'merchants' and in fact were wholesale import/export merchants, as Dublin was the country's main port for trade. As transport systems developed other ports opened up to imports and the focus of Dublin port changed to more local trade. Retail became important, having previously been considered socially inferior: John Bagot was the first retailer to act as president.

More of the professions began to be included. Solicitors, architects, engineers and accountants joined Chamber and banking and insurance were better represented. A large number of well-known Dublin businesses were established during this period – W. & R. Jacobs, Bewleys, Clerys (then McSwineys), Arnotts, Heitons – and their owners became major players in Chamber. The city did not have a strong manufacturing base with the exception of brewing and distilling, and these businesses, always well represented in Chamber, had become the major industries of the city. In 1865 Council looked into acquiring additional accommodation in Commercial Buildings and set up a committee to negotiate with the Commercial Buildings Company, many of whose directors were, of course, Council members. Two years later, after intense negotiations, amendments were approved involving additional accommodation with building works and furnishing amounting to £1000. The annual rent was increased to £310. The room previously occupied by the Underwriters' Association was added to the lease in 1874 for another £150 in rent and converted into a new reading room.

Many members of the Ballast Board were also Council members. The Board approached Council in late 1865 about proposed new charges necessary to raise £500,000 to develop the port and Council agreed not to oppose the Port Bill. But in January 1866 forty-three members with shipping interests requisitioned a general meeting to express their concern and Council appears to have withdrawn its support for the bill. Sixty-four members requisitioned a second meeting the following month, under the leadership of William Watson, director of the City of Dublin Steampacket Company, to keep up pressure on Council to act.

George William Frederick Howard, Viscount Morpeth, a popular chief secretary in Dublin, who received a roll signed by 160,000 people as a token of appreciation when he left that post.

Later, as the 7th Earl of Carlisle, he was twice Lord Lieutenant in Lord Palmerston's Whig governments, 1855-8 and 1859-64.

© National Portrait Gallery, London

This meeting raised the issue of a fairer representation of the interests of merchants on the Ballast Board, which agreed to form a mercantile committee to sanction increases in charges. As a result of these discussions, later in 1866 the Ballast Board proposed two new bills: the first was to give shipping and mercantile interests greater representation on the Board, the second to take the management of lighthouses from Dublin port and create a separate body for their management, the Commissioners of Irish Lights. The annual report for 1866 commented: 'The recent conflict of opinion between the merchants of Dublin and the Ballast Board, honourable alike to the independence and energy of the one party, and to the discretion and forbearance of the other, is too fresh in the recollection of Chamber to require more than a passing observation.' Discussions of the new bills continued for two years before the changes were passed in 1869.

Lawyers to Chamber

William Shannon, secretary to the first Chamber, was a notary public. The second secretary, Joseph Miller, was a lawyer. The revived Chamber did not initially use a lawyer but in 1823 Henry Staines (1775-1847), of 88 Abbey Street, acted for it in an unsuccessful attempt to get a charter. He continued to act on various issues until 1839, when Council expressed some dissatisfaction with his bills. After Staines, Chamber's preferred lawyer was William Neilson (1803-56), of 104 Middle Abbey Street.

When Neilson died suddenly early in 1856, Council decided to appoint official solicitors and chose D. & T. Fitzgerald of 2 Fleet Street. David (1812-76) and Thomas Fitzgerald (1820-1912) were brothers. Another brother, John David Fitzgerald, was a successful barrister (sometimes used by Chamber), judge and attorney general. D.& T. Fitzgerald also acted for the Commercial Buildings Company and was occasionally conflicted when issues arose between the two bodies. The firm moved to St Andrew's Street and by the turn of the century it was one of the most prominent in Dublin. It acted for Chamber for more than a hundred years and one of the firm's last actions on its behalf related to its move to Clare Street in 1964. The firm ceased to exist not long afterwards and Ivan Howe, its former partner, acted for the Chamber for the next few years.

The government began to run the telegraph service in February 1870 and within six months a special meeting was requisitioned that noted: 'In the opinion of this Chamber the management of the Telegraphic service in the country since it has been undertaken by the Post Office has been most inefficient.' Complaints included fitful and interrupted service, staff shortages and inadequacy of equipment. On behalf of Chamber, John Bagot entered into prolonged correspondence with the prime minister, William Ewart Gladstone, criticising the inactivity of the Postmaster General, the Marquess of Hartington, in dealing with Chamber complaints. (Obviously this inactivity was forgiven when in, 1887, Chamber presented an address to Hartington, who had become Lord Lieutenant in 1871, in support of his opposition to Gladstone's Home Rule Bill of 1886.)

The opening times of Chamber, particularly Sunday opening, began to be a bone of contention among members. From its establishment in Commercial Buildings in 1820, Chamber opened seven days a week. In 1863 a petition by some of the more evangelical members that Chamber close on Sunday was rejected. Opposing members resisted the encroachment of religion into the working of Chamber. Further petitions that Chamber should close on Sundays were voted down in 1900, 1904, 1908 and 1914. A recurring controversy with similar roots concerned the operation of a hostelry called the Bodega on Dame Street, which shared the main entrance to Commercial Buildings with Chamber and which aroused the opposition of members who belonged to the temperance movement.

David Fitzgerald, Chamber's law agent, raised the question of the organisation's legal standing when it presented petitions and motions to parliament. The honorary secretary, John Bagot, advocated that Chamber

Opening Hours

From 1828 Chamber was open 8am-5pm and again from 7pm-10pm and from 1851 open continuously. Sunday opening was 1pm-10pm. A clerk or porter was on the premises at all times: Chamber's single clerk must have had to work seven days a week until 1847, when Thomas Jameson retired and was replaced by two clerks.

There had been a complaint about 'the attendance, supervision and general management of Chamber and in the nature and arrangement of the books, papers and mercantile lists' and it was felt that 'Mr Jameson [was] no longer capable of discharging [his] duties.' Jameson died nine months later: poor health must have affected his work.

Closing time was partially due to late closing prices coming from London. Repeated proposals gradually led to restrictions on Sunday opening. From 1915 the rooms no longer opened on bank holidays and in 1918 they closed at 6pm to save on lighting due to war shortages, a decision that was never reversed. First Sunday and then Saturday closing came to pass.

John Bagot (1811-87)

John Bagot joined Dublin Chamber in 1832, about the time he began his business, a tea and wine merchants called Bagots Hutton in South William Street. He was also a member of Dublin Port and Docks Board, a director of Dublin Savings Bank and the Dublin Artisans Dwelling Company and auditor of the City of Dublin Brewing Company in Blackpitts.

In Council minutes he is first reported as agitating for reform of duty on spirits on behalf of the Spirit Grocers' and Tea Dealers' Association, of which he was president in 1846. Elected to Council in 1863, he was selected as honorary secretary after the death of Francis Codd in 1867. Chamber President William Digges La Touche stepped down in 1882 and Bagot served as president for three years. He appears to have been an efficient man, under whose direction Chamber was incorporated and membership reached its highest level for the 19th century.

Bagot lived in Clontarf. He was married twice and died at home of 'gout of the stomach'. In his obituary the *Nation* described him as 'a thorough going West Briton. He is a lover of the English connection.' Nevertheless, he produced a pamphlet entitled 'An Essay on Parliamentary Reform' in 1881, questioning the 'existing Parliamentary system operating in regard to Ireland'. After various amalgamations and takeovers, the firm of Bagots Hutton Kinahan went into voluntary liquidation in 1982.

Ferdinand de Lesseps (1805-1894), who spoke at a Council meeting in May 1857 about his proposed canal in the Isthmus of Suez, an idea of which Chamber members approved.

either become incorporated or obtain a charter and his was a very influential voice, as illustrated by Council's decision not to hold an AGM in 1873 when Bagot was confined to bed by a leg injury and unavailable to attend. Eventually Chamber was incorporated and the Board of Trade approved its new rules in 1878. Henceforth there would be only one vice-president and Council would include twenty-seven members of Chamber, nine of whom were elected each year for three years, as well as the Lord Mayor and high sheriff and the MPs for Dublin. Council members who missed five meetings without approval would lose their seat. John Bagot, the honorary secretary, and William Digges La Touche, who had succeeded Thomas Crosthwait as president when Crosthwait died in 1870, were re-elected to their posts and Patrick Sweetman (1803-85), a brewery owner, was elected vice-president.

PUBLIC TRANSPORT IN DUBLIN

Before the introduction of trams, public transport had been provided by private companies such as Wilson Omnibus Company, which ran six omnibuses under the 'Favourite' name, one leaving the city centre hourly for Terenure. A well-documented tragedy occurred in December 1861 when the horses stopped at the incline of Portobello Bridge and the omnibus rolled back, toppled and plunged into Portobello lock, drowning the six passengers.

Dublin Tramways Company opened the first tramway in 1872, running from College Green to Rathgar via Dawson Street, Harcourt Street and Rathmines. A pair of horses drew each tram on a track and the journey, a distance of four kilometres, took twenty minutes. The route was soon extended to Nelson's Column in Sackville Street, which became the central terminus. William Barrington set up the North Dublin Street Tramway Company in 1876, and a third company, the Dublin Central Tramways Company, was incorporated in 1878. Its directors included the Cork builder and railway contractor William Martin Murphy and his father-in-law James Fitzgerald Lombard. These three businesses amalgamated, the resulting Dublin United Tramways Company (DUTC) dominated by Murphy and Lombard, while Barrington emigrated to the US.

Werner von Siemens invented the electric tram in 1879 (his first tram ran near Berlin) and J. Clifton Robertson, engineer and managing director of the Dublin Southern Districts Tramways Company, electrified a line from Haddington Road to Dalkey in 1896. William Martin Murphy was not initially a supporter of electrification but later, realising its potential, he bought out the DSDC and began electrification of the DUTC lines. Although Dublin corporation was opposed to overhead wiring, its objections were overcome and the entire system electrified by 1901.

In 1923 buses began to compete with trams and the DUTC acquired the right to operate its own bus system in 1924, taking over twenty-five private bus companies in the next decade. The company gradually ceased tram operations and the last tram, to Blackrock depot, ran in 1949. In 1944 the government amalgamated the DUTC with the nationalised Great Southern Railways to form CIÉ.

Courtesy of the National Library of Ireland

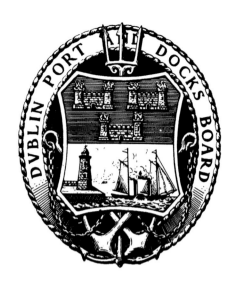

Men of business always had an interest in public transport, an area in which there was much development in the second half of the 19th century. Horse-drawn omnibuses, which had operated for many decades in Paris, arrived in Dublin. In 1858 a hackney from the centre of the city to Rathmines cost a shilling, while the omnibus cost threepence. Birkenhead, near Liverpool, was the first town in the UK to have horse-drawn trams on a rail system, a much smoother and more comfortable means of conveyance than omnibuses on cobblestones. In 1861 the appropriately named George Train proposed a tramway in Dublin but it was ten years before the Dublin Tramways Company Act was passed, supported by Chamber. The first tramway began operation on 1 February 1872, running from College Green, convenient to Chamber premises, to Terenure. Quaker businessmen were prominent among the early tram developers, as they had been with the railways. Chamber also supported an unsuccessful Dublin City Junction Bill, an attempt to link the various railway termini in Dublin, in 1873. Tramways and increased commercial traffic led to traffic congestion in the city and the corporation introduced the Dublin Traffic Regulation Bill in 1876, with much lobbying for Chamber support.

After Dublin Corporation was reformed in 1849, there was a period of relative harmony between the two bodies and several members of Chamber were elected to the corporation. Unionists and Liberal nationalists reached an informal agreement to rotate the mayoralty, an arrangement that remained in place until 1882. But Chamber vigorously opposed a number of bills raised by the corporation that would allow it to take control of the markets and the gas companies, effectively giving it a monopoly. The corporation became more nationalist as the franchise was extended, many of those elected being tenement landlords, publicans and small traders, while Chamber's natural constituency was the larger businesses and professions.

The Ballast Board, renamed the Dublin Port and Docks Board, under its reconstitution bill of 1869, sought to extend its remit to Howth. Chamber members with a shipping interest formed a committee to meet the board to discuss the bill, which they viewed positively, and agree some modifications. Council had clearly not learned from its previous experience with members on the subject of the Ballast Board and was surprised when five members resigned in protest at its next meeting, strongly opposing the bill. Council rescinded its support and agreed to resist the bill, so the five withdrew their resignation. The act that was eventually agreed provided the board

Anthony O'Curry (1797-1881)

When Robert Heron, one of the two clerks to the chamber, was seconded to the committee set up in 1850 to fight the Dublin Improvement Act, instead of the usual advertisement and interview for a temporary replacement, Anthony Curry was appointed 'after a full inquiry' and paid a guinea a week (he was not called O'Curry in Chamber until 1868).

Anthony O'Curry was born in County Clare, the younger brother of Eugene O'Curry, who worked with John O'Donovan and George Petrie on the Ordnance Survey. He too was a scribe of ancient Irish manuscripts and his brother got him work with the Ordnance Survey. His appointment to the post with Chamber was probably due to vice-president Charles Haliday, a friend of George Petrie and a member of the Royal Irish Academy, where Eugene worked after leaving the Ordnance Survey. When

Eugene O'Curry died, Haliday approached Anthony, his brother's executor, with a view to buying Eugene's archive for the Royal Irish Academy, to discover that he had been beaten to it by the Catholic University.

O'Curry served the Chamber well and retired in 1878 due to ill-health. Council generously voted him a pension of £100 per annum (his salary was £120 at the time he retired). He died on 4 August 1881 in his home, 108 Amiens Street, leaving his wife and three daughters in straitened circumstances. The pension died with him but Council agreed to contribute £10 to the public collection made for him through the *Freeman's Journal*, which described him thus: 'as librarian and curator of the Commercial Buildings' Newsroom, Dame Street; his genial and obliging disposition made him very popular.'

THE ASSOCIATION OF CHAMBERS OF COMMERCE

Ten chambers, Belfast Chamber and nine in England, founded the ACC in 1860. Initially none of the larger cities was represented, and while over the next ten years the majority of smaller Chambers joined, a number of major ones did not do so. In its early years the association's secretary, based in London, was part-time. Robert Bennett described its role – 'to collect information, transmit it to chambers at cost price, and to assist local chambers in gaining interviews with MPs, officials, etc' – so that the benefits of membership were greater for smaller chambers.

The ACC's early years were fraught with conflict over its role and priorities: its strength was its relationship with politicians. All its presidents, 1860-1912, were MPs or members of the House of Lords and local MPs received honorary membership, all of which facilitated its access to parliament. Dublin Chamber agreed to join the ACC in December 1869 at a subscription of five guineas and the other Irish chambers followed suit.

London Chamber of Commerce reformed in 1882 and joined the ACC, initiating a reorganisation. A full-time secretary was employed from 1888. In 1919 the organisation changed its name to the Association of British Chambers of Commerce (ABCC). Dublin Chamber normally sent delegates to the AGM, which was held in London about March of each year. There was also an autumn meeting, generally in a provincial centre, and this was held in Dublin in 1891 and in 1911. After the establishment of the Irish Free State in 1923 Dublin Chamber, along with the other southern Chambers, withdrew from the ABCC.

with additional borrowing powers for works to the docks but the Local Government Board was to do the audit rather than the Port and Docks Board's own auditors. The Vernon estate opposed the extension of the docks to Clontarf and succeeded by amendment to the bill in keeping them a thousand feet away.

Although Chamber claimed to be non-political, its unionist orientation became more obvious once Home Rule became a live issue on the political agenda. Gladstone's first Home Rule Bill of 1886 was easily defeated in the House of Commons but the Irish Party under Charles Stewart Parnell, committed to achieving Home Rule, subsequently held the balance of power there. The decades of Parnell's domination of Irish politics were a period of uncertainty and instability for Chamber.

In 1881 William Digges La Touche served his last year as president. When he resigned the honorary secretary, John Bagot, replaced him. La Touche died in 1882. He had been a director of the Munster Bank which collapsed due to fraud by one of its managers and high borrowings by its directors. The bank was resurrected as the Munster & Leinster Bank by one of the directors, the Cork brewer J.J. Murphy, and in time all the creditors were repaid.

William Ewart Gladstone (1809-95), four times Liberal Prime Minister, 1868-94. His introduction of two Home Rule bills for Ireland was a cause of concern for Chamber members.
© National Portrait Gallery London

VII

AGAINST THE TIDE, 1882-1902

The Council feel themselves imperatively called on, at the present crisis, to declare their opinion that any measure calculated to weaken the union at present existing between Great Britain and Ireland would be productive of consequences most disastrous to the trading and commercial interests of both countries.

Chamber of Commerce petition against
the Government of Ireland (Home Rule) Bill, 1886

For the first seven decades of the 19th century Dublin MPs served the city's merchants well because, in the limited franchise of the time, they were the main electorate. But Irish politics were changing. The Irish Party under Charles Stewart Parnell was more concerned with agitating for Home Rule and land reform than with commercial issues. From 1884 the number of MPs for Dublin doubled to four, with a fifth representing Trinity College, but the focus of attention of these politicians was increasingly their nationalist electoral base rather than merchants and traders. Dublin Chamber of Commerce, while claiming to have no political bias, declared itself to be a loyal and unionist organisation and as the support of nationalist MPs and corporation members was lost to the unionist population of Dublin it turned to Chamber as its 'de facto' representative to agitate for its concerns. Chamber might have fractured during this period and it is a testament to

Book listing the attendance at the Unionist Convention for Ireland (excluding Ulster), held in Dublin, 23 June 1892.

timeline

the skill of its leadership that it managed to walk the tightrope between the two sides of the national debate. Cork Chamber of Commerce, founded in 1820, split because Charles Stewart Parnell was annually re-elected president of the organisation, a reflection of its nationalist majority, and members opposed to Parnell founded the Incorporated Cork Chamber of Commerce and Shipping in 1883. The two Cork chambers did not reunite until 1952.

During the presidency of John Bagot, membership of Dublin Chamber rose to a high of 1215. At this time John Richardson Wigham began his twelve-year term as honorary secretary. Wigham, a unionist, a successful engineer, designer of a new system for the lighting of lighthouses and a leading member of the RDS and British Association for Science, was equally efficient in his work for Chamber. After William Digges La Touche, presidents served for three years and, as with Dublin Corporation, there appears to have been an effort to alternate the presidency between Protestants of various denominations and Catholics, although this did not mean any weakening in Council's unionist leanings. If a new Council member was coopted he tended to be of the same religion as the man he succeeded.

A Council meeting was cancelled after the murder of the Chief Secretary and Under-secretary in 1882 – the 'Phoenix Park murders' – 'in view of the terrible event which occurred on Saturday evening last, viz, the barbarous murder of Lord Frederick Cavendish, Secretary to the Lord Lieutenant and Mr Thomas H. Burke, Under Secretary'. One hundred and fifty members called for a special general meeting 'in order that an opportunity may be afforded to give expression to the feelings of unbounded horror at the atrocious outrage perpetrated yesterday evening in the foul assassination of the chief secretary and the under-secretary for Ireland.' Richard Martin,

Chamber vice-president, presented an address expressing the sentiments of the meeting to the Lord Lieutenant, Earl Spencer, in Dublin Castle.

Telecommunications were among the technological advances of the late 19th century. The telephone arrived in Ireland in 1880 and two years later Chamber applied to the National Telephone Company for an instrument and cabinet in the members' reading room. This innovation proved to be a bone of contention, as the Bodega continued to be. Walter Brown and William Wallace, both Methodists and supporters of the temperance movement, called on Council in 1883 'to use its best endeavours to free Chamber from the evil influences caused thereby' (apparently members spent too much time drinking in the Bodega before attending Chamber meetings). At the AGM the following January, when Council informed members that the Commercial Buildings Company could do nothing under the terms of the Bodega's lease, Thomas Wallace Russell proposed that Chamber should move premises. His proposal was defeated by 133 votes to 51. Eventually the Bodega got its own entrance by making a door out of the window to the right of the main entrance.

The question of the speeding up of the postal service remained to the fore in Council's deliberations. Little had changed since the completion of the rail and sea link in the 1850s. In 1884 the post office was due to enter into a new contract for the transport of mails from Holyhead to Kingstown. Council raised the concern that the tender made no reference to the specifications of the vessels to be used and lobbied the government and the Postmaster General in London to ensure that the provider would be required to use better and faster ships. When the contract came up for renewal again in 1896 Chamber redoubled its efforts, again organising deputations to the

1890
Opening of National Library and National Museum.

1891
Opening of Loopline Bridge.

Death of Parnell.

1892
Opening of first corporation electricity station in Fleet Street.

1893
Defeat of Gladstone's second Home Rule Bill in the House of Lords.

1894
First meeting of Irish Trade Union Congress.

1896
First film screening in Dublin.

Electric tramways begin from Haddington Road to Dalkey.

1898
Local Government Bill.

Registration Act gives women a vote in local elections.

THE CHAMBER AND THE TELEPHONE COMPANY

The first telephone company in England was set up in 1879. The Post Office had owned the telegraph company since 1870 and wanted to have a slice of the telephone business but did not have the money to invest in it. They managed to convince the courts that they were entitled to a licensing fee, and a charge of 10% of the profits was levied.

The United Telephone Company began business in Ireland in 1880, setting up a switchboard on the top floor of Commercial Buildings, initially with five subscribers. Due to lack of activity the boy employed to operate the switchboard was found playing marbles in the courtyard and dismissed. The staff in 1881 consisted of a lady operator, three clerks and a manager. The number of subscribers had quadrupled to twenty and the company provided service from 9am to midnight.

In 1882 the Telephone Company of Ireland took over from the United Telephone Company and William Fereday Bottomley (1842-91), a forty-year-old Mancunian electrical engineer, was installed as manager (or secretary as he was titled). In April of that year Council decided to instal a telephone in the reading room for the use of members. At this time there were two hundred and seventy subscribers and Chamber was allocated the phone number 56. The phone company charged an annual fee of £12 for unlimited service. So popular did the telephone prove that, in 1886, when the contract came up for renewal the company was willing, for the annual fee of £12, to provide free calls only to Chamber members who were subscribers, all others to pay for their calls. It recommended that two instruments be provided, one for subscribers and the other for non subscribers. Alternatively Chamber could pay £60 for free access for all. According to Bottomley, calls from the reading room were numerous and half were made by non-subscribers, 'some of

them having offices in the immediate neighbourhood of the Commercial Buildings'. Furthermore, he noted: 'The Council must be aware that the instrument…is much used at present – very often for frivolous purposes – by persons who really should have no right to use it, to the delay and inconvenience of those who have.'

Council accepted the first offer but the members protested, in particular with regard to the division of the membership into two classes. Council was advised by its law agent, D.& T. Fitzgerald, that as offer and acceptance existed it was in a contract with the telephone company. The members refused the arrangement and the following year Council asked the telephone company to remove the apparatus.

Clearly this position was untenable and after nine months, Council approached the telephone company to ask that the phones be reinstalled. The Telephone Company of Ireland now had 1300 subscribers and Chamber's new phone numbers were 2575 and 2576.

The National Telephone Company took over from the Telephone Company of Ireland in 1893 and in 1905 the Post Office, which was suffering losses to its telegraph business because of the arrival of the telephone, announced its intention of taking over the telephone companies in 1912. This came to pass after six years of a deteriorating phone service as a result of lack of investment by the phone companies.

THE
Telephone Company of Ireland,
LIMITED.

Lord Lieutenant and the Postmaster General and forming a joint mails committee in Commercial Buildings in conjunction with the RDS and Dublin Corporation.

The postal service would also benefit from the interconnection of the Dublin termini of various railway companies, which would facilitate more rapid distribution of mail throughout the country. Two proposals were presented to parliament: the first, known as the Loopline, was to connect the Northern Line in Amiens Street (now Connolly Station) with the Dublin, Wicklow & Wexford Railway Company station in Westland Row (now Pearse Station); the second, the City of Dublin Grand Junction Bill, would see the connection of the DW&WR Company station in Sydney Parade with the Great Southern & Western Railway company near Kingsbridge (now Heuston) Station, a more difficult route. Dublin Corporation objected strenuously to the proposed Loopline Bridge as it interfered with the view of the Custom House – an objection that has validity to this day – but Chamber support for it extended to sending the honorary secretary, J.R. Wigham, to London to attend the House of Lords committee that was considering the matter. The Loopline received approval but it took a number of years for the companies involved to reach agreement. In 1890, Wigham announced that, on behalf of Chamber, he had travelled from Kingstown to Amiens Street on the new Loopline in thirteen minutes, although the line did not come fully into use until 1895. Newcomen Bridge over the Royal Canal near the North Strand, which opened in 1892, connected the Loopline with the Midland Great Western and the Great Southern Railway Companies.

Council minutes of the period often contain brief resolutions that mask larger issues. Carlisle Bridge had been widened in 1879 to accommodate

1899
Outbreak of Boer War.

Establishment of Department of Agriculture and Technical Instruction for Ireland.

1900
Queen Victoria visits Dublin for the last time.

heavy traffic and William Watson, director of the City of Dublin Steampacket Company, and other members of Chamber had objected to the erection of a statue of Daniel O'Connell in Sackville Street in 1880, claiming that the base was so large that it would interfere with traffic. (They did agree that 'honour should be paid to the memory of an illustrious Irishman'.) As a result the base was reduced from 40ft to 32ft. In 1884 the corporation proposed renaming some of the city's streets and set up a committee to look at proposals (in the end only one name was suggested, Sackville Street to O'Connell Street). The following year the proposal to rename Sackville Street came before Council, which passed a resolution 'that it is the opinion of this Council that the project of renaming the streets of Dublin would, if carried into effect, be most injurious to the interests of the trading and commercial classes, and to the community in general, and that it would create a vast amount of commercial and postal confusion and inconvenience'. The objectors took the issue to court before Vice-Chancellor Chatterton, who ruled against the name change. In revenge the corporation renamed Lower Temple Street, in a disreputable part of the city, Chatterton Street. The names Sackville and O'Connell co-existed until the street was officially renamed after independence, with the majority of the population, now nationalist, adopting the name of the 'illustrious Irishman'.

Chamber again found itself at odds with Dublin Corporation when, in 1885, the Prince and Princess of Wales, the future Edward

VII and Alexandra, visited the city. Council noted that 'the announcement of the intended visit of the Prince and Princess of Wales to Dublin has been received with the most heartfelt pleasure and satisfaction by the members of the Dublin Chamber of Commerce.' Five hundred and thirty-four members, nearly half the membership at the time, signed a requisition that an address of welcome be presented to the visitors and that a citizens' committee be formed to organise a fitting reception as the corporation had refused to do so. Chamber president, Richard Martin, presented the address but his speech was not entirely positive: '...while we must admit that the outlook in this country is in some respects disheartening, we sincerely hope that the gloom at present existing is the "dark before the dawn"; and we earnestly pray that your Royal Highnesses may on your next visit witness a more prosperous and more contented Ireland.' At the time the country was in a state of economic depression. Martin was made a baronet for his efforts.

The flight of the better off and the middle classes from the city to the new suburbs gained momentum as the century progressed, encouraged by the arrival of the railway and tramway. Initially the railway line facilitated development along the coast south of Dublin, much of it a ribbon of villas. The tramways generally tended to provide services to established suburbs rather than initiate development in green-field areas. Most of those leaving the city for the suburbs favoured the adjoining townships of Rathmines and Pembroke, which accounted for 50 per cent of the population living outside the city boundaries, while 30 per cent lived in the coastal townships and Kingstown. Rathmines maintained a very low rate of two shillings in the pound. As a result rates in the city increased. Although their businesses were in the city, many Chamber members lived in the suburbs and the issue of rates was of lively concern to them. The corporation realised that the

Richard Martin (1831-1901)

A member of the shipping and timber importing family, Martin went to Canada and Scandinavia as a young man to learn the timber business, then worked in the family firm. With the backing of his father-in-law, Sir Dominic Corrigan, the Queen's Physician in Ireland, he began business under his own name in 33 Sir John Rogerson's Quay in 1864.

Martin became very wealthy, one of the biggest importers and ship-owners in Dublin and the holder of many directorships, including becoming deputy-chairman of the Royal Bank of Ireland, the first Catholic to hold the post. A unionist and deputy-lieutenant for Dublin, he was made a baronet in 1885 after the royal visit of that year. In 1893 he was a member of an anti-Home Rule crusade to London.

extension of city boundaries was its best option to increase valuation, by raising the rates of the outlying areas and reducing those of the city proper, but Chamber strongly opposed the corporation's efforts, particularly in relation to the wealthy townships of Rathmines and Pembroke.

The Royal Commission on Municipal Boundaries visited Dublin in 1879 and found in favour of the corporation, declaring that the townships were in fact suburbs, but the corporation did not have the funds to act on the recommendation and propose a bill. Meanwhile the Lord Lieutenant stalled calls for boundary revision by requiring that the city first be revalued, a step the corporation opposed: it now included many publicans and tenement landlords who feared revaluation because when a similar process had been carried out in England the value of public houses tripled. Belfast expanded to include its suburbs in 1891, technically becoming the largest city in Ireland, and finally, in 1898, the House of Commons passed the Dublin Municipal Boundaries Bill, despite objections by the townships. But the House of Lords amended the bill so that the only new inclusion in the city was working-class Kilmainham. Negotiations with the House of Lords resulted in the absorption of the townships of Drumcondra and Clontarf, to the north of the city, as these were limited in size and unable to fund their own sewage and water services. Rathmines and Pembroke held out until 1930, remaining a bastion of unionism. By the turn of the century the corporation had lost interest in further expanding the city boundaries.

Basically, as historian Mary Daly writes: 'Dublin local politics was grounded in sectional interests. Loyalty to either nationalism or unionism, class or creed took priority over the welfare of the city or its people.'

After the 1849 Improvement Act Chamber was initially satisfied with Dublin Corporation but as the century progressed, found that body becoming more and more nationalist. It behaved more like the representative parliament Ireland did not have than a local government body, readily debating national political issues while the city slid steadily into decline. Representatives of the minority unionist population, which now included Dublin Chamber of Commerce, opposed, almost reflexively, every attempt of the corporation to amend legislation, facilitate extra borrowing or carry out major infrastructural works such as drainage or water schemes.

Lord Mayor Edmund Dwyer Gray, a Protestant nationalist, MP for Dublin, pioneer in public health and owner of the *Freeman's Journal* – himself a member of Chamber – was critical of the organisation for its repeated interference in municipal affairs, observing: 'Whenever the corporation proposes any large schemes, there starts up an amount of opposition to it which very frequently paralyses to a considerable extent the power of the corporation. The Chamber of Commerce and amateur bodies which call themselves citizens' committees, and so on, start up and represent themselves as citizens of Dublin.'

The electorate of Dublin had tripled as a result of the 1884 Representation of the People Act, while the Reform Act of 1885 doubled the city representation from two to four MPs. The Registration Act of 1898 included women in the

Contemporary image from Le Monde *of the murder in the Phoenix Park on 6 May 1882 of the newly-appointed Chief Secretary, Lord Frederick Cavendish, and his permanent Under-secretary, Thomas Henry Burke, who had been a regular correspondent of Chamber.*

Chamber called a general meeting the following day to 'give expression to the feelings of unbounded horror at the atrocious outrage perpetrated yesterday'.

Courtesy of the National Library of Ireland

Frank Leah's cartoon of William Field. A butcher from Blackrock, Field was a nationalist MP for Dublin, St Patrick's Division, 1892-1918. He was twice blackballed before being elected a member of Chamber in 1892.

Field attended Council frequently as an ex-officio member by virtue of being an MP and was a very active spokesman for Chamber in Westminster.

electorate for municipal government for the first time. The result of all these changes was an increase in nationalist representation but the more nationalist the corporation became the more unionist Chamber appeared to be.

Council consisted of twenty-seven elected members and six ex-officio members: the Lord Mayor, high sheriff and four city MPs, all or almost all of whom would have been nationalist at this time. In 1889 a motion to exclude the ex-officio members from Council was proposed at the AGM. The Lord Mayor, Thomas Sexton (1848-1932), and William Martin Murphy, MP for St Patrick's Division, led the objections in the newspapers and the motion failed. Murphy's successor as Irish Party MP was William Field (1843-1935), a butcher from Blackrock, who was blackballed for membership twice in 1892 and eventually elected on his third attempt in 1893. Often contrarian to Council or majority opinion, Field was, however, Chamber's most active representative in parliament. He incurred the wrath of the unionist honorary secretary, John R. Wigham, for reporting events in Council to the *Freeman's Journal*, contrary to Wigham's 'official' account. Thirty-five applicants were blackballed between 1868 and 1894, many for political reasons, although some were elected on subsequent ballots. At the 1896 AGM it was noted that some selective blackballing at the membership ballots had led to the high sheriff, Joseph Hutchinson, being refused twice.

Chamber continued to present addresses to incoming Lord Lieutenants: one exception was Robert Offley Ashburton Crew-Milnes, 2nd Baron Houghton, a Liberal appointee of Prime Minister William Gladstone in 1892. He refused an address from Chamber as well as from the Methodists, as they had expressed a firm belief in the necessity of maintaining the Union.

William Field MP and Henry Joseph Gill, the high sheriff, proposed in Council that Chamber should remove the reference to the Union and make the address acceptable to the recipient but their proposal was defeated. Dublin Corporation had voted against giving Houghton an address. On his death in 1922 *The Irish Times* rather pointedly noted that 'socially, the Viceroyalty was a failure'. At Dublin Castle functions polite society shunned Lord Aberdeen, a later Liberal viceroy who was friendly to nationalists. Chamber clung to the necessity of maintaining the union as the 19th century drew to a close.

A Chamber member was accused of using insulting and abusive language to another at the AGM of February 1888. To compound matters the dispute was taken before a police magistrate, who refused to act as he deemed that the alleged offence had occurred in a private place. A special meeting was called to amend the rules to allow the removal of a member for 'conduct unbecoming'.

A sense that Chamber was no more than a gentleman's private club persisted among some of the members, including solicitor William Thomas Daniel, who used it as a poste restante for his letters and telegrams, much to the annoyance of Council. In the manner of a gentleman's club, Chamber continued to provide daily newspapers and a telegraph service for members, although a subcommittee set up to investigate the matter in 1889, with a view to making savings, reported that: 'State of the odds and sporting telegrams to the commercial reading room seems to us an unreasonable expenditure. Perhaps, as we are not sporting men, we may be prejudiced.' Council decided to maintain the provision of sporting intelligence. Another result of this investigation was the decision to present to the National Library copies of

William Thomas Daniel (1826-1910)

Daniel, a Catholic solicitor, practised in 88 Lower Leeson Street. He first came to notice as the leading objector to the proposed Sunday closing of Chamber in 1883 and again in 1904, when he threatened to sue Chamber for loss if it went ahead with the proposal. Chamber declined the challenge and kept the Sunday opening.

Daniel treated Chamber with similar insouciance in 1889 when Council rebuked him for using the reading room as a poste restante address, asking to be sent a copy of the rules and regulations in order to ascertain which rule he might have broken. When this was done he again prevaricated and questioned whether the Board of Trade had approved of them. Finally he agreed a date to attend Council but just before the appointed time he sent a letter from the Raven Hotel in Droitwich, a spa town in Worcestershire, claiming that he was in Droitwich on the advice of his doctor and unable to attend the meeting. The matter ended there.

Abraham Shackleton (1827-1912) of Shackleton's Flour Mills, Lucan, was a frequent contributor to Chamber meetings from the floor and something of a contrarian.

Described as 'a convinced nationalist and Home Ruler' and willing to state his views openly when they were distinctly unpopular, Shackleton was upright, religious and liberal. He was the uncle of the explorer Ernest Shackleton.

Shackleton ran twice for Council in the 1880s to ensure that there was a vote for the position.

newspapers fastidiously bound by Chamber over the previous seventy years.

Dublin Chamber took a keen part in the (British) Association of Chambers of Commerce after joining in 1870. The common agenda included the need for commercial education, something Dublin Chamber wholeheartedly supported. At the association's general meeting in 1891 Dublin Chamber's resolution that commercial education should extend to girls as well as boys was passed. The ACC autumn general meeting was held in Dublin that October. A subscription list in Dublin Chamber raised £1500, including a contribution of £500 from the president, the ship owner Michael Murphy. Meetings were held in the Royal University in Earlsfort Terrace, while entertainment included a *conversazione* ('meet and greet' in modern parlance) in the newly opened National Museum, a trip to Powerscourt and a banquet hosted by Michael Murphy in Leinster Hall on Hawkins Street.

An application to increase the membership subscription from thirty shillings to £2 was not passed until 1892, although proposed a decade earlier. It was by then necessitated by falling membership. Electric light arrived in the reading room in 1893. In the first year of the new century, Council asked retiring presidents to provide a signed portrait, beginning a collection that was hung in Council's rooms and included presidents back to William Digges La Touche; alas it has long since been lost.

Home Rule reappeared on the political agenda of the Liberal government and the Unionist Alliance organised a convention in Dublin in June 1892.

THE UNIONIST CONVENTION

Thirteen Council members attended the 'Unionist Convention for the Provinces of Leinster, Munster & Connaught' in June 1892:

Name	Business/profession	Business Address	Denomination
Edmund J. Figgis	Corn merchant	Dartry Road	Plymouth Brethren
William Findlater	Solicitor	Fitzwilliam Square	Presbyterian
Marcus Goodbody	Tobacco manufacturer	Blackrock	Quaker
John Malcolm Inglis	Iron and coal merchant	Donnybrook	Presbyterian
John Jameson Junior	Distiller	Malahide	Church of Ireland
Edward Hudson Kinahan	Wine and spirit merchant	Merrion Square	Church of Ireland
Charles E. Martin	Timber merchant	Fitzwilliam Place	Roman Catholic
Richard Martin	Timber merchant	Merrion Square	Roman Catholic
Thomas Pim	Railway director	Glenageary	Quaker
James Talbot Power	Distiller	Leopardstown	Roman Catholic
William Robertson	Banker (Bank of Ireland)	Roebuck	Church of Ireland
William Watson	Ship owner	Fitzwilliam Place	Church of Ireland
John R. Wigham	Hardware merchant	Blackrock	Quaker

The following fourteen Council members did not attend the Unionist Convention:

Name	Business/profession	Business Address	Denomination
John E. Barry	Corn and malt factor	Mountjoy Square	Roman Catholic
John Lloyd Blood	Brewery manager	Monkstown	Church of Ireland
David Drummond	Seed merchant	Orwell Road	Presbyterian
Edward M. Hodgson	Merchant	Dartry Road	Church of Ireland
Thomas Maxwell Hutton	Coachworks proprietor	Summerhill	Unitarian
Thomas S. McCann	Barrister	Lower Leeson Street	Roman Catholic
Andrew McCullogh	Wine merchant	Bray	Presbyterian (?)
John McEvoy	Soap and candle maker	Baggot Street	Roman Catholic
Marcus T. Moses	Tea merchant	Bray	Church of Ireland
Michael Murphy	Ship owner	Merrion Square	Roman Catholic
Thomas A. O'Farrell	Corn merchant	Lansdowne Road	Roman Catholic
Frederic W. Pim	Linen manufacturer	Blackrock	Quaker
George Smyth	Stockbroker	1-2 College Green	Church of Ireland (?)
A. William Wallis	Salesmaster	Blackrock	Church of Ireland

John Wigham sent an address on behalf of Chamber: '...as a corporate body we have no politics, yet we are essentially a unionist Chamber – not for any political end, not for any party purposes – but solely and simply because in defending the union but we are defending the commercial interests with which we are identified...we are threatened by such dangers to our trade as the proposals of Mr Gladstone or the separatist policy of the so-called Nationalist party.' Council minutes contain no mention of the address being discussed but half its members attended the convention, not including the president or the vice-president, Thomas Maxwell Hutton. In February 1893 Council discussed Gladstone's second Home Rule Bill and strongly opposed it: this was the Bill passed by the House of Commons but voted down by the Lords.

Michael Murphy died the week before the 1893 AGM and John R. Wigham replaced him after twelve years as honorary secretary. John Malcolm Inglis was secretary for the term of Wigham's presidency. With Wigham, who was strongly unionist, at the helm at a time of increasing support for Home Rule, Chamber saw its greatest drop in membership, by one-third from its

John Richardson Wigham (1829-1906)

Wigham, who served as honorary secretary and later as president of Chamber, was born in Edinburgh and came to Dublin at the age of fourteen as an apprentice to Joshua Edmundson, a hardware merchant in Capel Street who was married to his sister. He was a successful inventor, particularly of gas appliances, and designed a gas works for Kingstown as well as a new system of gas lighting for lighthouses, which was the subject of a legal dispute with the lighthouse board, Trinity House. Eventually he was awarded £2500 for the patent.

Wigham owned twenty-five patents, for, among others things, an oil-lit navigational buoy, sirens and fog signals. He was a member of the Royal Irish Academy and a leading member of the RDS science committee. Wigham was chairman of Blackrock District Council but as a Quaker he refused a knighthood. Described as an uncompromising unionist by the *Irish Times*, he did not seek re-election to Council in 1903 after a stroke that left him very incapacitated.

zenith in 1882. The issue was raised at the AGM of 1896, with the suggestion that membership was being offered only to those with 'Tory views'. Although no resolution was passed in response to this comment, neither was there any further blackballing of applicants. Despite political disagreements, Chamber allied itself with the corporation in 1897 to oppose a new Port and Docks Board Bill, advocating instead a revised bill that led to a reconfiguration of the board. The new board included six corporation nominees with the Lord Mayor as ex-officio, twelve members elected by mercantile traders and nine elected by ship owners. This board first met in 1899 with Sir Richard Martin, a former member of the old Ballast Board and past president of Dublin Chamber in the chair. But the bill had failed to deal with the issue of the financial renewal of the Port and Docks Board and the new board soon proposed another bill to parliament which was passed, after much negotiation, in 1902.

Abraham Lyon (1849-1923), who joined Chamber in 1892, was a frequent contributor from the floor at general meetings. A provisions agent, he was a nationalist councillor and later alderman for Clontarf on Dublin Corporation.

Courtesy of Colm Lyon

When Queen Victoria again visited Dublin in 1900 Chamber prepared a decorated loyal address, which a deputation led by the president, John Malcolm Inglis, presented at the Viceregal Lodge. Inglis received a knighthood in the subsequent birthday honours list but died of influenza before he could present a loyal address on the coronation of Victoria's successor, Edward VII, the following year. James Murphy, son of former president, Michael Murphy, replaced Inglis as president.

The 19th century had seen a great decline in Dublin since its pre-Union glory days as the second city of the UK. The census of 1901 gave the population of the city borough area as 290,638, 50,000 less than that of Belfast, although it had increased by more than 100,000 since 1820, when Dublin Chamber of Commerce was revived. The city now housed most of the poor while the better off lived in satellite townships, of which Rathmines and Pembroke had a population of 150,000, so Belfast's claim to be a more populous city was not true in reality.

As Chamber entered the new century the face of business was changing, just as the country was changing, to a more nationalist configuration. Chamber's failure to reflect this led to a decline in membership in favour of alternative organisations such as the Dublin Mercantile Association and the Family Grocers' and Purveyors' Association.

VIII

TO THE LOCKOUT, 1900-13

*Chamber used to be a somewhat lethargic Body, holding occasional meetings,
but doing very little more. Recently it has become far more active.*

William Martin Murphy at Chamber AGM, January 1914

Although Home Rule was still on the political agenda, by the turn of the
20th century members of Dublin Chamber were beginning to accept the
inevitability of Ireland's leaving the Union and the organisation's focus
returned to commercial matters. Of more pressing concern during this
period were falling membership, which continued for the next decade, and
the rise of trade unionism, Chamber being primarily an employers' body.

For the moment, however, the organisation continued to be a bastion of
unionism. In 1903: 'the announcement of the intended visit of their Majesties
the King and Queen to Dublin was received with the most heartfelt pleasure
by Council, and it was agreed that preparations should be made to give
their Majesties a cordial reception.' Council felt that such preparations
would best be carried out by a citizens' committee that would ideally be

*Galley motif of the Chamber
badge presented by William
Martin Murphy, 1913.*

formed by the Lord Mayor. But the corporation and the nationalist Lord Mayor, Tim Harrington, refused to cooperate, so Chamber president, James Murphy, assumed the role of organiser, under the chairmanship of the Earl of Meath, while the assistant secretary, Robert Middleton Perry, acted as secretary to the committee. Council unanimously mandated Murphy to present a loyal address to the royal visitors at Dublin Castle and he received a baronetcy for his pains. Edward VII visited Dublin again in 1904 and a Chamber delegation went to Kingstown to present a loyal address. A third address greeted the king's final visit in 1907 to attend the Irish International Exhibition in Herbert Park. Chamber paid James McConnell of Lower Sackville Street, illuminating and heraldic artist, five guineas for preparing the address.

Dublin Corporation continued to refuse to meet royal visitors or to pay its respects to the newly appointed Lord Lieutenant, so when the Liberal Lord Aberdeen (favourable to nationalists and Home Rule and in reality little liked by Chamber) arrived in Dublin in that position in 1906 it fell to Chamber and other establishment bodies such as the YMCA and Rathmines Urban District Council to welcome him.

When the visit of the new king, George VI, was announced in 1911, Chamber once again proposed the formation of a citizens' reception committee under the chairmanship of the Earl of Meath. But cracks were appearing in the organisation's unionist carapace. *The Irish Times* reported: 'A small body of Nationalists of extreme views yesterday caused considerable disorder at the Ancient Concert Rooms, at the meeting convened by John Mooney JP, President of Dublin Chamber of Commerce, and other influential citizens, for the purpose of appointing a committee to organise a fitting welcome to the King and Queen on the occasion of their coming visit to Dublin.' The report provided a list of the loyalists who attended, noting that about forty Sinn Féin members interrupted the meeting with sarcastic and heckling comments from the floor. Francis Sheehy-Skeffington proposed a nullifying amendment but this was defeated by a large majority, so John Mooney presented yet another illuminated address to the royal couple. Mooney, a miller and director of the Johnston, Mooney and O'Brien bakery, received a CVO (Commander of the Royal Victorian Order), rather than the baronetcy or knighthood bestowed on his predecessors. Council also agreed to decorate the front of Commercial Buildings and the citizens' committee paid for the decoration of the streets and a trip to the seaside for ten thousand poor children to celebrate the visit.

The proposal to hold an Irish International Exhibition was made at the Irish Industrial Conference in 1903, after the success of a smaller Cork Exhibition. It transcended political divisions as it was the Lord Mayor who asked for Chamber support on this occasion. William Martin Murphy, who was to be such a dominant figure in Dublin commercial life in the coming decade, was the main driver of the exhibition and James Shanks, a mineral water manufacturer and future president of Chamber, its chief executive officer. Chamber president, Marcus Goodbody, and Richard W. Booth were coopted on to the committee and a deputation from Dublin Chamber including Murphy, Shanks and Goodbody went to Belfast Chamber of Commerce to seek its support. Herbert Park was chosen as the site of the exhibition (nothing of the infrastructure remains but the bandstand and the pond). It was popular but made a loss of £100,000, which had to be financed by subscribers from among the commercial community who had pledged £150,000 to a fund toward its success.

1908

Registration of motor vehicles for the first time.

Opening of Dublin Municipal Art Gallery, the first in the UK to be dedicated to modern art.

The National University replaces the Royal University.

Introduction of pensions for people over seventy.

1911

Introduction of Parliament Bill in the House of Commons.

Founding of Dublin Employers' Federation with William Martin Murphy as president.

George V visits Ireland, the last royal visit of the 20th century.

1912

The Post Office takes over telephone companies.

Sinking of the *Titanic*.

1913

The Dublin Lockout.

Nassau Street decorated for the visit of the new king, George V, in 1911. As the nationalist corporation refused to mark the royal visit by erecting bunting, Chamber took on this task, establishing a citizens' committee.

Courtesy of the National Library of Ireland

In line with its policy of encouraging commercial education, Chamber welcomed the establishment of the School of Commerce in Rathmines. London Chamber of Commerce had begun to offer annual commercial examinations which were taken up by thirty-seven other British chambers and Dublin Chamber agreed to be a local centre for its Commercial Education Certificates from 1904. About fifty candidates from various commercial colleges sat the exam each year, although results were poor. In 1908 Chamber wrote to the Royal Commission on University Education, seeking the establishment of a chair of commerce in the new National University in Dublin. The commission asked Chamber to suggest a curriculum and when UCD initiated a commerce department the following year, Chamber stopped holding the London exams.

During the early years of the 20th century AGMs were frequently acrimonious, with some members critical of Council's running of Chamber. Prominent among those who raised issues from the floor were Alderman Abraham Lyon, William Field MP, Abraham Shackleton, solicitor William Thomas Daniel, John Lambert Jones, an auctioneer and valuer from Dartry and Thomas Neville Stack. The last raised, yet again, the issue of the Bodega, remarking, at the 1903 AGM, that 'although he had no objection to a good glass of whiskey himself...he objected to see men oscillating between the rooms of [the Chamber] and the cellars of the basement.' Charles Athill Stanuell, a solicitor, was in frequent correspondence with Council about a range of issues. In 1911 Bernard O'Reilly described some members of Council as: 'most amiable fossils – the most useless fossils'.

The issue of Sunday closing arose again in Chamber in 1904 and was debated several times over the next few years. On this occasion the campaign was spearheaded by John Lambert Jones and William Perrin, seeking, they claimed, 'respite from toil'. At the AGM of January 1908 William Martin Murphy opposed the proposal, noting that 'there were a great many people who thought that nothing should be done on Sundays but that their dinner should be got for them by their servants' and the motion was withdrawn. Murphy had joined Chamber in 1876 but, although he served on Council 1885-92, when he was ex-officio as MP for St Patrick's Division, he did not serve again until 1906, when he was coopted to fill the place of John Tyrrell, who had died.

Another perennial issue was raised by the Quaker members, miller Abraham Shackleton and stockbroker Jonathan Goodbody, who objected to Chamber's taking the sporting news by telegram at the cost of £35 per year. John Lambert Jones agreed, declaring at the 1905 AGM, 'Nothing could dissipate society more than gambling and racing and nonsense and smoking,' which raised a laugh but no support.

British politics were undergoing profound change. The Labour Party was founded in 1900 and the Liberals developed a more socially progressive programme during their long period in power 1905-1922, in contrast with the party's laissez-faire economic and social policies during the 19th century. Henry Campbell-Bannerman, who was prime minister 1905-8, had been Chief Secretary in Ireland

A "WARM" WELCOME.

Mr. Wm. M. Murphy, J.P., Chairman, Chief Executive Officer Shanks, and the members of the Executive Committee of the "Irish" International Exhibition are making preparations to give His Majesty a warm welcome. Kingstown Town Council are making the same.
If His Majesty brings something in his pocket "warm" is not the word.—*From Our Ballsbridge and South Coast Short-handed Writer.*

WILLIAM MARTIN MURPHY (1845-1919)

William Murphy (the 'Martin' was adopted later in memory of his mother, Mary Anne Martin, who died when he was four) was born near Castletownbere, County Cork. His father, Denis Murphy, was a builder. He was educated in Belvedere College, then apprenticed to an architect. On his father's death, when he was nineteen, he returned to west Cork and took over the family's contracting business. In 1867 he moved to Cork City and married Mary Julia Lombard, daughter of the successful Cork businessman, James Fitzgerald Lombard, who had a number of Dublin business interests. Murphy moved to Dublin in 1875 and joined Chamber the following year. In 1878, with his father-in-law, he set up the Dublin Central Tramway Company, his first venture into the transport business. His building company laid the lines. Subsequently Murphy was involved in railway and tramway construction in Britain, South America and Africa.

Murphy's other commercial interests included the ailing Clerys department store, which he bought with Fitzgerald Lombard, and the moribund *Irish Daily Independent*, which he relaunched as the *Irish Independent*, turning it into the highest-selling newspaper in Ireland. He was the driving force behind the 1907 Irish International Exhibition but when the king visited the exhibition he refused the knighthood offered to him.

William Murphy was Irish Party MP for St Patrick's Division, Dublin, 1885-92, and opposed Parnell when the party split over the latter's affair with Kitty O'Shea. He lost his seat to the pro-Parnell candidate, William Field, and failed to get elected in two further elections but was a supporter of T.M. Healy and the Sullivans, who formed the west Cork anti-Parnell clique in parliament, and used the *Irish Independent* to promote his views.

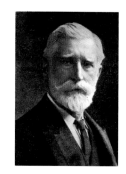

Although he did not seem to be a man given to frivolous pursuits, Murphy was a member of the Royal Irish Yacht Club and was a frequent sailor in Dublin Bay on his twenty-foot yacht *Eva*. He was the first captain of Milltown Golf Club and president of the Rathmines and Rathgar Musical Society. Working to the end, he died on 25 June 1919 in his home, Dartry Hall, Rathgar. He is buried in the O'Connell Circle in Glasnevin.

There is no doubt that Murphy was a thoughtful and intelligent man but he clearly had a stubborn streak and did not easily forgive or forget perceived slights. His wide-ranging address to the Chamber AGM in January 1913 was one of the most considered speeches of the day but his actions did not always live up to these reflections.

in 1884. He was a social reformer and a supporter of free trade and Home Rule. When he died in 1908, just nineteen days after resigning due to ill-health, H.H. Asquith, lukewarm on Home Rule but with a cabinet equally bent on reform, replaced him as prime minister. Much of the Liberals' legislative programme related to workers' rights and working conditions and, not surprisingly, chambers of commerce, which were mainly employers' bodies, generally disagreed with it. Other chambers throughout Britain regularly wrote to Dublin Chamber to ask for its help in opposing various pieces of legislation. For instance, Leeds Chamber of Commerce opposed the Coal Mines Regulating Act of 1908, known as the Eight-Hour Act, which limited miners' working hours, claiming that the bill would seriously limit production, increase the price of coal and (somewhat defying credulity) was not needed in the interests of the men. Belfast and Londonderry Chambers of Commerce objected to the 1908 Sweated Industries Bill which provided for minimum wages in clothing manufacture, as these cities had substantial linen industries.

The Liberals introduced state pensions in 1908 and, in 1911, workmen's compensation for injury, a Shop Bill, which regulated hours of employment for retail staff, and a National Insurance Bill. To pay for these innovations they increased income tax. Chamber opposed all the reforming Bills on the basis that they created a financial imposition on commerce. Employers' prevailing attitude to employees, whether benign or tyrannical, would have been autocratic and in the context of the times – and after a century of laissez-faire economics – the resentment Chamber members felt at what they perceived as government interference is understandable, however laudable the improvement in the lot of ordinary people may seem to modern-day readers. The issue came to a head when the House of Lords threw out

The Oliver Record Has Never Been Equaled.

The OLIVER Typewriter

THE STANDARD VISIBLE WRITER.

Advertisement for the Oliver typewriter of 310 Broadway, New York. Booth Brothers of Upper Stephen's Street were the Irish agents. The Oliver typewriter had keys above the roller that struck downwards, giving the machine the appearance of having wings, and was the first typewriter that allowed the user to see what was being typed.

The typewriter was patented in 1891 by a Canadian, Thomas Oliver (1852-1909), a Methodist minister in Iowa. The Chamber's machine, a type Number 3, was olive green, with three rows of white keys laid out in QWERTY format.

Asquith's 1909 budget, which included raising taxes. Council of Dublin Chamber sent the prime minister and the Lord Lieutenant a memorial to protest against it, putting Chamber firmly in the same camp as the House of Lords. The Lords' rejection of this budget led to a constitutional crisis and a general election, which saw the Liberals returned to power with the support of the Irish Party. The Liberals then passed the 1911 Parliament Act which curtailed the power of the Lords to veto bills passed by the Commons. In future they could delay legislation for no more than two years and budgets were exempt from their veto. The Lords had no option but to pass what was to them an unpalatable Act, as Asquith threatened otherwise to flood the house with Liberal peers.

Another consequence of the 1911 Parliament Act was to facilitate the passing of Home Rule, which had been Liberal policy since prime minister William Gladstone introduced a Home Rule bill in 1886. First defeated in the Commons, then, in 1893, by the Lords, Home Rule appeared to be inevitable when Asquith, in keeping with his electoral pact with the Irish Party, steered a new bill through the Commons in 1912. The Lords, predictably, voted it down but their veto could now last no more than two years so Home Rule in 1914 must have looked like a safe bet to observers, both nationalist and unionist. Chamber had had twenty-five years to get used to the inevitability of self-government for Ireland, however damaging members perceived it as being to their commercial interests, and there is no comment on the 1912 bill in Council minutes. With a commendable sense of realpolitik, Council had already agreed, in 1909, to send a 'précis' of its meetings to the *Sinn Féin* newspaper at the request of its editor, William M. Kenealy.

THE BODEGA

From its inception, Commercial Buildings incorporated some form of hostelry, coffee room or restaurant. There was originally a restaurant on Cope Street and a coffee room on Dame Street. Joseph Kavanagh opened the Metropolitan Dining Rooms in 1867 and they were later run by Harry Kilbey, from London. The Bodega Company Limited of London, which had several premises in England, then acquired the restaurant and Frenchman Foy Rivière (1834-1902) franchised the name in Dublin. The *Irish Times* advertisement for the opening in July 1882 described the premises: 'A most capacious and elegantly furnished grill room and cold buffet has been provided. The cooking is first class and the attendance is good.' The dining room was in the basement, accessed by stairs from the main entrance hall off Dame Street, which it shared with the Chamber of Commerce.

Temperance-minded members of Chamber immediately expressed dissatisfaction with this arrangement. This group, led by Thomas Wallace Russell, also undertook a prosecution of the manager, James Edward Larchet, for breach of the licensing laws in 1884. They alleged that he was providing libations to the Chamber reading room and the courtyard of Commercial Buildings, both of which areas were unlicensed. Under cross-examination Russell was accused, to laughter in the court, of frequently declaiming, *Bodega est delenda* (The Bodega is to be wiped out). The case was dismissed.

The Bodega established branches in Belfast and Cork, where the name survives. In 1896 it advertised: 'With commercial men the Bodega is a favourite resort during luncheon hours, and again when the dinner bell rings. The Bodega has a fine grill room, and an excellent table d'hôte daily commencing at half-past five.' The Bodega was sold in 1954 and Hugh Dolan reopened the premises as the Ouzel Galley Lounge on 11 February 1955.

THE BODEGA,
COMMERCIAL BUILDINGS,
DAME STREET
(Under Chamber of Commerce).
THE BODEGA
WINES,
WHISKIES,
CIGARS, &c
GRILL AND RESTAURANT ATTACHED.
TABLE D'HOTE, FROM 5.30 P.M.,
2s 6D.
SANDWICHES IN 100 VARIETIES.

Above: *Advertisement for the Bodega which ran in* The Irish Times *in the 1890s.*

Left: *Bodega postcard from a later date.*

© Irish Historical Picture Company

At the beginning of the 20th century standard Greenwich Mean Time was not used in Ireland, although it had been introduced throughout Great Britain in 1880 because of the necessity of standardising transport timetables. Chamber agitated for the introduction of uniform time in Ireland and supported Charles Craig's private members bill of 1913 to this end but it was unsuccessful. It was only at the end of summer time in 1916 that GMT was introduced in Ireland because of wartime exigencies.

The continuing fall in Chamber's membership numbers was a recurring concern at Council meetings. In 1907 Council investigated the possibility

James Larkin (1876-1947)

James Larkin was born in Liverpool and worked from the age of eleven, eventually getting employment on Liverpool docks. In 1905, as a foreman docker, he lost his job because he joined his men on strike. The National Union of Dock Labourers (NUDL) recognised Larkin's organisational abilities and brought him into the union, sending him to Belfast in January 1907. By June he had called a general strike in Belfast port in response to the failure of selective strikes and the employers' use of strikebreakers. The moderate NUDL was unhappy with the way the strike had accelerated and negotiated a settlement, much to Larkin's annoyance. Larkin went to Dublin and established the Irish Transport and General Worker's Union (ITGWU), and in May 1911 began a newspaper, the *Irish Worker*, in which he expounded socialist and syndicalist ideas. In September the union went on sympathetic strike in the Great Southern & Western Railway, refusing to handle timber from merchants W. & L. Crowe, who were in dispute with its workers. The strike ended badly for the ITGWU and the railway company reinstated only 90 per cent of the strikers.

After the Lockout of 1913 Larkin went to America, where his style of oratory was less appreciated, returning to Dublin briefly in 1916 to find that James Connolly had led the Irish Citizen Army into the Rising. In America he supported the Communist Labour Party and a clampdown on communism resulted in his spending four years in prison for criminal anarchy. On his release in 1923 he returned to Dublin, resuming his position as general secretary of the ITGWU. He fell out with the ITGWU and established the Workers' Union of Ireland, taking two-thirds of the Dublin membership of the ITGWU with him. He won a Dáil seat for the Irish Communist League in 1927 and was later an Independent and a Labour TD. He was also a member of Dublin Corporation. He died in 1947 after a fall through the floor of Thomas Ashe Hall.

Larkin had a tendency toward exaggeration in his public speaking, and described his nemesis, William Martin Murphy, as 'the most foul and vicious blackguard that ever polluted any country'.

of reducing Chamber's rent by surrendering the reading room and in the same year Council agreed to waive readmission fees for individuals rejoining Chamber. In 1910 the decline was reversed, with an increase in membership of fifteen, and numbers improved over the next ten years. From 1910 elections were held for Council, whereas previously the nine retiring members were usually returned unopposed. By now the organisation had debts of £2000 and was obliged to sell half its remaining Bank of Ireland shares to meet them. The 1906 annual report told members that Chamber had acquired some modern office equipment in the form of an 'Oliver' typewriter, purchased for £19/16s, and in 1911 a shorthand typist was engaged.

In 1913 William Martin Murphy wrote of the advantages of joining Chamber for a small annual subscription of £2: 'They have the use of these fine rooms in a post centrally positioned, and excellent telegraphic service of financial and general news, together with a supply of newspapers, magazines and reference books, more generous than can be found elsewhere in Dublin. There is, moreover, a quiet and comfortable writing room upstairs, with a free supply of stationery for the use of the members. In fact, there will be found here nearly all the conveniences of a club.' It would appear that the requirement to be subjected to a ballot had become a formality, as anyone wishing to join had only to complete a postcard and the secretary would look after their nomination.

Trade unionism advanced in the early 20th century after years of repression and political and legal restrictions. Many of the early unions were for workers in specific skilled trades, such as the Dublin Operative Bakers and the Operative Stonecutters of

Portrait by Margaret Crilley (1886-1961) of William Martin Murphy.

Crilley was a student of William Orpen, whose portrait of Murphy – similar but without the chain – Dublin Chamber presented to the subject as a token of its esteem. Crilley's copy still hangs in Chamber.

CHAMBER'S BADGE OF OFFICE

The formal chain and badge worn by presidents that William Martin Murphy presented to Chamber in 1913 was designed and manufactured by West & Company, 18-19 College Green. It was made of 18-carat solid wrought gold. The heavy chain could be detached from the badge and a ribbon in St Patrick's Blue used instead for travelling.

Wests incorporated accoutrements of the Ouzel Galley society into the design. The enamel badge shows the ship in full sail as in the painting of 1752 and the mounting includes the Chamber logo and shamrocks. The links include a smaller enamel badge, also decorated with shamrocks, carrying the city's arms and the ominous motto *Obedientia Civium Urbis Felicitas* (The obedience of citizens makes a happy city). The chain of 'SS' links incorporates the Ouzel Galley medals with the ship and Equity, Mercury – the Roman god of commerce – and harps.

George N. Jacob donated the insignia to the Association of Chambers of Commerce of the Irish Free State in 1927 and Chamber had Gunnings silversmiths make a chain for Dublin Junior Chamber. Both are still in use today.

In 1952 Thomas Laurie presented medal replicas of the badge of the president's chain to Chamber. These were in solid silver gilt, hung on a silk ribbon with an ornamental bar, enamelled with the words 'past president' and the year. Each surviving past president received one. A similar medal is still presented to presidents when they complete their term of office.

Ireland. But the Irish Transport and General Workers Union (ITGWU), which James Larkin established in 1909, was open to unskilled labour, as much of Dublin labour was at this time. The Liberal government had passed an act freeing the unions from liability for damages incurred during strike action and a number of minor strikes were resolved early in the century, generally in the favour of employers.

In the ITGWU Jim Larkin used the tactic of sympathetic strikes, whereby workers of other businesses refused to deal with a company in which strike action was ongoing. A strike of timber carriers and labourers, many of them ITGWU members, began in August 1911 and the following month more than seven thousand employees of the Great Southern and Western Railway went on a sympathetic strike that lasted for nineteen days. At a special general meeting of Chamber the timber merchant William Crowe, whose company was one of those affected by the industrial action, commented that 'settlement of the railway strike would not get rid of the evil that brought it about'. His words, although rather extreme, would prove prophetic. The company refused to yield and the strikers returned to work on the employers' conditions. William Martin Murphy was a director of the Great Southern & Western Railway and as a consequence of this dispute formed the Employers' Federation to face down labour unrest. Many of the strikes related to union issues, particularly union recognition and the refusal of staff to work with non-union labour. Labour disputes became progressively more militant, a militancy that reached a climax in August 1913.

William Martin Murphy replaced William Anderson, managing director of the Dublin United Tramways Company, as Chamber vice-president when Anderson died in 1910. He was elected Chamber president in 1912 and re-

The inscription on the back of the chain reads: 'Presented to the Dublin Chamber of Commerce, 3 February 1913, by William Martin Murphy, MP for St Patrick's Division, Dublin, 1885-92. President of the Chamber 1912-13.'

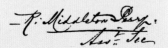
elected the following year, the first president with nationalist leanings. In February 1913 he presented a chain to Chamber, remarking: 'When attending public functions in the capacity of President of the Dublin Chamber of Commerce, during the past year, it struck me that the representative of so important a body should have some badge of office to be worn on such occasions.' There is no indication that Murphy was deliberately selected as president for these years of industrial unrest but he was the most prominent businessman of the period and, although considering himself a good employer, had every intention of confronting the 'menace' of trade unionism and syndicalism, especially the idea of one large union, the ITGWU.

1912 was the calm before the storm. In 1913 there was a bewildering number of strikes among all classes of workers: even the schoolboys in Rutland Street National School struck. At Chamber AGM on 28 January 1913, William Martin Murphy, in a considered and wide-ranging speech, advocated a policy towards workers that might be described as one of enlightened or self-interested benevolence, warning that while there had been industrial peace the previous year, members should 'not therefore... think that "all is well", and so neglect to consider with sympathy the condition and wages of employees, especially those in the lowest grade who are so seriously affected by any rise in the price of food. Apart from its justice the policy of looking after the condition of your labour, particularly low-paid labour, will be found to pay from a business point of view.' He had been an employer for nearly fifty years and 'never had to face a strike of workmen directly employed by myself'. This was soon to change. Murphy was nothing if not stubborn – he knew his business and would not allow Larkin or anyone else to dictate to him – and adamant in his opposition to his employees becoming members of the ITGWU.

THE LOCKOUT

On 15 August 1913 William Martin Murphy arrived at the dispatch department of the *Irish Independent* and told the workers that they had to chose between the company and the union. Forty men and twenty boys were laid off and pickets were placed on the newspaper. The boycott of the *Independent* newspapers spread to the Dublin United Tramways Company dispatch department and distributors Eason and Son. On 17 August Murphy dismissed two hundred workers for refusing to handle the newspaper and thirty employees of Easons came out in strike in sympathy with their co-workers in the *Independent*. On 23 August dockers who were members of the ITGWU refused to unload a ship carrying goods intended for Easons. On Tuesday 26 August 1913 about a third of the DUTC conductors and drivers stopped their trams at 9.40am. Murphy was prepared for this and although there was some immobilisation the trams were soon back in action. The DUTC power station in Ringsend continued to operate. On 3 September, the employers, feeling that they had the upper hand, agreed to require their employees to pledge not to join the ITGWU, an action which brought support from England for the workers and extended the dispute.

The strike quickly descended into violence both by police and by workers. Trams were attacked and those who continued working were subject to violence. A number of these employees carried arms to protect themselves. A ricochet from a sidearm fired by a pursued van driver hit Alice Brady, who died from tetanus several days later. Strikebreakers who were brought in to replace the strikers were particularly subject to violence. One of these, Thomas Harten from County Meath, who worked in Tedcastles, was beaten to death. Police protecting the deliveries and trams were stoned. The violence increased on both sides. On Sunday 31 August the police baton-charged a mass meeting and two strikers, James Nolan and John Byrne, subsequently died of their injuries. The union did not have sufficient funding to provide strike pay for more than a month but English unions contributed to the cause. The economic strength of the employers eventually won the day and the strike came to an end in February 1914. The Lockout was soon overshadowed by the outbreak of the First World War in August 1914.

Strikers during the Lockout express their views on William Martin Murphy.
Courtesy of the National Library of Ireland

When, in February 1913, Messrs Barmak Ltd., bedding manufacturers of Fumbally Lane, off New Street, wrote to Chamber seeking its assistance in regard to 'interference' by the ITGWU, Council replied that the company should refer to the Employers' Federation as 'Council had no machinery for dealing with such cases.' In the light of heightened industrial tensions the Lord Mayor, Lorcan Sherlock, set up an informal conference comprising four members from Chamber – Richard K. Gamble, James Shanks, William Wallace and William Martin Murphy – and four from Dublin Trades Council. A meeting in July approved the formation of a conciliation board but Murphy, who was unable to attend, disagreed with the proposal and had Chamber delegate its involvement to the Employers' Executive Committee of the Dublin Employers' Federation. The conciliation board never really took off.

It is important to remember that Dublin Chamber of Commerce had been established as a lobby group for business. Over the preceding century it had attracted members who did not own their own businesses – professionals, agents for insurance companies and branch managers of larger companies – but it remained overwhelmingly an employers' body. It is therefore not surprising that the Employers' Executive Committee set up offices in Commercial Buildings to manage the employers' response for the duration of the Lockout.

Over the next four months William Martin Murphy was usually in the chair at Chamber meetings – on 1 September he 'was received with considerable applause when he rose to open the quarterly meeting' – but in general the organisation preferred to distance itself from the conflict and defer to the Employers' Executive Committee.

Chamber members were not all in agreement about the proper response to striking or locked-out workers. Two motions were proposed for a special general meeting held in November to discuss the Lockout. Richard Jones, an egg and butter merchant, proposed to endorse the position of the Employers' Executive Committee but a conflicting motion by the Rathmines draper, Edward Lee, suggested that as a gesture of goodwill the employers should withdraw their requirement that workers sign an undertaking not to join an union. Council recommended that these motions should not be discussed, as they could 'cause a great deal of ill feeling and division in Chamber'. The annual report for 1913 noted with obvious relief that 'Council did not find it necessary to take any official part in the struggle, as the question was being dealt with by a special committee delegated by the general body of the employers to look after their interests.'

The Lockout was at its most intense between September and November 1913 and slowly fizzled out as hardship forced the men to return to work. It was over by February 1914. Larkin's strategy of sympathetic strikes unified the workers but also unified the employers, whose economic strength won the day, although at considerable cost, both financial and in terms of public perception.

The year of the Lockout brought another controversy to Dublin that, thanks to W.B. Yeats's poem, 'September 1913', occupies an enduring place in Irish history. Hugh Lane, the London gallery owner and art collector and nephew of Lady Gregory, had offered to Dublin his valuable collection of mostly French 19th- and early-20th-century paintings on the understanding that a gallery would be built for them. The corporation exhibited the pictures on a temporary basis in Clonmell House in Harcourt Street and Lane

'That...whilst determinedly opposed to the principle of sympathetic strikes with their attendant disastrous effects to Employers and Workers, [we] are of opinion that the employers in the interests of peace and goodwill ought to withdraw the agreement they have asked their workers to enter into...'

Edward Lee's opposing motion

commissioned the British architect Sir Edward Lutyens to prepare a design for a new gallery. Lutyens's proposal was for a bridge to span the Liffey in the place of the Halfpenny Bridge or Metal Bridge as it was then known (it was still a toll bridge at the time, which put it beyond the means of the working classes), which would house the gallery as well as a pedestrian thoroughfare. Rather surprisingly Sinn Féin supported the proposal while unionists and the Ratepayers' Association opposed it. William Martin Murphy led public objections in a series of letters to the *Irish Independent* from January 1913: he felt that the gallery was a vanity project for Lane; he doubted the ability of the corporation to carry it out; he considered it a waste of ratepayers' money and said he would prefer to see 'one block of sanitary houses at low rents replacing a reeking slum, than all the pictures Corot and Degas painted.' Murphy's objections were somewhat disingenuous: deplore as he might the living conditions of the poor, he opposed any attempt by the corporation to raise money either by increasing rates or borrowing, even if such funds were destined for housing.

The campaign against the municipal gallery simmered on for the first half of 1913 but it was not until shortly before the beginning of the Lockout that twenty-one members of Chamber requested a special general meeting to oppose the project. This was held on 12 August and Murphy was in the chair; after the meeting a memorial objecting to the proposed gallery was prepared and sent to the Lord Mayor and the Dublin Port and Docks Board, which had responsibility for bridges over the Liffey. Chamber would countenance no replacement for the Halfpenny Bridge other than a vehicular bridge and objected to the waste of public money on the gallery.

The gallery never did go ahead. Lane died when a German submarine torpedoed the *Lusitania* off the Old Head of Kinsale in 1915, leaving his bequest unresolved, and Yeats castigated Murphy and the merchants of Dublin for greed and philistinism:

What need you, being come to sense,
But fumble in a greasy till
And add the halfpence to the pence
And prayer to shivering prayer, until
You have dried the marrow from the bone?
For men were born to pray and save:
Romantic Ireland's dead and gone,
It's with O'Leary in the grave.

W.B. Yeats, 'September 1913'

In 1927, eight years after the death of William Martin Murphy, Council adopted a resolution, prompted by the Friends of National Collections of Ireland, that the Hugh Lane pictures should be in Ireland.

IX

A TUMULTUOUS DECADE, 1913-23

The Sinn Féin Rebellion broke out with startling suddenness on Easter Monday, April 24th, and for a period of about a week murder, fire and pillage were rampant in parts of the City. Many hundreds of lives were lost, and great damage was done to both public and private property amounting to several million pounds. The outbreak found the authorities quite unprepared, and it was some days before an adequate force of troops could be brought into the city to quell the disturbances...

Comment on the 1916 Rising in the Chamber report for that year

After the difficulties and conflicts of 1913 the mercantile community of Dublin may have expected matters to return to normal but the Lockout proved instead to be an entrée to a decade of tumult, after which Ireland would be a different place both politically and commercially.

In 1911, in an effort to encourage more involvement by the membership, Council member James Shanks, proposed that vacancies on Council should be filled by votes from Chamber as a whole. But this suggestion was not acted on. During William Martin Murphy's second presidency, in 1913, it was Shanks who had proposed that the articles of association be changed so that the president and vice-president would not be eligible for re-election until a year had lapsed. This motion was passed and future presidents, with the exception of Thomas Laurie, served for only one year. In 1919 it was decided

McConnell Art Studio, which produced Chamber's formal addresses.
Courtesy of the National Library of Ireland

timeline

1914

Passing of Home Rule Bill in the House of Commons but suspended for the duration of the war.

Howth gun-running.

Outbreak of the First World War.

1915

Sinking of RMS *Lusitania* off Kinsale.

Gallipoli offensive sees many deaths among the Royal Dublin Fusiliers.

1916

Easter Rising in Dublin followed by execution of leaders.

Prime Minister Asquith visits Dublin.

Battle of the Somme.

Greenwich Mean Time (GMT) extended to Ireland.

1917

US enters the war.

that the position of honorary secretary be replaced by that of deputy vice-president, which meant that the management of the Chamber was given to the employed secretary. The unwritten policy of alternating presidents of different religions continued until 1919, when the War of Independence and then the Civil War saw Chamber trying to strengthen its position by electing prominent businessmen to the post, irrespective of religion. Membership numbers rose to a high in 1919 only to fall back in 1924.

At the AGM in January 1914 William Martin Murphy was applauded as he rose to speak, observing that Jim Larkin had hoped (in vain) to establish 'a cooperative commonwealth, of which, no doubt, he was to be the "Cromwell"'. In the same month Council decided not to subscribe to the *Daily Citizen*, the organ of the British Labour movement, but by March, following a request by member Alfred C. Aykroyd, a wool merchant, it had reversed this decision. At the meeting it was proposed that a subcommittee be formed 'to afford the citizens of Dublin and businessmen of Ireland an opportunity to express their appreciation of the great public services rendered by our ex-President, Mr William Martin Murphy, during the recent prolonged labour troubles.' A portrait by William Orpen was commissioned and, accompanied by an illustrated address, presented to Murphy in 1915. Chamber also commissioned a copy by Margaret Crilley, painted under the direction of Orpen; in this Murphy is wearing the presidential chain.

Clontarf solicitor James Brady, a Sinn Féin supporter, maintained his position as a contrarian at Chamber general meetings, in which task he was joined by his son James Vincent, also a solicitor. Brady senior, while much in agreement with William Martin Murphy, objected to the statement in the annual report for 1913 that Chamber did not involve itself with the recent disputes and proposed unsuccessfully to have it removed. His was the sole vote against the adoption of the report. James Brady lost two sons during one week of the First World War and another was assassinated during the War of Independence.

In July 1913 the HMS *Dublin* visited Kingstown. Edward H. Andrews proposed that Chamber make a presentation to the ship's complement (crew), as this was the usual custom in any city after which a ship was named. The nationalist Lord Mayor, Lorcan Sherlock, refused to do this, so Chamber set up a citizens' committee, as it had done before in similar circumstances, which the Earl of Meath agreed to chair. The presentation was postponed due to the Lockout and again in April 1914 after the Curragh Mutiny, on the suggestion of the Earl of Meath.

Richard Keene Gamble, a barrister and director of Brooks Thomas and son-in-law of Sir Maurice Brooks, was elected president at the 1914 AGM. There is no comment about the impending war in the 1914 minutes but the president, vice-president, Patrick Leonard, and honorary secretary, Edward H. Andrews, all attended the International Chamber of Commerce gathering in Paris in June 1914. At the quarterly meeting in September, after war had been declared, Richard Keene Gamble commented that the Paris meeting was one 'in which the members met under the shadow of the cloud of war which had spread over the larger part of the European Continent'. It was not for Chamber 'to discuss the causes of the outbreak or the awful responsibility of the aggressor'. He went on to consider how best the organisation might assist the British Empire in the conflict. Chamber encouraged members to facilitate employees to enlist by ensuring, wherever possible, that their positions remained open until they returned.

1918
German submarine sinks RMS *Leinster*.

Signing of armistice and end of the First World War.

Sinn Féin wins seventy-three seats in general election.

1919
War of Independence begins.
First meeting of Dáil Éireann in Mansion House, Dublin.

1920
Formation of Black and Tans in January and Auxiliaries in July.

Curfew midnight-5am imposed in Dublin from 20 February.

Bloody Sunday.

1921
Burning of Custom House.

Truce on 11 July and Anglo-Irish Treaty signed 7 December.

1922
Dáil approves Treaty on 7 January.

1922

Anti-Treatyites seize Four Courts and Civil War begins.

Death of Arthur Griffith and Michael Collins.

T.M. Healy appointed first Governor-General of Irish Free State.

1923

Separation of fiscal systems of the United Kingdom and Irish Free State.

Civil War officially ends on 24 May.

Irish Free State joins the League of Nations.

This was the Council's last real chance to tap into its traditional unionist core, by placing itself fully behind the war effort. Edward Andrews was prominent in the recruitment drive. A special meeting of Council, shortly after the war began, approved the opening of a subscription list for the provision of an ambulance for the front. £333/15/9 was raised and £300 spent on the ambulance, with the remainder given to the Irish Motor and Cycle Ambulance Fund. Chamber held a recruiting meeting in early March 1915, at which Major General L.B. Friend, commander of the forces in Ireland, spoke. Andrews remarked, with some truth, that 'the war would not be a walkover; they would be put to the pin of their collar to win it. They were going to sacrifice hundreds of thousands of lives, but they would do so willingly, and be victors in the long run.' The War Office wrote: 'the patriotic action of the Chamber of Commerce is noted and greatly appreciated.'

In May 1915 Chamber passed a vote of confidence in Earl Kitchener, regretting 'that a section of the English press should have been allowed to repeat unwarranted and harmful statements'. Horatio Herbert Kitchener, whose image was on the famous 'Your Country Needs You' poster, was Secretary for State for War and had been blamed for shortages in munitions at the front. A year later Council expressed sincere sympathy when Kitchener drowned – the ship on which he was travelling to Russia was torpedoed and sank.

In October of that year Chamber supported the formation of a commercial 'pals' company and Council returned the subscription of Lieutenant Edmund Mahony because he had enlisted. Mahony, the son of James Mahony, a corn merchant and former Council member, was killed in France just before the end of the war. As the war continued, votes of condolence on deaths at the front became more frequent. The annual reports during the war years included a roll of honour, enclosed in a black box, with lists of members and their relatives who were lost, and a similar roll was erected in the members' room of Chamber.

War did not mean that Chamber forgot about business. The first mention of war-related difficulties was in relation to the shortage of aniline dyes, synthetic red and purple dyes used in the clothing and textile industries that were almost exclusively manufactured in Germany. A government proclamation on 9 September 1914 had banned commerce with 'alien enemy'. It wasn't just dyes that were affected by the ban: up to 80 per cent of toys were of German manufacture. Council raised a complaint early in the war that there was no military supplies depot in Ireland to which goods could be delivered. This meant that Irish manufacturers had to include the cost of transport to England in their tender price, putting them at a disadvantage.

Chamber's advertisement appealing for funds to send an ambulance to the front, Irish Independent, *14 October 1914*.

An Ambulance for the Front

Very early on in the war Arthur H. Huet of the Dunlop Tyre Company made contact with Chamber. A director of the parent company in London, Arthur Philip DuCros (1871-1955), had set up a scheme to collect subscriptions to provide ambulances for the front. He raised £50,000 in this way to provide three ambulance companies, which he undertook to maintain at his own expense but somehow he managed to give the impression that he had paid for the ambulances himself. For this he was knighted in 1916. It was said of him that he had difficulty telling the difference between company and personal assets.

DuCros, a colourful character, was born in Ireland and elected Conservative MP for Hastings in 1908. He was a vocal opponent of votes for women and the suffragettes burnt his home in St Leonard's in 1913.

On 7 October 1914 Huet asked Chamber to raise £300, enough money for one ambulance, which would bear the name, 'Dublin Chamber of Commerce'. £333/15/9 was raised within a week and the ambulance was quickly reported as being at the front. The excess of £33/15/9 was given to the Irish Motor and Cycle Ambulance Fund towards an ambulance to ferry wounded soldiers from Dublin port to hospital. DuCros gave annual updates to Chamber on the performance of the ambulance until it was withdrawn to England in January 1918 because of difficulty in obtaining spare parts.

Aniline Dyes

Aniline, also called phenylamine or aminobenzene, is an organic compound with the formula $C_6H_5NH_2$, which is abstracted from coal tar. It was developed by German scientists during the first half of the 19th century and a number of German companies, with state aid, effectively monopolised the market.

At the outset of the First World War, 90 per cent of the world's synthetic dyes were produced in Germany by companies whose names we still recognise: BASF (Badische Anilin und Soda Fabrik) founded in 1861 and AGFA (Aktien Gesellschaft für Anilin Fabrikation) founded in 1873, both of which have 'Anilin' in their name. The embargo on German products at the outset of the war caused what was known as a 'dye famine', which was relieved by the British and the Americans developing their own aniline dye industries. Chlorine, a by-product of the manufacture of aniline dyes, was used in the production of poison gas during the war.

Following agitation the Ministry of Munitions established a samples room in 12 Nassau Street.

Neither was there a munitions industry in Ireland but Chamber lobbied successfully and the National Shell Factory in Parkgate Street and the Dublin Dockyard War Munitions Company were established in the city. There was increased taxation on alcohol, which Lloyd George saw as affecting munitions production; this was an issue that revived temperance divisions in Chamber. Council objected to the increase in tax affecting Dublin's leading industries of brewing and distilling but the Methodist member, Richard Booth, put forward an amendment in support of the government.

The single vexed issue raised during the early months of 1916 was in relation to workers in Dublin port, who had been on strike in support of pay demands. Chamber members were not the only ones surprised when, on Easter Monday, 24 April 1916, the Irish Volunteers and Irish Citizen Army took over the GPO and read the Proclamation of the Irish Republic. The city came to a standstill until the Rising was suppressed six days later. Fifteen leaders were executed after courts-martial, 3-12 May. During this period a special meeting of Council was called to discuss what was called the 'recent crisis'. A resolution was passed and forwarded to the king, the prime minister, the Lord Lieutenant, Dublin MPs and the newspapers, which assured 'His Gracious Majesty of the loyalty of the commercial community to his person and his throne' and recorded 'their abhorrence of the dreadful scenes of murder, carnage and destruction resulting from the action of a section of the community in the city.' Council could not resist accusing the Liberal administration (to which Chamber was naturally hostile) of facilitating the Rising by 'gross and unpardonable laxity, long continued, of the administration of the Irish government'. The statement concluded with the more pragmatic and self-interested desire that the Treasury should fund without delay the reconstruction of buildings and property.

At an enquiry into the Rising in June, the evidence of Chamber president, Richard W. Booth, suggested that one of its causes was labour unrest as a result of Jim Larkin's being allowed to continue in his agitation by an administration seeking compromise rather than enforcing the law. In any event the Rising made Chamber aware that there was no uniformity of political opinion in Dublin, despite the ongoing war.

The dust of the Rising having settled, Chamber held a special meeting at the end of June in order to revive a citizens' committee to make a presentation to HMS *Dublin,* which had not long before taken part in the Battle of Jutland. The sum of £560 was subscribed, which procured a rose bowl for the captain, a silver inkstand for the warrant officers, a full set of brass instruments for the ship's band purchased from Messrs Butler & Sons, and several gramophones, records, footballs, games and cricket outfits to be presented to the men. A number of silver cups for gunnery, rowing, sailing and so forth were also included. The officers and crew presented the ship's ensign to Chamber in return, complete with gunfire damage from the Battle of Jutland. Council was unsure what to do with the flag but in 1917 George Black Thompson, a wine merchant, had a presentation case made and suitably inscribed for it, so that it could be displayed in the members'

View from Nelson's Pillar of the ruins of Clerys and the Imperial Hotel after the 1916 Rising, both businesses associated with William Martin Murphy.

Council's condemnation of the Rising concluded with 'the opinion that the funds necessary for restoring the buildings and property of unoffending citizens destroyed in the course of the rebellion should be provided by the Imperial Treasury without delay.'

Murphy helped to organise the compensation claims of businessmen affected by the Rising and it is probably the case that firing from HMS Helga destroyed Murphy's businesses.

By permission of the Royal Irish Academy
© RIA

HMS *Dublin*

HMS *Dublin* was launched in April 1913 and based in the Mediterranean at the beginning of the war. In May 1916, she took part in the Battle of Jutland, at which she received some damage. The battle was the only full-scale naval action of the First World War as the smaller German fleet avoided further contact. HMS *Dublin* survived the war and was sold for scrapping in 1927.

The flag presented to Chamber was kept in the conversation room in its glass and wood case. Not surprisingly such a symbol of empire became a security concern in the 1930s and the flag was removed to Christ Church Cathedral. More recently the flag was on display, still in its case, in the National Maritime Museum in Dún Laoghaire.

conversation room. Richard Caulfield Orpen, brother of the painter, William Orpen, designed the case.

The Corinthian Club borrowed the flag to hang at a dinner held in 1917 for the Irish Convention, which been called together to propose a constitution for Ireland when the Home Rule Bill came into effect after the war. It represented parliamentary nationalists, unionists, the labour movement and business, although Sinn Féin were not involved, as the use of the Royal Ensign at the dinner might indicate. Chamber was represented by honorary secretary, Edward Andrews, a unionist, while the president, Matthew Minch, a nationalist, attended the convention as chairman of Kildare County Council. The convention's report, issued in March 1917, was full of exceptions and exclusions, the Ulster unionists disagreed with much of it, and in any case it was made irrelevant when Lloyd George introduced Home Rule with a Conscription Act for Ireland in April 1918.

HMS Dublin, *which was launched in 1913, took part in the Battle of Jutland in 1916.*

Left: The presentation case with the flag of HMS Dublin. *Its dedication plaque, originally kept in Chamber, is now in the possession of the National Maritime Museum, Dún Laoghaire.*

Below: *The flag today.*

© The National Maritime Museum

The 1916 Rising had coincided with a decline in enlistment. Conscription had been enacted in the rest of the United Kingdom in 1916 but the Irish Party had convinced Lloyd George that it would be counterproductive to introduce it in Ireland. In December of that year, Council adopted Edward Andrews's somewhat anodyne motion: 'In order to win the war as quickly as possible it is, in the opinion of this Council, absolutely necessary for government to organise the entire nation so that its full working powers, both in men and women, be made available.' The 1918 Conscription Act for Ireland aroused considerable opposition and never came into effect.

Shortages caused by the war were of more concern to business as the fighting in France dragged on. Government control of shipping limited transport to Ireland and resulted in a reduction in coal supplies, which were essential for the production of electricity and gas. In 1918 Chamber premises, which were now lit entirely by electricity, closed at six in the evening, as the corporation had begun restricting electricity supply. Timber imports were also regulated. In addition, the war had led to inflation: wages and salaries were increasing. The lease on Commercial Buildings was due for renewal in December 1917.

Alfie Byrne (1882-1956), Lord Mayor of Dublin 1930-39 and again in 1954-5. He was also an independent TD for Dublin constituencies, 1922-28 and 1932-56. He is photographed with President W.T. Cosgrave (1880-1965).

Courtesy of the National Library of Ireland

Following negotiations, Council felt that they could not meet the 50 per cent increase in rent sought and surrendered the reading room.

Chamber continued to support the war effort, despite diminishing support among the Irish population as a whole. Council arranged for the governor of the Bank of Ireland to speak on the advantages of war loans, an evening to which the Lord Mayor, MPs and city and township councillors were invited. Maurice Dockrell took the opportunity to attack 'the farmers of Ireland [who] owed a very great debt of gratitude to the general public, which found the money for them to buy out the landlords', because their sons were not enlisting. In a continuing effort to encourage enlistment Captain Stephen Gwynn MP addressed Chamber in 1918 on the invitation of president Edward Andrews.

Partly as a result of the threat of conscription, support for an independent Ireland was growing among the general populace. Despite this, in May 1918 Edward Andrews proposed to present the usual address of welcome to the incoming Lord Lieutenant, Viscount French. There were three objectors at the Council meeting: two MPs, Alfie Byrne and William Field, ex-officio members of Council, and Fonso J. Carton, an egg merchant, (known as 'Eggs Carton'), who had been elected to Council the previous January. The motion passed, with three votes of opposition, but a requisition supported by twenty-two members called for a special general meeting. A report of the meeting appeared in the *Irish Independent* and at the subsequent Council meeting Edward Andrews expressed his displeasure at the leaking of the story, which breached Council rules, as well as which he considered the report to be inaccurate. At the requisitioned meeting in Commercial Buildings the opposition, led by Byrne and Carton, were shouted down. According to the *Irish Independent*, 'Alderman Byrne, amid a deafening uproar, sprang on a chair and, gesticulating wildly, cried out, "I claim you must listen to minorities." The uproar increased rather than subsided and Alderman Byrne threw the chair on the floor. A member approached him in a very threatening manner and a collision appeared imminent, all of the members having risen and joined in the general yelling.' Council prevailed and the motion, 'That it is inopportune at the present time for the Council of this Chamber to present an address of welcome to His Excellency the Lord Lieutenant,' failed. The whole Lord French affair had been very divisive and the changed political situation meant that Council made no attempt to honour the final Lord Lieutenant, Viscount FitzAlan of Derwent, with an address, on his arrival in 1921.

The end of the First World War was approaching. At a general meeting on 17 October 1918 a vote was passed to congratulate 'Marshall Foch the Generalissimo of the Allied armies in France for the magnificent progress made in France and Flanders'. By coincidence a Council meeting was held

Twenty-two Chamber Members

The members who objected to the presentation of an address to the new Lord Lieutenant Viscount French and requisitioned a general meeting in 1918:

David Archibald

Joseph Arigho JP

James Brady

James Vincent Brady

Alfred Byrne

Ado Carton

Fonso J. Carton

Michael Joseph Cooke, JP

James J. Doran

M.J. Halligan

James J. Halpin

William Francis Hooke

Richard F. Jones

Michael F. Judd

J.M. Kavanagh

Peter Paul Leonard

M.J. Moran

James Joseph Nagle

Samuel J. Nolan

William Nolan

E.J. O'Donnell

Malachi J. O'Reilly

The Commercial 'Pals' Company

In 1915 Council agreed to sponsor the raising of a 'pals' company (comprising men from the same area, employment or sports association) for the war. A committee headed by Sir William Fry raised £500 and Edward H. Andrews and William Crowe, two subsequent Chamber presidents, were very much involved in the recruitment. The company was trained in the Curragh and in February 1916 formed the nucleus of the new 10th battalion of the Royal Dublin Fusiliers. The battalion was in the Royal Barracks (now Collins Barracks) on Benburb Street when the Easter 1916 Rising broke out and was involved in suppressing it, with four of its members killed. In August 1916 the 10th battalion was sent to France, where it joined the 63rd Royal Naval Division. In November of that year it suffered 50 per cent casualties at the Battle of Ancre, which was the last big battle of the Somme offensive before the winter. The battalion was disbanded in February 1918.

ROLL OF HONOUR.

The Council have to announce that the past year has unfortunately seen additions to the Roll of Honour. Several gallant gentlemen have fallen, and the Council beg to tender their sincere sympathy to the relatives in their sad bereavement.

The following deceased gentlemen were sons or brothers of Members of the Chamber :—

Henry Campbell Anderson, R. Rossington Barnett, Edward Ellard Brady, Matthew Brady, Richard G. Brewster, Fredk. G. Brien, R. B. Burgess, Osborne Samuel Burke, Vincent Connell Byrne, Leo. F. Byrne, Geo. David Louis Clancy, Geo. Chaigneau Colvill, M. L. Cooper, E. C. Darley, Robert Blacker Douglas, Kearsley M. Drummond, George Grant Duggan, John Rowswell Duggan, W. G. M. Eager, N. J. Figgis, Charles A. Findlater, H. S. Findlater, Brendan J. Fottrell, R. M. B. Gamble, Owen Frederic Goodbody, Edward Stokes Hatte, J. Bagnall Lee, J. G. M'Cormick, J. H. G. M'Cormick, Eric Newland M'Mullen, Edmund J. Mahony, Eric Manly, W. F. A. Matthews, A. B. Mayne, Edward Chaytor Millar, Alan L. Ramsay, Gerald C. Rooney, R.M.; Richard Rooney, R.E.; Wilfrid A. Sidford, Joseph M. Simington John Humphrey, F. Vernon, Kenneth Moss Wallace, E. Theaker Weatherill. Chas. Robt. Wilson, M.C.; George Henry Wilson, M.C.; Arthur Hone Wilson, Maurice Wookey.

The final roll of honour published in the annual report for 1918, recording the names of members and their sons who died in the First World War. A similar roll of honour hung in Chamber.

on Armistice Day, 11 November 1918. A telegram of congratulations was sent to General Haig, commander of the British forces, but – a reminder of the reality of war – two names were added to Chamber's Roll of Honour, bringing the total to forty-eight: fourteen serving members, the remainder sons and brothers of members.

There was a general election in December 1918 but Council minutes make no mention of it other than noting the receipt of a letter from the Irish Association for the Prevention of Intemperance, seeking support for a prohibition on the sale of alcohol on election day. Sinn Féin won a large majority of the seats, except in Ulster. Neither did Council comment on the outbreak of the War of Independence or the first meeting of Dáil Éireann in January 1919. Normal commerce continued to be affected by wartime restrictions. Shipping controls still limited coal and timber imports, so they had become more expensive. Salaries generally were increasing and in January 1920 Chamber almost doubled the salaries and wages of its staff. The subscription, which had been at £2 for many years, was raised to three guineas.

William Martin Murphy was still an active member of Council and attended his last meeting on 16 June 1919, ten days before his death. His portrait in Chamber was draped in black and a resolution of condolence was sent to his son, William Lombard Murphy, who was invited to replace his father on Council.

On 29 November 1919, the IRA shot dead thirty-eight-year-old Detective Sergeant John Barton near Commercial Buildings. Council's condemnation of the killing is the first mention in the minutes of the War of Independence, which had begun in January of that year. The motion sent to the Lord Lieutenant concluded: 'The Council feels that the time is now arrived when it is the duty of all classes to express their indignation at such cowardly and inhuman acts which are doing such incalculable injury to our city and country.' A few weeks later, after a failed attempt on the life of Lord Lieutenant French, Chamber president, William Wallace, sent a telegram to French to deplore the assassination attempt. Viscount French introduced the Black and Tans into the conflict in January 1920.

***Left:** A solder indicates where Viscount French's car was shot at in an assassination attempt, 19 December 1919.*

Chamber president, William Wallace, sent a telegram to French: 'To convey to Your Excellency my horror at the dastardly attempt on your life today, and hasten to express thankfulness at your providential escape.' French's reply expressed: 'Sincerest thanks for your kind congratulations on my escape from the dastardly assassins, who are doing their best to bring disgrace on our country in the eyes of all Christian Lands.'

***Right:** Sir Ian Macpherson, Chief Secretary, with John Denton Pinkstone, Viscount French of Ypres and of High Lake (County Roscommon) (1852-1925), Lord Lieutenant 1918-21. French was the recipient of Chamber's final address of welcome, a source of contention among members.*

Courtesy of the National Library of Ireland

By now Chamber had been forced out of its traditional comfort zone and into political uncertainty. When a British Labour Party delegation visited Dublin in 1920, Council could not agree to send representatives to meet them. At the same time it felt that a motion by Francis Usher to express confidence in the administration of Viscount French would give rise to unpleasantness in Chamber and the secretary was directed to persuade Usher to withdraw it.

The ongoing War of Independence gave rise to frequent mentions in the reports of the difficulty in carrying on business under the prevailing conditions of lawlessness. A comment by Lloyd George that he would meet with the 'responsible people who would make a deal to get peace to accept Dominion Home Rule for Ireland', reported in *The Irish Times* on 26 July 1920, led to a special meeting of Council three days later which adopted a resolution that it 'views with horror the crimes and reprisals which are rapidly making life intolerable in Ireland and calls upon all Irishmen of goodwill to use their utmost efforts to prevent the re-occurrence of these outrages.' Therefore 'the Council asks the government to give a pledge in parliament to concede a measure of complete self-government for Ireland subject only to the restrictions mentioned in the PM's recent speech, viz: that Ireland should remain within the Empire and that Ulster should not be coerced.' Council condemned the burning of Cork in January 1921 and its report for 1920 commented: 'Murder and assassination have stalked daily through the land.'

An *Irish Times* editorial strongly supported Council's resolution: 'The issue is no longer between Union and Home Rule, but between any tolerable form of government and no government at all.' Chamber no longer had any faith that Lloyd George could impose law and order on the country. As if to emphasise this, a few days later Francis Hugh Brooke, agent to the Fitzwilliam Estate, chairman of the Dublin & South Eastern Railway and a director of the Bank of Ireland, was shot dead by a group of armed men in his office in Westland Row. Brooke was an adviser to Viceroy French and a member of the Privy Council.

Council also had difficulty countenancing a partitioned Ireland because it would separate the southern unionists from the larger cohort of unionists in Ulster. A special committee and a delegation to a meeting of the Irish Chambers of Commerce discussed the impending Government of Ireland Act and Chamber objected to the proposed partition and the duplication of functions within the act. Nevertheless in December 1920 the Act was passed, giving Ireland two Home Rule parliaments. Southern unionists were dissatisfied but Andrew Jameson, a moderate unionist who had been elected to Council in 1919, was very effective in dealing with the resurgent nationalists. He was also a leading supporter of a proposed Irish National War Memorial for the Irish dead of the recently-ended war, first mentioned in Council in August 1919. In 1921 Chamber's choice of then vice-president Jameson as its new president was significant as he would have been regarded as the most pragmatic kind of unionist, willing to accept compromise but respected by both sides. The 1921 Chamber report commented: 'One of the regrettable effects of Partition is that it would deprive the southern Irish parliament of the steadying influence and business training of the men of Ulster.'

A truce between the combatants in the War of Independence came into effect on 11 July 1921. British proposals for an Irish settlement were

William Maunsell Calwell (1886-1967)

William Maunsell Calwell was born in Dublin in 1886. He joined the Royal Dublin Fusiliers on the outbreak of the First World War and was promoted from the ranks, to lieutenant in 1916 and captain the following year. He was awarded a military cross for conspicuous gallantry in September 1918 for taking command of half his battalion and successfully withdrawing the men when they were in danger of being cut off.

In 1921 Calwell was appointed secretary to Chamber in the place of the deceased Robert King Irvine. An efficient man of high reputation, he was effectively poached by J.C.M. Eason in 1925. He became a director of Easons, succeeding Jack Eason as managing director in 1950. Calwell remained involved with Chamber, joining as a member in 1928 and managing the King Irvine Fund.

Andrew Jameson (1855-1941)

Scots-born Andrew Jameson came to Dublin to work in the family brewing business, Jameson & Pim, and joined Dublin Chamber. In the 1890s he was a member of the Irish Unionist Alliance and later the Irish Unionist Anti-Partition League. When Jameson & Pim was absorbed into Watkins Brewery in 1904 Jameson became chairman and managing director of the family distillery. In 1921 he was appointed to the Privy Council and given a New Year Honour, 'Right Honorable'. During the Civil War he and James Green Douglas met Éamon de Valera in an attempt to bring the conflict to an end. He served as Chamber president in 1922 and was Jamesons' representative on Council 1922-38. President W.T. Cosgrave attended his funeral.

Jameson's obituary in *Time* magazine described him as the 'pink-cheeked, buffalo-hunting chairman of Jameson & Son Ltd', a reference to a hunting excursion with Teddy Roosevelt in Texas in 1876. Aleck C. Crichton, Chamber President in 1974, is the grandson of Andrew Jameson.

presented in July and treaty negotiations began in London in October. Dáil Éireann asked Chamber for its opinion and it responded that it objected strongly to Clause 5 of the settlement, which proposed that there would be no restrictions on trade between the two islands. Chamber preferred an Irish parliament to have full control over its own trade, which Professor Edward P. Culverwell, in a letter to *The Irish Times*, saw as striking evidence of confidence by a loyalist body in an Irish parliament. Clause 5 was omitted from the Treaty when negotiations concluded, on 5 December 1921. A special meeting of Council on 30 December discussed the Treaty and recommended acceptance of it. A copy of the resolution was sent to Arthur Griffith, Éamon de Valera, the speaker of the Dáil, and the press. The Lord Lieutenant was no longer relevant. John Good, a past president, and James Shanks, who proposed the resolution, were very active in promoting the settlement.

A domestic problem interrupted Council's consideration of the Treaty when it was discovered that a Chamber clerk, Louis H. Donne, who had been employed since 1894, had disappeared, along with a number of the receipt books. The embezzlement came to light when William Calwell was appointed secretary after the death of Robert King Irvine. King Irvine had been ill and had missed the irregularities in the books. Donne was never prosecuted or found. Accountants Craig Gardner were called in to investigate and not surprisingly their report suggested that professional auditors should be appointed. Until then two honorary auditors had audited the books every year. The incumbents, J. Denne Bolton, secretary to Rathmines UDC, and flour merchant George Byrne, resigned and Craig Gardner became Chamber's auditors. Today this position is held by PriceWaterhouseCooper (PwC).

Due to the extraordinary political circumstances, Council broke its own rules by making an unsuccessful attempt to persuade Andrew Jameson, who had been appointed to the new Free State senate, to continue as president for another year. Instead William Hewat of Thomas Heiton & Company took over the presidency. The issue of Chamber becoming politically involved was raised again prior to new Dáil elections but it was agreed that it would be unwise to depart from the principal of non-intervention in political matters. Likewise, when it was suggested that a 'Treaty fund' be raised to help defray the costs of the pro-Treaty candidates, Council demurred.

In March 1918 it was proposed that the articles of Chamber be amended to allow nominees of various trade bodies to hold a seat on Council. James Vincent Brady claimed that a vote on this issue would be illegal and said that he would take proceedings if it were held. A ballot of the entire Chamber went ahead nevertheless and the proposed change was passed by 266 votes to 111. The article was first enacted in 1922 and over the next few years Jamesons Distillery, W. & R. Jacob, the Irish Banks Standing Committee and Irish Motor Traders all nominated a Council member in addition to the twenty-seven elected members. Andrew Jameson and George Jacob resigned their Council seats and were reappointed as nominees of their companies. These new members tended to be more pragmatic and flexible than the august patriarchs of traditional family businesses and better able to respond to the changed commercial environment. Over the years a number of Chamber presidents came from among company nominees.

Andrew Jameson, Chamber president in 1921, an eventful year.
Courtesy IDL Archive

Commercial concerns, from which Chamber had been distracted for a number of years, were back on the agenda, including railway strikes, additional charges on freight to Ireland and a postal strike. The Council made representation to the provisional government in Dublin to persuade it that taxation in the Free State should not differ from that of the UK. Chamber representatives attended the meeting of the Association of British Chambers of Commerce in London for the last time and were to the fore in encouraging the formation of an Association of Chambers of Commerce of the Irish Free State in 1923. This operated from Commercial Buildings from November of that year and John Good was its first president.

In April 1922 the anti-Treaty 'Irregular' forces occupied the Four Courts in the first action of the Civil War. At the end of June the courts were destroyed after they were bombarded by Free State forces and mined by anti-Treaty soldiers. Gunfire broke one of Chamber's plate-glass windows during the affray. The Civil War, which was to paralyse the new state until the following May, had begun. In a short time, the part of O'Connell Street that had not been destroyed in the Rising was damaged by Free State forces trying to dislodge anti-Treaty soldiers. In August 1922 condolences were offered on the death of Arthur Griffith and a special Council meeting was called following the death of Michael Collins. A statement was issued: 'That this Council deeply regrets the tragic death of General Michael Collins while fighting gallantly in the cause of order.' Chamber was represented at both funerals. The instability of the Civil War gave rise to fears about security and Chamber ordered that the president's chain be put in the vaults of the Bank of Ireland for safe-keeping.

A formal letter from the Bank of Ireland noting Council's resolution that the president's chain should be kept in the bank vault due to fears for security arising from the uncertain atmosphere of the Civil War.

James Shanks (1845-1926)

James Shanks was born in Belfast. He joined the firm of Messrs Wheeler & Company, a British mineral water and bottling works, and moved to Dublin in 1869 to run their new plant in Townsend Street, which he subsequently took over.

In 1893 *The New York Times* reported: 'Perhaps the finest looking man who stepped ashore from the *Compania* yesterday was the Right Honorable the Lord Mayor of Dublin, James Shanks…well built, and has a ruddy complexion and heavy mustache…he was addressed in ultra fashionable attire, and spoke in a cheery, hearty way.' As Lord Mayor, Shanks was attending the World Fair in Chicago. He was a Home Ruler and supported Parnell after the split in the Irish Party.

With accountant Robert Gardner and hotelier Henry Jury, Shanks built the International Grand Hotel in Bray. It was loss-making and sold in 1904 for £34,000. He acted as chief executive officer of the Irish International Exhibition in Herbert Park in 1907. Serving on Council from 1912, Shanks was among the most active members and persisted in drawing attention to the appalling housing situation in Dublin. Chamber awarded him its first honorary membership when he retired from Council in 1924.

The conflict made commerce difficult. There were robberies, disruption to the railway and communications infrastructure, a reduction in trade and increased taxation to pay for the war effort. Prices were still rising. The report at the end of the year remarked: 'The course of events during 1922, with its long tale of criminal destruction of life and property, will, no doubt, have due historical record, and will make painful reading for lovers of their country.' In April 1923 custom barriers were put in place between the Free State and the UK, despite attempts by Chamber to secure a derogation.

Civil War hostilities ceased on 24 May 1923. Despite its previous decisions not to become involved in politics, the disruption and uncertainty caused by the Civil War made Chamber revisit its policy and in July it supported the formation of a businessman's committee to put forward candidates

The mayoral crest of James Shanks, from the oak room of the Mansion House.

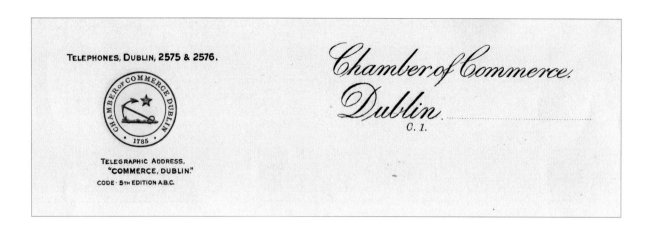

TELEPHONES, DUBLIN, 2575 & 2576.

CHAMBER OF COMMERCE DUBLIN
1785

TELEGRAPHIC ADDRESS,
"COMMERCE, DUBLIN."
CODE · 5TH EDITION A.B.C.

Chamber of Commerce
Dublin
C. 1.

Chamber letterhead from 1920. It still carries the erroneous founding date, even though this had been corrected in 1913.

for the general election in 1923. Four candidates were selected for Dublin constituencies, of whom the president, William Hewat, and past president, John Good, were elected. Old habits die hard: Chamber presented an address of welcome to T.M. Healy on his appointment as the first Governor-General of the Irish Free State in June 1923.

James Shanks was president in 1923. Remembering William Martin Murphy's comments at the time of the Lockout about the dreadful state of tenement housing (and, indeed, Murphy's stated preference for housing over an art gallery), Chamber became involved in preparing a policy for housing reform in Dublin. The collapse of two tenement houses in Church Street on 3 September 1913, killing seven, had served to emphasise the dangerous condition of housing in Dublin. Shanks spearheaded the campaign on housing, raising the subject at Council meetings each year, even during the war. In 1914 Council nominated Shanks and Horace Plunkett as part of a deputation of the Citizens' Housing Reform League to meet the Prime Minister in London to seek state intervention in the provision of housing in Dublin.

Activity on the issue was limited for the duration of the war but Council raised the topic of housing again in 1919. James Shanks had a prominent role on Council and after his retirement due to ill health in 1924 Chamber awarded him its first honorary membership.

To its credit, Chamber had survived the tumultuous decade of revolution and the establishment of the Free State, relatively intact and coherent, ready to revert to concerning itself solely with the commercial life of Dublin.

X

IN THE NEW STATE, 1922-32

The government has shown a willingness to hear the views of the Council on all matters relating to trade and commerce.

Annual Report for 1926

The proclamation read on the steps of the GPO on Easter Monday 1916 declared: 'The Republic guarantees religious and civil liberty, equal rights and equal opportunities to all its citizens, and declares its resolve to pursue the happiness and prosperity of the whole nation and of all its parts, cherishing all the children of the nation equally, and oblivious of the differences carefully fostered by an alien government, which have divided a minority from the majority in the past.' A provisional constitution and a democratic programme, which included some of the social concerns of the Labour party, were read at the opening of the first Dáil in 1919. The idealism of these documents seemed to die with the Treaty and pragmatic politicians were in control of the first governments of the Free State, perhaps rendered more cautious and conservative by the Civil War that marked the first year of the

Masthead from the Dublin Chamber of Commerce Journal, *which was first published in 1927. It ceased publication after two years but was revived in 1952.*

1924

Free State Army mutiny. Minister for Industry and Commerce, Joseph McGrath, resigns in protest.

Dissolution of Dublin Corporation and appointment of three commissioners to run Dublin.

Railway Act amalgamates seventeen companies into the Great Southern Railway Company.

1925

Shannon Electricity Act launches construction of hydroelectric station in Ardnacrusha.

1926

Inauguration of 2RN (later Radio Éireann).

1927

Assassination of Minister for Justice, Kevin O'Higgins.

state's existence. The Catholic hierarchy that, in general, opposed the War of Independence, was firmly on the side of the Treaty and Catholic social values soon came to define the new state, so that the unionist adage, 'Home Rule is Rome Rule' was proved correct. Nor did the Free State initially do much to improve the lot of the poor of Dublin and other cities, whose housing conditions remained largely unchanged. Within a short period of time the government introduced censorship, removed power from the local authorities and attempted to limit the role of women to the home. When Fianna Fáil came to power in 1932 it introduced a marriage bar restricting women's employment in the public service, most of the provisions of which remained in place until after Ireland joined the EEC in 1973. Éamon de Valera's 1937 Constitution rearticulated the Catholic ethos of the state.

The Senate in the Free State's new bicameral parliament had been designed to include representatives of unionism and the minority Protestant population, giving them a forum for expression and some limited influence. Much of the wealth of the country remained in Protestant hands, something that was reflected in Dublin business and consequently in Chamber's membership. In 1922 Chamber was asked to nominate six individuals for the new Senate and in all nine members of the first Senate were members of Dublin Chamber, including Bryan R. Mahon, Andrew Jameson, James G. Douglas, Horace Plunkett and James Perry Goodbody.

The aim of Chamber was to promote the commercial and manufacturing interests of the city but over the previous decades it had allowed itself be distracted by national and world political issues to the detriment of its declared mission, so that bodies such as the Dublin Mercantile Association had taken over some of Chamber's functions. Council had frequently drawn attention to the fact that Dublin's distance from the administration in London was detrimental to its economic wellbeing and gradually came to realise that a government in Dublin gave it far more influence and access to decision-making and decision-makers than it could ever have had in the old régime.

An area in which the priorities of Chamber diverged from those of government was in commemorating the dead of the First World War. From 1919 Chamber had facilitated the collection of funds for the Irish National War Memorial and by 1924 £20,000 had been raised from among its members. The English architect, Edward Lutyens – also architect of the ill-fated bridge gallery for the Hugh Lane collection – designed the monument but the Free State government was not enthusiastic about the project and there was difficulty in obtaining a suitable site. Eventually a plot was acquired in Islandbridge, by the river Liffey, and work began on Lutyens's design in 1932. The memorial was completed six years later.

There is no doubt that the formation of the new state discommoded certain members of Chamber and in the uncertain climate of the early 1920s some professionals chose the familiarity of England rather than the unknown quantity of the new Ireland. Solicitor William Fry (1858-1939) had been a very active member of Council from 1905, prominent on many deputations, and had unsuccessfully run for vice-president in 1918 and 1919. In 1920 he resigned because he had moved to live in London. Similarly John Mackie (1876-1940), an accountant, resigned his Council seat because he set up an office in London. Mackie was, however, a liberal and supporter of Home Rule, and returned to Dublin and to Council when his firm amalgamated with Craig Gardner.

1927

Éamon de Valera and Fianna Fáil TDs sign the oath of allegiance and enter Dáil Éireann.

1928

Introduction of new currency for Irish Free State, at parity with sterling until 1979.

1929

Wall Street Crash on Tuesday 29 October.

1930

Local Government (Dublin) Act restores the corporation but under a city manager. New city boundaries include Rathmines and Pembroke.

1931

UK abandons the gold standard.

Free State Custom Duties Act imposes duties to prevent the dumping of goods.

1932

UK enacts Import Duties Act.

Fianna Fáil wins its first election and assumes power with Labour.

J.J. Crowe (1886-1929)

John Joseph Crowe was born in Longford, the fourth of nine children of an RIC policeman. In 1905 he began work as an assistant clerk in the War Office, then spent twenty years in the Department of Agriculture. After independence he chose to move to Belfast with the Northern Irish Department of Agriculture rather than remain with the new government.

In 1925 Crowe was chosen by ballot to succeed William Calwell as secretary of Chamber, at a starting salary of £350 per annum. From September 1928 he suffered from recurring illness and in January 1929 he went to Switzerland for health reasons, for which Chamber gave him six months' paid leave. He died in Arosa in March and was survived by his wife and daughters.

For Jacobs, one of Dublin's largest employers, political uncertainty was a factor in the company's decision to open a factory in Liverpool in 1922. George N. Jacob, the director, was no supporter of Home Rule but became reconciled to the new dispensation and served as Chamber president in 1926. Membership of Council changed considerably at the time of the formation of the new state but some of the change was coincidental, occasioned by the deaths of a good number of the old guard, such as William Goulding (fertiliser manufacturer), Frederic W. Pim (drapery and manufacturer), Robert W. Kennan (sugar merchant) and former presidents Minch, Mooney, Wallace, Malone, Murphy, Gamble and Goodbody. These departures left a large number of vacancies to be filled by new blood in Council, as former presidents tended to hold their seats on Council for life.

William Hewat of Heitons, who was president when the Civil War began, struck a negative, even apocalyptic note in his speech at the AGM in May 1922: 'The Provisional Government's attempt to function had been a conspicuous failure. Everywhere in Ireland there was fear – fear to purchase anything, fear to have anything for sale, fear of violence, fear that your life's work may be destroyed before your eyes, fear of being driven from your home.' But after the Civil War had ended and relative normality returned, Chamber soon grew accustomed to presenting resolutions and sending deputations to the new government ministers in Dublin, while ministers were invited to speak at Chamber's general meetings. In turn ministers invited Chamber to send representatives to several enquiries. In July 1924 members gave evidence at the Greater Dublin Commission of Enquiry which the government established after it suspended the corporation and installed three commissioners to run the city, maintaining that the corporation was being mismanaged and mentioning allegations of misconduct by certain councillors in the allocation of corporation houses. The commission recommended that the local authority should be under the direction of a city manager but the government did not put its recommendations into effect until 1930.

Chamber strenuously objected to an early proposal to amalgamate the main railway companies because of its innate aversion to monopolies and because it saw such an amalgamation as a step towards nationalisation. Several Council members were directors of railway companies but the railways themselves were loss-making and the government offered unification of the system as the solution. President William T. Cosgrave commented intemperately – and unjustly – during a debate in the Dáil: 'If there is one class in the community more responsible than another for the disorder that has taken place during the last two years, it is the so-called businessmen.' The Great Western Railway Company, which was formed in 1924, incorporated seventeen railway lines – all but the cross-border Great Northern Line – and the spat was soon forgotten. Cosgrave himself attended Chamber general meetings from time to time.

Council of Dublin Chamber in the courtyard of Commercial Buildings, early 1929. Front from left: J. Hubbard Clark, Sir Walter Nugent, Chamber president John Mackie, David Barry and assistant secretary, P.L. Prendeville, author of the first history of Chamber. Prendeville was deputising for secretary J.J. Crowe, who was on sick leave in Switzerland. Back from left: William Lombard Murphy, Michael O'Dea, William Crowe, Jack C.M. Eason and William P. Sherriff.

Chamber of Commerce Journal

P.L. Prendeville (b. 1907)

Patrick Lionel Prendeville was the eldest son of a drapery assistant from Kimmage and took a BComm degree in UCD on a County Dublin university scholarship. He was appointed assistant secretary to Chamber without competition, on the recommendation of his professor, Bernard F. Shields.

While working for Chamber Prendeville researched and wrote the organisation's first history, a thesis entitled *A History of the Dublin Chamber of Commerce, 1760-1860, with an Introduction to the Chamber of Commerce Movement*. This thesis, for which he earned a first-class-honours MComm, was never published but is available to read in UCD.

Prendeville had to deputise for the secretary J.J. Crowe because of the latter's illness, but after Crowe's death, he was not considered for the job, being still only twenty-two. Around 1932 he left Chamber to take up a lecturing position in UCD.

The Shannon Hydroelectric Scheme

A Drogheda-born science and engineering graduate, Thomas A. McLaughlin (1896-1971),worked for Siemens-Schuckert and devised a hydroelectric scheme for the River Shannon. Cumann na nGaedheal's Minister for Industry and Commerce, Patrick McGilligan, drove the project, unusually ambitious for a conservative government, through the Oireachtas.

The first contract was in place in August 1925, less than a year after McGilligan had brought the proposal to government. Siemens brought plant and machinery from Germany and employed up to 4800 men during the construction phase. The scheme started to produce electricity in October 1929 and the new government awarded Siemens-Schuckert a second contract in July 1932 to provide an additional 25-MVA turbine. This was commissioned in 1933.

During this period Council frequently discussed administrative difficulties in relation to tariffs and taxation, what might be termed teething problems, that arose as a result of separating the new state from the UK. The Free State Minister for Finance, Ernest Blythe, spoke at a general meeting on taxation and visited Council to discuss the subject.

There were almost a hundred and sixty different companies supplying electricity in the new state and the Shannon Hydroelectric Scheme was first mooted in 1924 as a means of consolidating the country's fragmented electricity infrastructure. The scheme also involved the creation of a national grid. Chamber objected on two grounds: that the cost of £6.5 million was too high for the new state to bear; and that existing providers, particularly Rathmines Urban District Council, had expended a great deal of money on their own generating facilities, which would now be redundant. The core of the issue was the effective nationalisation of the electricity supply: as with the railways, nationalisation was anathema to Chamber. Council even went

A visit to the site of the Shannon Hydroelectric Scheme in Ardnacrusha led by Chamber president, David Barry (on the left), with Patrick McGilligan, Minister for Industry and Commerce, to his left.

Courtesy of the National Library of Ireland

so far as to get opinion as to the legality of the project but decided not to proceed when it was pointed out to them that there was general support for it in the Dáil and throughout the country. The Minister for Industry and Commerce, Patrick McGilligan, met Council members several times to try to allay their fears. When, shortly afterwards, the government signed a construction contract for the Shannon scheme with the German firm of Siemens-Schuckert, some Chamber members were unhappy that a British firm had not been given the chance to tender for the project, conscious too that Siemens-Schuckert had produced aircraft used against Britain during the First World War.

Ardnacrusha had the capacity to generate twice the then needs of the whole state and to justify its existence economically it would have to take over all existing generating facilities, including those of Dublin and its townships. When Dáil Éireann passed the Electricity (Supply) Bill, 1927, Chamber issued a resolution: 'That we, the members of the Dublin Chamber of

Commerce, representing the ratepayers of the city, protest emphatically against the policy embodied in the Electricity (Supply) Bill, 1927, under which the distribution and sale of electricity in the city are to be taken over by the Shannon Electricity Board.' British Fascists, Irish Free State Command, (with offices at 52 South King Street) also protested: 'We are not opposed to just measures being carried into law, but we view with grave concern a measure such as the Electricity Supply Bill, which is based on State socialistic principals.' Public meetings of protest were held in Rathmines UDC and in Chamber, on 12 April 1927, Chamber president, George Jacob, described the Shannon Bill as 'legalised robbery', including clauses 'which strike an the very root of civilised society'. After three further general meetings Chamber felt that it had no option but to accept the bill, subject to two guarantees: that should the scheme fail the old power stations of the corporation and Rathmines and Pembroke should not be returned in a dilapidated state; and that Dublin consumers should benefit from the new station's lower distribution costs.

The Irish Times, still the voice of the establishment, editorialised: 'We sympathise with Chamber's difficulties, but…it has condoned the principal of confiscation, as applied by the state to civic property; and this, surely, is a very serious responsibility for the most representative body of business men in Dublin.' It finished by cruelly suggesting: 'The Chamber of Commerce has failed, and now the last word lies with the Senate.' David Barry, the Antrim-

ASSOCIATION OF CHAMBERS OF COMMERCE OF THE IRISH FREE STATE.

TELEPHONES 23281 & 23282.
TELEGRAMS.
"COMMERCE, DUBLIN."

**COMMERCIAL BUILDINGS,
DAME STREET,
DUBLIN.**

*Letterhead of
the Association
of Chambers of
Commerce of the
Irish Free State.*

IRISH ASSOCIATIONS OF CHAMBERS OF COMMERCE

The Association of Chambers of Commerce of the Irish Free State was incorporated on 24 August 1923. Its first president was Dublin Chamber's former president, John Good, Its offices were in Commercial Buildings and William M. Calwell, secretary to Dublin Chamber, was its secretary. From its inception the association prepared an annual budget submission on behalf of its members. Two years after the enactment of the 1937 Constitution its official name was changed to the Association of Chambers of Commerce of Ireland. Because of its size, Dublin Chamber tended to lead the way in the association and it was not until 1967, when it moved out of Commercial Buildings, that it employed its own full-time secretary.

In 2005 the association rebranded itself as Chambers Ireland with a new logo, which by 2010 had been adopted by many member chambers around the country – although Dublin Chamber continued to use its own. Staff numbers increased from eleven in 2003 to twenty-eight in 2007 to implement state and EU projects but this strategy ran into difficulties. A deficit resulted so staff numbers had to be reduced and the debt tackled.

There are now forty-four accredited members of Chambers Ireland, which has offices is in Newmount House, Lower Mount Street, Dublin, The association supports chambers throughout Ireland and provides a national policy voice on their behalf.

*A group photographed in the
courtyard of Commercial
Buildings at the meeting of the
Association of Chambers of
Commerce of the Irish Free State,
1928. George N. Jacob (in the
centre, wearing a watch fob) was
president of the association.*

Chamber of Commerce Journal

born manager of the British and Irish Steampacket Company and vice-president of Chamber, went so far as to resign briefly from Council because of its decision to accept the Shannon Bill but in October 1928, as president, it was he who led a Chamber excursion to view the marvels of Ardnacrusha. Five hundred people paid a guinea for the trip, which included a first-class ticket on a special train to Limerick, 'a light luncheon, dinner and motor conveyance from Limerick'. Patrick McGilligan went as a guest of Chamber. After the trip Barry was more amenable and announced that 'the Minister could rely on the members of Chamber doing their best to make the scheme a success. The visit to the scheme had impressed the members of Chamber with the importance of the undertaking.'

Membership increased to a high of nine hundred in 1927 before falling back. Chamber spent £300 on improving the premises and bought a set of Malton Prints and Brooking's 1728 *Map of Dublin* from McCambridges to hang in the members' conversation room. (They still adorn the walls of Chamber.) A coffee bar was initiated in the reading room and photographs of the refurbished premises used in an advertisement in *The Irish Times*. A brochure, probably Chamber's first, appeared in 1926, giving an account of its work, and Chamber approached editors of the national newspapers to ask them to give greater coverage to its proceedings. In the same year the first annual Chamber dinner was held in the Royal College of Surgeons dining room. Tickets cost two guineas and one hundred and eighty people attended, including the Governor-General and the Chief Justice, as well as presidents of other Chambers. At the third annual dinner in the Mansion House in 1928 – the last until 1949 – ladies were welcome.

UCD had introduced a Commerce degree in 1908, with the support of Chamber, and Council now focused its attention on having Trinity do the same. After many years of effort, including the appointment of John Good as Chamber representative on a committee on the board of Trinity set up to create the faculty, TCD finally opened its School of Commerce in 1925. In keeping with its policy of support for commercial education, Council advised employers to favour graduates of the schools of commerce if possible and when, in 1927, Council decided to employ an assistant secretary, it selected a UCD graduate, P.L. Prendeville, on a salary of £150 per annum.

On 1 January 1926 a state radio station, 2RN, which would eventually become Radio Éireann, began broadcasting from Little Denmark Street, moving to the reconstructed GPO in 1928. The Minister for Industry and Commerce asked Chamber to provide commercial news and, in November 1931, *The Irish Times* reported: 'Mr. J.R. Clark, secretary to the Dublin Chamber of Commerce, in a broadcast from the Dublin wireless station on Tuesday, made an appeal to the British Chambers of Commerce to advise the British public to give preference to Irish Free State goods.' This was Chamber's first recorded use of modern mass media and the first time the secretary acted as its spokesperson.

Chamber president, J.C.M. (Jack) Eason (1881-1976), and other officers attended the funeral of the assassinated minister for Justice, Kevin O'Higgins, in January 1927 and Council passed a resolution of 'abhorrence of the dastardly crime committed'. There was great public excitement when Colonel James C. Fitzmaurice of the Irish army and two German colleagues crossed the Atlantic from Baldonnel aerodrome. Jack Eason

David Barry (1873-1938) was born in Ballycarry, County Antrim. He joined Chamber when he first arrived in Dublin in 1912 and served on Council from 1921 until his death and as president in 1928.

Barry was MD of the British and Irish Steampacket Company and, although a unionist, he represented the more pragmatic strand of Chamber, accepting the political changes that had taken place in Ireland. He is buried in Ballycarry, where his gravestone – unique among those of former Chamber presidents – notes his Chamber presidency.

DUBLIN CHAMBER OF COMMERCE,
(INCORPORATED).

COMMERCIAL BUILDINGS, DAME STREET,

DUBLIN, 12th OCTOBER, 1929.

NOTICE OF MEETING.

The October Ordinary General Meeting will
be held in the Chamber at 3 o'clock, p.m.,

on

MONDAY, 21st OCTOBER, 1929,

when an Address will be given by

Dr. W. C. DWYER,

CITY COMMISSIONER,

on

OUTDOOR RELIEF.

By Order,
J. R. CLARK,
Secretary.

Chamber notice of the October 1928 general meeting, to be addressed by one of the three city commissioners who ran Dublin, 1926-30.

sent a congratulatory telegram to W.T. Cosgrave, noting: 'this magnificent achievement redounds to the credit of all concerned, and adds to the prestige of our country.' Council received an indignant deputation from the Law Society in May 1929, asking Chamber to oppose new legislation requiring solicitors to pass an examination in Irish. Council deferred any decision on the issue.

Three commissioners had replaced Dublin Corporation's elected representatives since 1924 and, after they stood down, in 1931, Chamber president, James J. Halpin, presented each of them with a motor car and an inscribed silver cigarette case in appreciation of their efforts at an event in the Shelbourne Hotel. The gifts were funded by subscription by ratepayers, the money collected by Chamber. It is true that the commissioners managed the city efficiently but they did not really attempt to solve any of its major problems, as this would have involved expenditure and necessitated increasing the rates. For instance when the city received an offer of a free trial of new-fangled traffic control lights to help alleviate traffic problems, they overruled accepting the offer. For this reason they were popular with the businessmen in Chamber.

The Local Government Act of 1930 reinstated the corporation and the city area under its control now included Rathmines and Pembroke, something Chamber had opposed for decades. Now it passed without mention. The act installed a manager to run each corporation or council, a system that remains in operation to this day. As a result of lobbying by the mercantile community, the act also created a commercial constituency – five seats in a council of thirty-five – with an electorate confined to business ratepayers. Chamber was entitled to nominate four candidates and three were successful in the subsequent election: John Hubbard Clark, Charles E. McGloughlin, chairman of the Port and Docks Board, and Sir Thomas W. Robinson. The commercial constituency lasted only five years.

Chamber's annual reports from 1927 onwards were positive about the economic outlook. In 1929 bank deposits were showing an increase but the cost of living index was falling behind that of the United Kingdom. Chamber president, Sir Walter Nugent, a senator and director of Great Southern Railways, observed at the May general meeting that 'the Irish Free State had now reached a period of well-defined progress.' Economic progress of any kind would prove to be short-lived: in October 1929 the stock market in Wall Street crashed. The UK took measures to deal with the crash that had a knock-on effect on Ireland's economy, removing the gold standard and imposing duties on imports. The positive outlook of the 1929 report was definitely missing from that of the following year, which announced:

John Good

John Good (1867-1941)

John Good was born in 1867, the son of Matthew Good, manager of the Dublin Dockyard Company of Ringsend. He was apprenticed to his uncle, James Pile, a builder, and started business on his own account in 1890. J. & P. Good, which he founded with his brother Peter in 1897, was one of the foremost contractors of its time: it built Rathmines Town Hall and the Burton building on the corner of Dame Street and South Great George's Street.

Good served on Council from 1915 until his death and was president in 1920. He was a member of Pembroke UDC from 1918 and stood unsuccessfully on the Unionist ticket in Pembroke District in the 1918 general election. He served as an Independent (Businessmen) TD for South Dublin, with Chamber's support, 1923-37, his Dáil contributions concerning the construction industry and business matters. His brother pre-deceased him and their firm ceased trading after his death.

WOMEN IN CHAMBER

In 1919 Dublin Corporation wrote to Council to invite it to 'nominate five persons, some of whom to be women, to represent the Chamber' on the committee it was about to form to enquire into profiteering by business as a result of the recent war. After a couple of days' consideration Council 'authorise[d] the secretary to nominate five gentlemen to act.' Dublin Chamber had no women members at that time, although none of the organisation's rules prohibited them, and it was not until 1926 that it got its first woman member. She was Alice Emilie Yeates (1856-1943) from Manchester, widow of Arthur Mitchell Yeates, owner of the prominent Dublin opticians Yeates & Company, with premises on the corner of Grafton and Nassau Streets. Mrs Yeates did not presage a tidal wave of women members. During the 1930s and 1940 there was only a handful of women on each year's membership list, while in the 1950s the number usually just exceeded ten.

In 1956, at the launch of Dublin Junior Chamber, the election of a woman, E. Beryl Gavin, as secretary was still unusual enough for the then Chamber president, J. Harold Douglas, to remark: 'In particular he welcomed Miss Gavin, who was the sole representative of the ladies.' Beryl Gavin was both private and constituency secretary to Maurice Dockrell TD.

The first women on Council were ex-officio, as Lords Mayor of Dublin: Kathleen Clarke, the first woman to hold that office, 1939-41; Catherine Byrne, 1958-9; Carmencita Hederman, 1987-8. Claire Shorthall, Junior Chamber president for 1984, was also an ex-officio member. Eileen Galligan, of the House of Ireland, was the first woman to be elected a member of Council, in 1987.

Belfast Chamber of Commerce elected a woman president, Irene Calvert, as far back as 1965 but she has been the only woman so far to hold the office. In 1968 she became a member of Dublin Chamber when she was executive manager of the Great Southern Hotels Group. Jeannette McDonnell was president of Limerick Chamber in 1993 and 1994 but Cork Chamber did not have its first woman president until Gillian Keating began her term in 2013, In contrast, Dublin Chamber of Commerce has had four female presidents, Mary Finan the first in 1996. Chamber established a women in focus group under Senator Mary White in 1997; it concluded that women members represented only 15 per cent of Chamber members and that their attendance at Chamber functions was lower again. Chamber's current CEO (from 2000), Gina Quin, is the first woman to have held this position.

Four women presidents of Dublin Chamber. From left: Mary Finan (1996), Áine Maria Mizzoni (2005), Margaret Sweeney (2008) and Imelda Reynolds (2011).

The Refurbished Chamber

The Irish Times of 25 February 1926 commented on: '...the main reading room of the Dublin Chamber of Commerce, which has been refurbished in a modern fashion. It would be interesting to know what the original Ousel Galley committee would think if they visited the scene of their former labours and witnessed the changes that have taken place since it looked after the welfare of Dublin commerce...The main room on the ground floor has been totally refurbished. Owing to its size it was necessary to treat it as two separate rooms divided by a passage leading to the second and third floors. The spaces on either side of the passage are covered with Donegal carpets in the centre of which are placed magnificent mahogany tables 11'x4'. The seating accommodation consists of armchairs in hide and velvet. New writing tables have been constructed specially to fit in with the scheme of alterations, while the electric lighting has received careful attention. On the second floor a coffee room has been provided, where light refreshments may be obtained from 11am daily, while on the third floor suites of offices have been constructed for the accommodation of the staff. These improvements add considerably to the comfort of the members, and with the other advantages which the Chamber offers, there should be considerable additions to the membership list during the current year. The furniture, carpets, etc., were supplied by the well known Dublin firms, Messrs. Millar and Beatty and Messrs. Anderson, Stanford and Ridgeway, Grafton Street.'

The piece included an advertisement for the chamber and another for Siemens-Schuckert, to whose appointment as contractors of the Shannon scheme Chamber had objected.

'The past year has been one of widespread depression both in industry and agriculture. Apart from repercussions of the financial crisis in the United States of America, the commerce of the world has been dislocated by the phenomenal fall in wholesale prices.' Despite this the report opined that the Free State had escaped relatively unscathed. Soon the crash of 1929 would take second place to a homegrown cause of economic decline.

Éamon de Valera had founded Fianna Fáil in 1926 from the majority of anti-Treaty Sinn Féin members who no longer wished to continue the policy of abstention from the Dáil. In 1927, after the reality check of the assassination of Kevin O'Higgins, Fianna Fáil TDs took the Oath of Allegiance to the king, one of the most bitterly resented clauses of the Anglo-Irish Treaty of

1921, and entered the Dáil for the first time. After the general election of March 1932 the party formed a minority government with Labour support.

It was all change from the previous ten years. Chamber had traditionally been politically neutral, ostensibly at least, but it had supported the businessmen party contesting the 1923 general election and the 1930 corporation election. John Good was elected for Dublin South in the 1932 general election. Council member and incoming president, Henry Morgan Dockrell (son of Sir Maurice Dockrell, the only unionist elected in the south of Ireland, apart from Trinity College, in the 1918 general election), won a seat for Cumann na nGaedheal in 1932. All this meant that Fianna Fáil looked on Chamber with suspicion, as supporters of the former government party and as closet loyalists, if not unionists, with the result that relations between Chamber and the new government were notably lacking in cordiality. Chamber had to build bridges with the new administration in order to make its voice heard again on commercial matters.

XI

THE PROTECTIONIST YEARS, 1932-65

The Council of Dublin Chamber of Commerce regards with increasing anxiety the effect on the trade of the country of the present unequal monetary struggle with Great Britain.

Minutes of Council meeting, 21 November 1932

For the next three decades protectionism dominated Irish economic life. The very name Sinn Féin ('ourselves alone'), the founding party of independence, connoted self-sufficiency. During its decade in power, 1922-32, Cumann na nGaedheal, the pro-treaty offshoot of Sinn Féin, had somewhat supported the idea but rebuilding after the Civil War, the Wall Street Crash and the subsequent economic depression concentrated its energies on commercial survival. It was forced, like many other governments, to impose tariffs in an attempt to protect domestic commerce. Under the leadership of Éamon de Valera, Fianna Fáil were much more committed protectionists, something that became evident immediately the party came to power for the first time, after the general election of 1932.

Chamber logo in use during this period.

timeline

1932
Eucharistic Congress in Dublin.

Beginning of Economic War
with UK.

1933
Fianna Fáil win a second general
election with an overall majority.

1935
Cattle and Coal agreement
between the UK and Ireland
somewhat alleviates the
Economic War.

1936
Outbreak of Spanish Civil War.

1937
Passing of the new Irish
constitution.

1938
Anglo-Irish agreement ends the
Economic War and returns the
treaty ports to Ireland.

1939
Outbreak of Second World War.

In its general election campaign in February 1932, Fianna Fáil proposed an eight-point programme. Two of their proposals in particular had a negative impact on the country's economy over the next three decades: to retain the land annuities in the state treasury; and 'to organise systematically the establishment of the industries required to meet the needs of the community in manufactured goods', a policy that led to protectionism. The land annuities were farmers' repayments on loans the British government had advanced them to buy their land under different land acts, 1891-1909. The new state had agreed to collect these payments for Britain but de Valera, in an act of patriotic folly, withheld the payment due on 1 July 1932. The British government immediately placed restrictive tariffs on Irish produce – primarily agricultural – in an effort to recoup their losses; so began the Economic War, which lasted for six years. In retaliation, the Irish government passed the Emergency Imposition of Duties Bill, which taxed British coal. The fight would always be an unequal one, as more than ninety per cent of Irish exports went to Britain, while less than ten per cent of Britain's exports came to Ireland. The value of Irish exports to Britain fell from £43.5 million in 1929 to £18 million in 1935.

There rapidly followed a series of Dáil bills to counteract British impositions, introducing bounties for exporters to match the tariffs and a Price Control Bill: these bills were introduced with such speed that the Council of Dublin Chamber often did not get the chance to comment on them. The Control of Manufactures Act was particularly alarming in the eyes of Council, requiring new and expanding manufacturers to receive a licence from the minister. Licences were to be issued only to citizens of the Free State or to those who had lived in the country for the previous five years and the majority of shareholders in any new business had to be Irish.

As with the country, so with Chamber, which suffered from declining membership between 1927 and 1943. In an attempt to save money it decided to let out the large room on the ground floor and advertised secretarial services at a modest fee. In 1938 its lease in Commercial Buildings was due for renewal and Council decided it could no longer afford the large room. Instead 'a fine room with nine windows overlooking the quiet courtyard has been provided, heated by coal fires, better lighted, and better ventilated than the old room, making it more comfortable.' Chamber maintained its offices on the second floor with a committee room but the entrance to the premises was no longer from Dame Street but from the courtyard. The annual rent was reduced to a third of what it had been.

In 1932 the big event in Dublin was the Eucharistic Congress, which the Cumann na nGaedheal government had planned but which took place after the change of government. As had happened with royal visits in an earlier period, Dublin commercial interests were asked to contribute toward the decoration of the city. A round tower was placed on College Green beside Chamber's premises (where the contentious statue of King William of Orange had stood until it was blown up on Armistice Day 1928), but Chamber refused to subscribe towards the decoration of Commercial Buildings for the Congress. An observer might have seen an indication of the changed political climate in the action of Gardaí who approached Chamber in the lead-up to Armistice Day 1933 to suggest that for the security of the premises it would perhaps be wiser if the flag of HMS *Dublin* and its display case in the members' reading room be removed or covered up. Council took no immediate action but in 1940 delivered the ensign to the Dean of Christ Church to exhibit in the cathedral with 'the other historical relics of the city'. There do not appear to have been any celebrations for the one

1943

Founding of the Central Bank.

1945

Ending of Second World War.

1948

First coalition government passes the Republic of Ireland Act and Ireland leaves the Commonwealth.

1950

Establishment of the Industrial Development Association.

1951

Incorporation of An Córas Tráchtála to promote exports.

1952

Establishment of Bord Fáilte to promote tourism.

1957

The Treaty of Rome establishes the European Economic Community.

hundred and fiftieth anniversary of the foundation of Chamber, in 1933.

1958

T.K. Whitaker, Secretary of the Department of Finance, helps to create the *First Programme for Economic Expansion.*

1959

Election of Seán Lemass, former Minister for Finance, as Taoiseach.

1961

New state television service, RTÉ, begins broadcasting on 31 December.

1965

Anglo-Irish Free Trade Agreement.

Much of Fianna Fáil's early legislation focused on creating new industries in Ireland, some with the assistance of foreign expertise and money. The Minister for Industry and Commerce, Seán Lemass, established the Industrial Credit Corporation (ICC) in 1933 to provide funding for such new industries. Companies wishing to trade in Ireland had to manufacture in Ireland. Cadbury, Rowntree and Clarnico Murray opened factories in Ireland to manufacture confectionery, cars sold in Ireland had to be assembled in the country, mostly by newly-established Irish companies under a licence (John O'Neill, Chamber president 1936, and F.M. Summerfield, president in 1950, were the proprietors of two such car assemblers), and shoe companies such as J.H. Woodington of Bristol and Padmore & Barnes of Northampton also opened Irish operations. Ever more tariffs protected indigenous businesses. Introduced in response to the Great Depression that followed the Wall Street Crash and continued as part of the Economic War, by 1939 tariffs covered nearly two thousand items. Protectionism was not a one-way street, as Irish businesses wishing to trade in Britain had to open plants in Britain to avoid punitive tariffs. Guinness and Jacobs were two such companies.

From Chamber's point of view the advantages of protectionism soon compensated for the losses of the Economic War. Agricultural exports were the greatest losers but new industries emerged in what would now be called 'agribusiness', such as Comhlucht Siúcra Éireann (the Irish Sugar Company) in 1933 and Irish Tanners Ltd in Portlaw in 1935. Older established businesses also benefited by reduced competition in the home market. At the end of 1935 there was a degree of normalisation in the Anglo-Irish commercial relationship with the signing of the first so-called Coal-Cattle Pact –

supported by Chamber – whereby Britain agreed to increase its importation quota of Irish cattle in return for Ireland importing only British coal.

Chamber's relationship with the new government also normalised. The organisation had representation on a number of boards and committees and ministers often spoke at its general meetings. In February 1936 Council sent a message of sympathy to Taoiseach Éamon de Valera on the death of his son Brian in a horse-riding accident in the Phoenix Park and later that year a message 'expressing the Council's pleasure at the successful outcome of the operation on his eyes'. Nonetheless John Hubbard Clark, the outgoing president, submitted to the Minister for External Affairs a message of sympathy from Chamber to the British royal family on the death of George V, also in February 1936. That year's Chamber report listed the abdication of Edward VII as one of the three outstanding events of 1936 – the others being the Spanish Civil War and monetary agreement between the governments of France, Britain and the US.

Éamon de Valera's 1937 constitution confirmed the special position of the Catholic Church in Ireland. Chamber had a large constituency of Protestants of various denominations and Jews, who faced increased Catholic influence in all walks of life. When the eminent judge, W.E. Wylie, spoke to Chamber in 1941 about his Guild of Goodwill, which ran restaurants supplying cheap meals and provided fuel

Typical attendance at a Chamber meeting in Commercial Buildings, 1950s. It is noticeable that there is only one woman (wearing a hat) in the audience.

Chamber of Commerce Journal

'The outbreak of war in Europe made the year 1939 memorable in Eire for the emergency legislation by which the government took control of external financial transfers, immigration, emigration, the exportation of goods, and internal prices.'

Chamber report, 1939

'Notwithstanding the increased intensity of the war, conditions generally in this country during 1942 were better than might have been expected, but the outlook for 1943 is unpromising.'

Council report, 1942

'Fighting continues in Europe and Asia on an unprecedented scale, but after four years of war the situation in Eire is more favourable than might have been expected. With demand always in excess of supply, many businesses report a good year's trading.'

Council report, 1943

for the poor, he received a very positive reception and many members supported the guild. But the Archbishop of Dublin, John Charles McQuaid, responded to Judge Wylie's non-denominational guild by establishing the Catholic Social Services Conference, which a number of Chamber members also supported.

The Economic War ended in 1938 with an Anglo-Irish agreement, by the terms of which the Irish government paid £10 million to settle all outstanding debts from the land annuities. In return Britain restored the treaty ports to the Free State. The agreement gave Ireland the same favourable status with the United Kingdom as the other Dominion countries had received under the British Import Duties Act of 1932 and guaranteed that Irish impositions would not place British goods at a trading disadvantage. Chamber welcomed the settlement although it noticed that afterwards there was some stagnation of business in general.

In quick succession the Depression and the Economic War had affected the Irish economy. In less than a year it would have to face the adverse effects of a worldwide conflict. Europe was marching inexorably toward war. The Chamber report for 1938 noted that the crisis concerning the German annexation of parts of Czechoslovakia that was temporarily resolved by the Munich Agreement between Hitler and Chamberlain had an inflationary effect on prices. After the outbreak of war, in September 1939, business had a new government department to deal with – the Ministry of Supplies, headed up by Seán Lemass. The war, and particularly the German threat to shipping, meant that supplies were harder to obtain. This in turn caused a reduction in manufacturing, resulting in some companies accumulating reserves. This problem was exacerbated when the British prime minister,

J.R. Clark (1885-1967)

John Robson Clark was born in Newcastle upon Tyne, joined the Board of Works as a clerk in 1904 and a year later was assigned to the Registry of Deeds in Dublin where he worked for seventeen years.

During the First World War Clark was a sergeant in the Black Watch Highlanders. He chose to retire from the civil service at the foundation of the state and attended the College of Commerce in Rathmines, coming first in Ireland in the corporate accountants exam.

Clark succeeded J.J. Crowe as Chamber secretary in 1929 after serving for four years as secretary to the Association of Chambers of Commerce. Clark lived in Rathmines and was an avid sailor in the mermaid class and a member of the National Yacht Club. He retired from his job with Chamber in 1948.

Winston Churchill, put a squeeze on Ireland by limiting its supplies of foodstuffs, fertilisers and fuel in an effort to force the government to allow the Allies to use of the old treaty ports. The government set up Irish Shipping to augment imports, an initiative of which Chamber approved. Thomas F. Laurie, originally from Manchester, and Esso MD in Ireland, was president in 1938. When war started he was seconded to the Petroleum Board in London.

Fuel shortages limited internal transport: trains, often fuelled by turf, ran at much reduced speeds and Dublin tram services were restricted. In 1942 Chamber suggested to government that horse-drawn barges be reintroduced on the Grand Canal. Eleven such barges had been built by the end of the year and were reported as being successfully in use. Full rationing did not come until 1942, affecting tea, butter, sugar and fuel. Perhaps because Dublin business people had become used to difficult trading conditions during the Economic War they do not appear to have been too discommoded by the

J.R. Clark.

inconveniences of the early 1940s: as the war progressed Chamber reports were surprisingly positive. The demand for goods exceeded supply so the government had to take steps to prevent inflation, issuing price control orders and setting up a Price Control Commission that oversaw company profits. There were not many complaints from Chamber as members were well aware of the calamities that affected the people of mainland Europe. In 1944 the Chamber report commented: 'It was with difficulty that supplies of raw material for certain of our industries were procured and freighted, but sufficient was obtained to prevent any more serious shortage than in previous years and for this, as well as for our continued immunity from the intense suffering and misery which the war, now in its sixth year, has brought to the greater part of Europe there can be only humble gratitude to God.'

During the war Chamber managed to reverse the decline in membership that had persisted since 1927. Council gave credit for this to tea merchant David Coyle, who was president in 1943. Since then Chamber numbers have grown strongly every year.

P.J. macDwyer

P.J. MacDwyer (1897-1958)

Patrick John MacDwyer was born in Tyrone and grew up in Killeshandra, County Cavan, where his father was a sergeant in the RIC. He was educated in St Patrick's College, Armagh, and while he worked for Chamber he took courses in UCD.

MacDwyer joined Chamber as a clerk in 1925 and was appointed secretary to Chamber on the retirement of John Robson Clark in 1948. He was also secretary to the Association of Chambers of Commerce. He had been secretary for ten years and in Chamber's employ for thirty-three years when he died at the age of sixty-one. At the 1954 AGM, the president, P.J. Loughrey, said: 'In particular I cannot fail to refer especially to our secretary Mr P.J. MacDwyer, whose meticulous attention to detail and whose experience and guidance had proved so helpful to me in discharging my duties.'

CHAMBER MEMBERS IN THE SECOND WORLD WAR

Council member James Bell Hollwey, who had been an artillery officer in the First World War and was a major in the British office reserve, was called up on the outbreak of war. He was director of the shipping line George Bell & Company of Burgh Quay and had been on Council since 1937. Serving with the 92nd Light Anti-Aircraft Regiment, he was promoted to Lieutenant-Colonel in 1942. He returned to Council after the war and served on it until 1971.

Three future Chamber presidents also served during the Second World War. Philip R. Walker (1915-1982), Chamber president in 1962, was a captain in the Inniskilling Fusiliers in Burma. Aleck C. Crichton (b. 1918), president in 1974 and Jocelyn (Jack) Elliot Armstrong (1903-2001), president in 1959, both directors of Jamesons, were also Lieutenant-Colonels in the British Army. Crichton, who was in the Irish Guards, landed in France on D-Day and was injured a few weeks later. Armstrong, a career soldier since 1923, was in the Bengal Lancers and served mostly in India. Both Hollwey and Armstrong used their military rank in civilian life. In 1958 Chamber included fifteen men with military rank.

GEORGE BELL & CO
LTD.
CHARTERED SHIP BROKERS & STEVEDORES
INSURANCE & FORWARDING AGENTS

CORN EXCHANGE BUILDINGS
BURGH QUAY
DUBLIN·C·5

11th August, 1939.

The Secretary,
The Chamber of Commerce,
Dame Street,
    Dublin.

Dear Sir,

    This is to advise that I will be unable to attend any meetings of the Chamber until early November as I have been called up for a period of service in England.

            Yours truly,

Letter from James Bell Hollwey (1893-1975) informing Chamber that he would be unable to attend Council meetings because he had been called up for duty in England. Hollwey's wife was a daughter of William Hewat, Chamber president in 1922, and except for his period of war service he was a Council member continuously, 1937-71.

From left: Philip R. Walker (1915-82), Jocelyn Elliot Armstrong (1903-2001) and Aleck C. Crichton (b. 1918).

The Dublin Chamber of Commerce

(INCORPORATED)

TELEPHONE: DUBLIN 792811

TELEGRAPHIC ADDRESS :
"COMMERCE · DUBLIN"

CODES: A.B.C. 5TH & 6TH EDNS
BENTLEY · LOMBARD · MARCONI

COMMERCIAL BUILDINGS

DAME STREET

DUBLIN

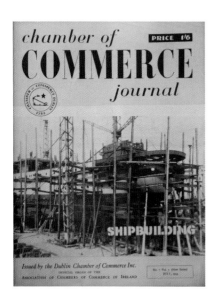

Above: *Letterhead used by Chamber during the protectionist years.*

Below: *The* Chamber of Commerce Journal *was revived in 1952. It was issued monthly by Dublin Chamber on behalf of the Association of Chambers of Commerce of Ireland.*

As early as October 1942 de Valera spoke about post-war reconstruction at a Chamber general meeting. Colonel The O'Callaghan 'forecasted that after the war there might be an army of Paul Prys and Nosey Parkers called planners. All liberty would disappear and life would become unbearable.' The May 1944 general meeting also focused on post-war planning. A member, J.J. O'Leary, had represented Ireland at an international business conference in Rye, New York, to discuss postwar international trade. O'Leary worked for Cahill's printers and on return he had a report of the conference's proceedings printed for his fellow members. War in Europe continued for another year, its ending welcomed by the same Council report that noted the first use of the atomic bomb in Japan.

The immediate post-war period saw a big increase in imports but a much smaller increase in exports. Inflation followed. The Ministry of Supplies was dissolved; emergency powers and price controls were revoked and replaced by the Services and Supplies Act in 1946. Labour disputes, which had been suppressed by the emergency powers during the war years, quickly resurfaced. Very cold weather, heavy and prolonged snowfalls throughout the country and inadequate fuel supplies characterised the beginning of

1947. In Dublin tram and bus drivers went on strike, as did bank staff throughout Ireland. In 1946 the government set up the Labour Court to deal with wage claims. Since 1936 the population of Dublin had increased by 100,000 to more than 500,000.

In 1948 Fianna Fáil lost power to an inter-party government led by John A. Costello. Now that the war was over Council's attention reverted to industrial relations, transport, Dublin port and rates but its constant cause for concern was the government's dependence on borrowing to balance the books. Revenue in 1950 was £7 million and expenditure was double that figure, while the trade deficit was running at £123 million. Chamber objected to the government's heavy expenditure of loan funds, noting that since the foundation of the state there had been an unbroken series of unbalanced budgets. The return of a Fianna Fáil government in May 1951 did not improve matters. Council reported that 1952 was a most difficult year and that 'one of the most disturbing elements of our economy is the growth of government expenditure...[which] has increased faster than the national income. The general apathy to the seriousness of the position as it affects the national economy and daily lives of citizens in deplorable.' The government's price control strategy had failed and it was becoming obvious to Chamber that protectionism was no longer working.

G.H.C. Crampton, president in 1952, commenting on a report by the Irish Business and Employers' Confederation (IBEC) on Ireland's industrial potential, said that the country's industries were overprotected. A sense of estrangement, a feeling among Chamber members that government did not have the interests of business at heart, was reflected in the selection

George Hugh Cecil Crampton (1901-76), managing director of G&T Crampton Limited from 1949 and Chamber president, 1952.

Crampton served on Council from 1941 until his death.

of business leaders rather than ministers to speak at general meetings. Between October 1953 and October 1954 guests included T.J. O'Driscoll, chairman of Córas Tráchtála (the newly founded Irish Exports Board), J.F. Dempsey, general manager of Aer Lingus, and John O'Neill, joint MD of Irish Shipping.

In 1949 the first inter-party government had established the Industrial Development Association (IDA) in an effort to attract overseas investments. That coalition returned to power in 1954 but it was as ineffective as the intervening Fianna Fáil government in managing the economy. The country suffered a balance of payments crisis in 1955, which Council reported as an unhealthy internal boom, and the government reacted by increasing import tariffs and giving a tax exemption on profits from exports, which proved to be a significant inducement for overseas industries to set up in Ireland. The country's population had remained static since the foundation of the state. Business too tended to remain static and the appointment of business leaders was often nepotistic, as protectionism meant that they had little

Chamber annual dinner, 1965. Irene Calvert, president of Belfast Chamber of Commerce, is seen here with Taoiseach Seán Lemass (left) and Dublin Chamber president E.C.G. Mulhern.

Chamber of Commerce Journal

need to compete. Emigration was the solution to endemic unemployment. The world was changing as Europe reconstructed itself after the war but Ireland remained in a state of depression. However, the atmosphere of the time does not emerge in Chamber reports because, although business was not improving, neither was it visibly deteriorating.

On 17 February 1949 Taoiseach John A. Costello was guest of honour in the Gresham Hotel at the revived annual dinner, an event that has continued until the present day. Post-war inflation led to a 50 per cent increase in Chamber's wages bill and membership fees increased by a guinea to four guineas in 1947 and to five guineas in 1956. The same year the Chamber general meeting approved the provision of a pension fund for its employees and established a Junior Chamber of Commerce, open to businessmen under forty. Its first meeting was held on 12 October under the chairmanship of Chamber president, Alex O'D. Shiel.

Éamon de Valera returned to power in 1957 but when he was elected the President of Ireland in 1959 Fianna Fáil's deputy leader, Seán Lemass, became Taoiseach. The secretary of the Department of Finance, T.K. Whitaker, and his officials had prepared a white paper, *The First Programme for Economic Expansion,* in 1958. It advocated an end to protectionism in favour of free trade. The paper was enthusiastically adopted by Seán Lemass, who abolished the cornerstone of protectionist policy, the Control of Manufactures Act, which he had introduced in 1932. Chamber too supported the programme.

On the signing of the Treaty of Rome in 1957 Chamber commented prophetically: 'The term Common Market – applied to the Community – may in a sense be misleading for the aims of the six countries go far beyond the creation of a mere customs union, in fact their aims are economic, financial, political and social.' The Common Market, more correctly the European Economic Community (EEC), consisted of France, Germany, Italy, Belgium, Netherlands and Luxembourg. Chamber was attracted to the idea of the EEC and Nita Watts, a senior economist with its research division, spoke at Chamber AGM in 1957. Britain responded by proposing a European Free

Above: Taoiseach Seán Lemass with Niall (left) and Vincent Crowley, after he addressed Dublin Chamber.

Below: Thomas F. Laurie (1894-1981), MD, Esso Ireland, who, uniquely, served as Chamber president on three occasions.

Chamber of Commerce Journal

Junior Chamber Council meeting in Commercial Buildings, 1960: the president, centre front, is Patrick J. Loughrey. Stephen Mackenzie is on his right and E. Beryl Gavin, honorary secretary, on his left.

Chamber of Commerce Journal

DUBLIN JUNIOR CHAMBER

Dublin Chamber launched Dublin Junior Chamber in Commercial Buildings on 12 October 1956, with the president, Alex O'D. Shiel, in the chair: the aim was to provide the commercial and industrial leaders of tomorrow. Membership, aged between eighteen and forty, reached a hundred in its first year. Junior Chamber has been accommodated by Dublin Chamber, firstly in Commercial Buildings and later in Clare Street, and from 1959 its president has been an ex-officio member of Council.

The Junior Chamber idea quickly caught on in Ireland and within a few years most Chambers of Commerce had a branch. Junior Chamber International (JCI) was founded in the US in 1944 and Dublin Junior Chamber immediately became affiliated to it. In May 1960 Dublin Junior Chamber hosted the 7th European Congress of JCI in Dún Laoghaire, with a hundred and fifty guests. The World JCI conference took place in Dublin in 1970.

Junior Chamber mirrors Chamber, organising talks and seminars on business matters. At one such event in TCD in March 1981 three masked men rushed in when British Leyland executive Geoffrey Armstrong was speaking and shot him in the legs before making their escape. Ostensibly their action was in sympathy with the H-Block protests. Armstrong recovered and an Italian, Giovanni Maritonni, was found guilty of the offence a year later.

Junior Chamber instituted the Entrepreneur of the Year competition, now run by EY accountants. The organisation suffered a hiatus at the start of the 21st century and its president no longer sat on Council but in 2005 its position on Council was reinstated. Junior Chamber remains an active networking body for younger business people in both the Irish and international organisations, promoting community projects and personal and business development.

Trade Area (EFTA) comprising European countries not in the EEC. Ireland was interested in joining EFTA but needed a derogation on tariffs as the country was less developed than its neighbours. When EFTA was finally founded in 1960 Ireland did not join but the Taoiseach negotiated an Anglo-Irish Trade Agreement consolidating Irish trade with Britain, irrespective of EFTA. In 1961 Ireland applied to join the EEC, along with Britain, and, although the applications were unsuccessful because of the intervention of French president Charles de Gaulle, politicians and business people alike accepted the principle of future membership.

Chamber objected to the introduction of PAYE in 1960 and a turnover tax (now VAT) four years later because it felt, with some justification, that the government would use the business community 'as a collecting agency for government revenue with its concomitant obligations' and that companies should be compensated for this 'arduous task'. The new taxes led to labour agitation for wage increases, something that Council also complained about. But in general the opening up of the economy had a positive effect on business.

The Harbour Act of 1946 re-organised Dublin port and entitled Chamber to nominate four members of the board. Metal transport containers as we know them today were developed by the US army to carry military goods during the Korean War. In 1955 the standard interlocking container was patented in the US and quickly adopted throughout the world because it was easier to handle and less prone to pilferage (a recurring concern of Chamber). Dock workers strongly resisted containers being introduced in Dublin port as being likely to make many of their number redundant. Council met the Minister for Transport to discuss the issue.

Certificates of Origin

In 1934 the Irish government announced that, forthwith, imports would require a certificate of origin, forming part of the export documentation and indicating the country in which a product was manufactured or produced. Marseille Chamber of Commerce first issued certificates such as these at the end of the 19th century. The Geneva Convention in 1923 allowed competent bodies to provide these certificates and chambers of commerce were considered to be such. Dublin Chamber began issuing certificates in 1935: the number issued rose steadily until the 1960s.

In 1964 ATA (temporary admission) carnets were introduced through the international Chamber; Dublin Chamber became the licensed issuer of ATA carnets for Ireland. These allow the export of items intended to be returned within a year, such as broadcast equipment or goods for trade forums and exhibitions. Chamber's export services department now provide both certificates of origin and ATA carnets, which are a source of revenue for the organisation.

In earlier decades the government, by means of a number of parliamentary acts, had effectively nationalised the railway system under the Great Southern & Western Railway Company. In 1945 Córas Iompair Éireann (CIÉ) was formed when the GS&WR was amalgamated with Dublin United Transport Company. The 1950 Transport Act amalgamated CIÉ and the Grand Canal Company and in 1952 the struggling Great Northern line was acquired by the two states. CIÉ was loss-making and the government had raised motor tax to subsidise the railways, as Chamber reported in 1952: 'Motor duties up and now pay £11m per annum…expected to subsidise CIÉ losses.' Chamber had objected strenuously to the government's attempt to create a transport monopoly under a railway bill of 1955 by permitting only CIÉ to convey goods, arguing that traders should be permitted to make their own transport arrangements (the bill permitted companies to transport only their own goods and not use other providers). The near monopoly of rail, road and canal services had been granted on the basis that it would be more efficient but in fact it made matters worse. The perennial increases in city rates in the 1950s and the 1960s were another regular cause of complaints by Chamber and city traffic, parking restrictions (the first parking meters were installed in 1964 'viewed with alarm by some members as impeding access to premises') and litter were issues about which Chamber had discussions with the corporation.

Chamber president, Philip Walker, Vincent Crowley (left) and Eamonn Andrews at Andrews's 1960 talk to Chamber about Ireland's new television service.

Chamber of Commerce Journal

In the 1960s Ireland advanced socially as well as economically. RTÉ, the national television service, was launched in 1960 and Eamonn Andrews, its first director, spoke at the Chamber general meeting in May although, soon after the service began, the Federated Union of Employers, with

Chamber support, complained that the station favoured trade unions over employers in its coverage.

After a hundred and forty-four years, Dublin Chamber of Commerce moved from Commercial Buildings. Council negotiated 'very satisfactory arrangements with the Commercial Buildings (Dublin) Ltd when the lease in Chamber's holding in the Commercial Buildings could not be renewed.' Chamber acquired the former Irish Sugar Company offices in 7 Clare Street, a purchase that put it into debt for the first time in its history, and in November 1964 the reading room was transferred to the new premises. The Minister for Industry and Commerce, Jack Lynch, performed the official opening on 25 February 1965.

At the end of 1965 Ireland signed the Anglo-Irish Free Trade Agreement with the UK. It was the first of a series of agreements that opened up the Irish market, culminating in EEC membership. In the face of a free market the nature of Irish business was changing but Chamber welcomed the changes. However, most of the protected industries fared badly in the open market, as three decades of protectionism had left them unprepared for competition.

7 CLARE ST

No 7 has ambitious early and mid-twentieth alterations made for the Dublin Chamber of Commerce. It retains an original stair, joinery and plasterwork overlaid by Georgian Revival ornament, the latter most evident in the rear ground-floor room.

Christine Casey, *The Buildings of Ireland: Dublin (2005)*

In 1744 James Fitzgerald (1722-73), the 20th Earl of Kildare (and 1st Duke of Leinster from 1766), Ireland's premier peer, took a lease of lands belonging to the Molesworth estate on which to build his town house, Leinster House, in what is now Kildare Street, to the design of the German immigrant architect, Richard Cassels (Castle). Until then most housing for the upper classes had been constructed on the estates of Luke Gardiner and Humphrey Jervis to the north of the city but Kildare's supposed boast that the fashionable world would follow him southwards proved true.

The Merrion estate was owned by the old Norman Fitzwilliam family and stretched along the coast, from St Stephen's Green to Bray. William Fitzwilliam, brother of the head of the family, Viscount Fitzwilliam, came to Dublin to look after the estate, ably assisted by the estate agent, Bryan Fagan, a Dublin distiller, succeeded after his death in 1761 by his wife Elizabeth and later by his daughter Barbara. The arrival of the Earl of Kildare in the area facilitated the possibility of maximising the rental income of the Merrion estate by developing it for housing. Merrion Lane,

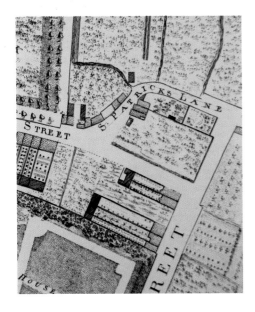

Kildare's mansion was on the boundary between the city and the country and Fitzwilliam's plan to form a square to the rear of Kildare's house would remove Lord Kildare's rural aspect. In an attempt to block the development of Merrion Square, Kildare ordered Cassels, his architect, to build a wall restricting the route to Clare Street. Bryan Fagan informed William Fitzwilliam that Thomas Manning and the other leaseholders were unhappy with this development and met the Earl of Kildare and Cassels on site in an effort to resolve the issue. Although in the wrong, Kildare attempted to pull rank but the matter was eventually settled in the Fitzwilliams' favour. William Fitzwilliam wrote in a letter to his brother in 1758: '[I] shall be glad to see his wall thrown down and the approach to Clare Street put into the shape designed.' There seems to have been a kind of building boom in the 1750s: Fitzwilliam wrote to his brother that they

now Merrion Street, was first to be set, from about 1750. Fitzwilliam proposed a new square to the rear of Leinster House which was to be accessed by 'a new intended street to lead from Patrickswell Lane [the old name for Nassau Street] to be called Clare Street.' Clare Street was named, along with two other streets, after Denzil Holles, Earl of Clare, who was related to the Fitzwilliams. In 1751 Fitzwilliam let the north side of Clare Street to Thomas Manning, a cabinet maker and timber merchant, and the south side to the Reverend John Kearney, an ancestor of President Obama and future Provost of Trinity College, with the proviso that they would develop it for housing.

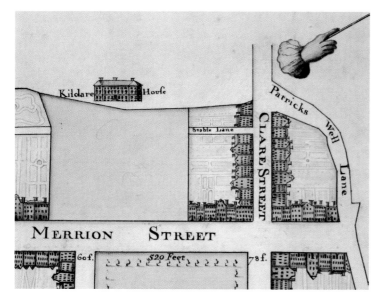

Proposed plan for Clare Street which Jonathan Baker drew for Lord Fitzwilliam in 1764. Apart from a number on Merrion Street, the houses were not yet built. The preponderance of 'Dutch Billies' and gables to the street is reminiscent of older styles, which were not used in the buildings of the new streets.

Reproduced courtesy of Trinity College Dublin

should set as many leases as possible while people were so enthusiastic: 'I think the present building madness can never hold.' Ten years later a shortage of money affected construction.

The estate was concerned that Clare Street should be paved and built upon in order to encourage the setting of the plots on the north side of Merrion Square. It paid the Reverend Kearney £64 for paving his part of Clare Street and building a range or low boundary wall around his site and the original leaseholders were given peppercorn leases for the first five years in order to encourage them to build on the site. In Thomas Manning's

case he was charged £5 for the first seven years. Leases were for ninety-nine years and specified the design of house to be built on the site. This is what gives Georgian streets such as Clare Street their distinct uniformity.

In an effort to stimulate development Fitzwilliam provided stone from his quarry in Ticknock and bricks produced on his estate in Old Merrion at a good price. Brickmaking involved digging a suitable clay, forming the bricks in moulds or 'stools' and cooking them in kilns; it was a dirty business. In 1772 parliament prohibited brick manufacture within two miles of the city and the

Merrion fields were closed but not before the houses on Clare Street, including Number 7, were created.

In 1765-7 the Wall family built the house, four storeys over basement, on a plot 25ft x 128ft, sublet by Thomas Manning. It had a number of residential occupants. Patrick Wall died before the building work was finished but his wife and son completed it before selling it to James Sheil in 1767. Sheil kept it only two years before he sold it to James Carrique Ponsonby of Crotto House in Kerry; in 1770 it passed from him to his father-in-law Charles O'Hara (1715-1776), MP for Sligo. In 1779 O'Hara's executor sold the house to another MP, James Tydd (1742-1803), who represented Maryborough in the Dublin parliament. Barrister William Ball bought the house from Tydd's widow for £1000 in 1803: 'with stables, outhouses, offices, yards, backsides, watercourses, sewer ways, cellars, vaults, passages, gutters, sinks, privys, lights and apartments thereto belonging'. Ball had new stables constructed to the rear, to the design of Sir Richard Morrison, a pupil of James Gandon. Known as 'Index Ball' for his work in publishing seven volumes of statutes of the Irish parliament,

Ball was also a writer of songs, including a number lampooning the revolutionaries of 1798 which can be found in the National Library.

Ball died in 1824 and four years later his daughters sold the house to Jane Affleck, 'milliner and dress-maker to his excellency the Lord Lieutenant'. Henceforth the house was a place of business as well as a home. Affleck died in 1848 and left the house to Jeremiah MacCarthy, Daniel O'Connell's tailor, who let it to the Christopherson sisters, milliners and dressmakers from Cockermouth, Cumbria. After the death of Esther Christopherson in 1880, Mac-Carthy's daughter, Jane Affleck MacCarthy, who was married to John Arthur Baker, a dental surgeon, moved into the house. In 1890 the Bakers sold 7 Clare

Stable Lane

Clare Street

Floor Plan of 7 Clare Street as it was originally built.

Street on to a physician, Henry Colpoys Tweedy (1847-1917), who used the house as a surgery as well as a home. Tweedy retired to England in 1900 after his eyesight began to fail and a dentist, Frederick Edward Davies (1869-1951), bought the house. In about 1925 Davies and his family moved out of Clare Street and the house ceased to have a residential function, although Davies continued his dental practice there. When he retired in 1939 he put the house up for sale and Comhlacht Siúcra Éireann, the Irish Sugar Company, established by Seán Lemass in 1933, bought it for £2000.

7 Clare Street today.

In 1946 the company engaged Michael J. Costello, a retired lieutenant-general, as managing director, and in 1950 it demolished some of the return and mews buildings and built a first-floor extension to the rear of the house, containing a map room used to plan the sugar-beet campaign, apparently along military lines. The Irish Sugar Company subsequently expanded its business by developing Erin Foods and moved to a new purpose-built office block in Earlsfort Terrace in 1964.

As the owners of Commercial Buildings had decided to demolish the complex and redevelop the site, Dublin Chamber had to move premises. In truth Chamber's accommodation in Commercial Buildings was somewhat higgledy-piggledy and the building in general in need of repair. Chamber bought 7 Clare Street from Comhlacht Siúcra Éireann for just over £22,000 and occupied the offices and reading room from November 1964 after a scheme of painting and decorating. The organisation's brass plate was moved from Commercial Buildings to Clare Street for the official opening on 25 February 1965.

A common failing in Dublin's Georgian houses is deterioration of the brickwork, particularly at the parapet, near the top of the building, and in 1977 Chamber was advised to replace the entire façade. The president, Eddie Kelliher, wrote to the members: 'I am sure that you agree that the Chamber is right in setting an example, by maintaining its share of the fabric of our city. Furthermore, even if our premises were not designated as a preserved building, No 7 Clare Street, is a first-class headquarters from which to conduct the Chamber's responsibility of representing the business community of Dublin, and furthermore should be kept in top condition.'

Unfortunately the original variegated red-stock brick was replaced by a more modern, mono-chromatic machine-cut brick. The restoration work cost £44,000, which was mostly funded by doubling the membership fees for that year. Chamber has continued to maintain its headquarters and many of the features of the original house are well preserved.

Right: The committee room in Clare Street, decorated to reflect its original style.

Far right: The Chamber plaque that Dermot O'Toole designed in 1960 for Commercial Buildings. When Chamber moved to 7 Clare Street it was re-erected and is still in use today.

THE DUBLIN CHAMBER OF COMMERCE 1783

XII

EUROPE AND THE OPEN MARKET, 1966-83

The 'Sixties' have been classified as the best decade since the founding of the state, as regards economic progress, political stability and prosperity. And this is true. The growth of industry, the buoyancy of exports, the relative constancy of employment and the marked improvement in the overall standard of living; all this coupled with the spectacular upsurge in tourism revenue and the consequent growth in our airline and shipping traffic could be said to have stamped on the Ireland of the Sixties the mark of success.

Chamber Report for 1969

In 1966 the state celebrated the fiftieth anniversary of the 1916 Rising, Seán Lemass resigned as Taoiseach and Jack Lynch (1917-99) replaced him. The Minister for Education, Donogh O'Malley (1921-68), announced his intention to introduce free second-level education in 1967, and increased expenditure on third-level education helped to supply an educated workforce for businesses investing in Ireland, both native and foreign. The economic policies of the previous ten years had resulted in an increase in employment, a reduction in emigration and the return of Irish families, mostly from Britain. However, industrial relations remained troubled. In 1966, as well as labour disputes in Dublin port, long-running strikes by bank officials and Electricity Supply Board (ESB) workers proved costly for business. *The Irish Times* reported a speech by Chamber vice-president J.R. Dick at the AGM in February of that year that evoked the memory of the Lockout: 'While

Chamber's bicentenary logo, introduced in 1983 and used for three years.

timeline

1966

The IRA bombs Nelson's Pillar.

Celebration of fiftieth anniversary of the 1916 Rising.

The Munster and Leinster and Provincial banks and Royal Bank of Ireland amalgamate to form Allied Irish Banks.

Seán Lemass retires and Jack Lynch becomes Taoiseach.

1968

Violence flares in Northern Ireland after civil rights protests.

1969

British troops arrive in Northern Ireland as violence escalates.

1971

Decimalisation of Irish currency.

The Catholic hierarchy lifts its ban on Catholics attending TCD.

1973

Ireland joins the EEC, along with the UK and Denmark.

this year they were celebrating the anniversary of 1916 it would have been nice to think that in 1963 – fifty years after a year of distressful relations in this country – we would have been able to celebrate the beginning of a new era of industrial relations. It was anything but [he said]. Little had changed in the negotiations taking place today since 1913 and last Monday the whole country had nearly ground to a halt.'

Chamber contacts outside Ireland expanded at this time, with trade missions from the US, Japan and London and formalised regular meetings with counterparts in Belfast, Newry and Dundalk to discuss cross-border issues. In 1968 Dublin Chamber, in conjunction with Cork Chamber of Commerce, inaugurated annual meetings with London Chamber of Commerce to explore the implications of free trade and in 1976 Dublin Chamber joined the International Chamber of Commerce.

The annual report for 1968 noted that Ireland's prospects of becoming a member of the EEC in 1970 were receding although it had given business a boost that year. Britain devalued its pound by 15 per cent as a result of an economic downturn and the Irish government had to follow suit. Dublin had changed little over the previous decades and still had its intact Georgian core but the city now became the focus of commercial development. Chamber began to take a much greater interest in the management of the city and its infrastructure. The first *Draft Development Plan for Dublin* was published in 1967 and, based on this, Chamber advocated the construction of a new Liffey crossing east of Butt Bridge to alleviate traffic congestion. City rates were still rising rapidly and Council noted with displeasure that the Dublin rate had nearly doubled in ten years. In 1968 a deputation from Council conveyed to the city manager the desirability of the roll-out of parking meters (he promised 2400 by July 1969) as well as requesting the corporation to erect multi-storey car-parks.

In April 1968 it was announced that decimal coinage would be introduced on 15 February 1971, called D-Day, and Chamber was involved in consultation about this as well as the introduction of metric measurement. Inflation was rising as a result of the developing economy and, according to Chamber, because the government was granting wage increases to prevent strikes. Wages increased by 13 per cent in 1969 and again in 1970 and Chamber called for more government action on industrial relations: 'It is not the function of the Chamber of Commerce to meddle in trade union matters or in the general field of industrial relations but it would be fatuous to suggest that a Chamber of Commerce declare itself indifferent to the overall effects of the widespread industrial strife.'

At the end of the 1960s Chamber began to modernise its management systems, announcing: 'the work of bringing the Chamber up to date and particularly to equip it to take its place in the world wide and European Chamber of Commerce movement, was commenced early in 1969.' The new position of executive director was created and John O'Brien, former president and director general of the Federated Union of Employers, was appointed. The position was in response to Ireland's imminent entry to the EEC, in which it was perceived that European Chambers of Commerce had a pivotal role.

Chamber suffered from the inflation that affected the economy as a whole and in 1969 had to cover losses for the previous year from its remaining Bank of Ireland shares, as well as doubling the membership fee. That same

1973

Fine Gael-Labour coalition wins general election.

Yom Kippur war between Israel and Arab countries results in an oil embargo which causes an energy crisis and inflation.

1974

Loyalist car bombs kill thirty-three people in Dublin and Monaghan.

End of marriage ban for women working in the civil service.

1976

An IRA landmine kills British Ambassador, Christopher Ewart-Biggs.

1977

Fianna Fáil returns to power with a twenty-seat majority.

1979

Ireland joins the EMS.

Charles Haughey becomes Taoiseach.

1981

Two short-lived minority governments.

1982

New coalition government led by Garret FitzGerald.

1983

Devaluation of Irish pound by 5 per cent.

year it began to organise members' lunches at which significant political and commercial figures spoke. Four or five were held each year, occasionally incorporating a site visit, and they were well attended. The prospect of accession to the EEC, the development in Ireland's economy and Chamber's own modernisation brought about an increase in membership.

Ireland was finally admitted into the EEC on 1 January 1973, along with the United Kingdom and Denmark. The resulting open market exposed the remaining protected Irish industries to competition, although derogations postponed the day of reckoning for some. Before accession Chamber attended meetings of Chambers of Commerce and Industry of Europe. The Association of Chambers of Commerce of Ireland had established the Irish Business Bureau in Brussels in 1971 in conjunction with Dublin Chamber, the Confederation of Irish Industry and the Federated Union of Employers. Patrick Jordan was its first director. In June 1972 the Bureau organised a familiarisation tour of the EEC institutions for representatives of Irish business organisations but on Sunday 18 June the BEA Trident carrying twelve Irish delegates, including Chamber president, Michael W. O'Reilly, crashed in Staines, south of London, shortly after take-off for Brussels, killing all one hundred and eighteen passengers and crew on board. The deaths of the twelve leading businessmen had a significant impact on the Irish business community.

The Yom Kippur War of 1973 had a drastic effect on the world economy, when the Arab nations of OPEC, led by Sheik Yamani, began an oil embargo in response to American aid to the Israelis. Oil prices had been increasing anyway since the US pulled out of the post-war Bretton Woods Accord and no longer pegged the dollar against the price of gold. Great Britain and the

THE STAINES AIR CRASH

On 18 June 1972 a delegation of fifteen Irish businessmen left Dublin for Brussels to attend meetings organised by the Irish Business Bureau. Twelve of the party flew to Heathrow to connect with British European Airways Flight 548 to Brussels. Barely four minutes after take-off the Trident stalled, fell from the sky and crashed near Staines, killing everyone on board.

The businessmen who died were: Michael J. O'Reilly, president. Dublin Chamber of Commerce; Owen Lochrin, vice-president, Chambers of Commerce Ireland; Con A. Smith, Renault Ireland; Edward Gray, Michael Sweetman and Fergus Mooney, Confederation of Irish Industry; Ivan Webb, Irish Employers' Confederation; Hugh Kilfeather, Córas Tráchtála; Guy Jackson, Guinness; Edward Coleman, Irish Steel; Michael Rigby-Jones, Irish Ropes; and Melville Miller, Rowntree Mackintosh.

A plaque outside the Council room in Clare Street commemorates the tragedy and on the fortieth anniversary of the crash, a memorial plaque and benches were unveiled in Herbert Park after a service at Donnybrook Church.

Left and below: The memorial to the twelve Irish businessmen who died in the Staines air crash on 18 June 1972, unveiled in Herbert Park in 2012, includes three benches, three oak trees and a memorial plaque.

Below left: Photograph from the Chamber of Commerce Journal of the 1982 president, Michael W. O'Reilly, who, with eleven other Irish businessmen, died in the Staines air crash on 18 June 1972.

other industrialised nations followed suit shortly afterwards, paper money was printed freely and inflation inevitably followed. Oil prices rose as the dollar, its transaction currency, devalued. In 1973 Chamber warned: 'In the short term inflation might seem attractive but in the long term it is one of the most devastating elements to encounter,' and the following year commented on the extraordinary change that the oil crisis had brought: 'The economy which had been expanding over the past fifteen years, was severely threatened from outside by world events and within by self-generated inflation and by lack of security.'

After many years of Fianna Fáil government, the Fine Gael-Labour coalition that came power in 1974 was greeted by unemployment running at 13 per cent and inflation at 17 per cent and was forced to adopt deflationary and cost-saving policies. This inflation and the loss of protective barriers after Ireland joined the EEC were the death-knell of the last remaining protected industries. Particularly badly hit were clothing and shoe manufacture. There was ongoing labour unrest, with high wage demands and agreements to counteract the effects of the inflationary economy, which seriously impinged on Dublin commerce. Anybody who lived in Ireland during the late

John O'Brien (1910-83)

John O'Brien was born in Dublin and graduated from UCD. He also qualified as a barrister. In 1937 he was appointed the first full-time secretary of what became the Federated Union of Employers and much of his career was with employer organisations. From 1945 he was an advisor to the International Labour Organisation (ILO) and an employers' delegate to the organisation, 1947-60.

Dublin Chamber employed O'Brien in the new post of executive director from 1969 in an attempt to modernise its organisation and prepare it for the challenge of joining the EEC. O'Brien was president of Dublin Chamber in 1961 and the Association of Chambers of Commerce of Ireland in 1967 and 1968 and served on Council 1952-68 and 1973-80 as a past president.

1960s and the 1970s will remember how frequently ESB and CIÉ strikes disrupted everyday life.

Another serious issue was domestic in origin. The conflict in Northern Ireland, which had its roots in the civil rights protests of the late 1960s, had rapidly escalated and by the 1970s had begun to spill over the border. On 17 May 1974 three car bombs exploded in Dublin, killing twenty-seven people and injuring hundreds of others. A fourth bomb, in Monaghan town, killed a further seven people. Council sent a delegation to the Taoiseach, Liam Cosgrave, on 22 May and to the Fianna Fáil leader, Jack Lynch, on 28 May to seek better security for Dublin. In July the Minister for Justice, Patrick Cooney, addressed a Chamber lunch on the subject of security in the state. A further consequence of the Northern Troubles was an increase in what Chamber called 'lawlessness', as paramilitaries began to fund their activities by means of armed robberies. In addition, Dublin was frequently brought to a standstill by protest marches, which created difficulties for business. Chamber called for more Gardaí in the city and a meeting with the Minister for Justice elicited the promise of twelve hundred extra Gardaí.

Rampant inflation had driven up Chamber costs and membership fees. In 1966 Chamber expenditure was just short of nine thousand pounds; ten years later it had nearly quadrupled. In 1975 membership reached a new high of almost thirteen hundred. Chamber lunches had an attendance of about two hundred and the annual dinner drew an attendance of almost four hundred at this time. Charles Haughey, then Minister for Social Welfare, addressed Chamber in 1978 but did not do so again until be became Taoiseach. During the 1970s two Chamber presidents were elected TD – James Gallagher for Fianna Fáil in 1972-3 and Paddy Belton for Fine Gael in 1977. Belton was

The Irish Business Bureau

The Irish Business Bureau opened in November 1971 in 77 Rue Joseph II in Brussels, a collaboration between the Association of Chambers of Commerce of Ireland, the Federated Union of Employers and the Confederation of Irish Industry to provide a point of access for Irish business in Brussels in the lead-up to Ireland's accession to the EEC. Dublin Chamber, as the largest member of the Association of Chambers of Commerce, was a major contributor to the running costs of the IBB.

The Bureau was initially under the directorship of Patrick Jordan and, from 1980, headed up by Aidan O'Boyle. In 1986 management of the Bureau passed to Peter Brennan (Chamber president in 2010).

In 1993 the FUE and CII merged to form the Irish Business and Employers' Confederation (IBEC), which assumed sole responsibility for running the Irish Business Bureau.

Lord Mayor of Dublin in 1978. When it was discovered that the brick façade of Chamber's premises would have to be replaced at a cost of £44,000, the membership approved the doubling of the annual fee at the 1978 AGM.

In the 1970s Chamber became more focused on the fabric and environment of the city. The 1974 report commented that Dublin was a city with many natural scenic and architectural advantages which were being lost through lack of planning, vandalism and traffic congestion. The first flush of economic growth in the 1960s had led to some pretty awful commercial developments in the city centre, of which Hawkins House, on the site of the Theatre Royal in Hawkins Street remains the outstanding eyesore. By the 1970s the need for the preservation of Dublin's Georgian heritage and more planned development was widely recognised. Another recurring environmental concern was the polluted state of the River Liffey.

Justin B. O'Connell (1929-2003) came from Phibsboro and was educated in St Vincent's Glasnevin and Cistercian College, Roscrea. Before he joined Chamber as assistant secretary in 1952 he was a trainee clerk in the costings section of the Irish Sugar Company in Carlow.

On the death of P.J. MacDwyer in 1958, O'Connell became secretary to Chamber and served in this capacity until his retirement in 1988.

Chamber was enthusiastic about CIÉ's proposed new rapid rail system for Dublin. In fact it wished to encourage better public transport to alleviate the gridlock in Dublin traffic. Another project the organisation promoted – even accepting that it would be tolled – but that was long in development was what is now called the East Link Bridge. Chamber set up the Inner City Redevelopment Advisory Committee, which assessed problems and proposed solutions in the areas of commerce, housing, employment and youth welfare and presented its report to the Taoiseach in 1978.

The coalition government's efforts to bring some discipline to the Irish economy began to pay off. Inflation had fallen to single figures, although

The Dublin Chamber of Commerce

(INCORPORATED)

TELEPHONE: DUBLIN 64291

TELEGRAPHIC ADDRESS :
"COMMERCE · DUBLIN"

CODES: A.B.C. 5TH & 6TH EDNS
BENTLEY · LOMBARD · MARCONI

7 CLARE STREET

DUBLIN 2

wage increases were still high. But the coalition lost power in 1977. Fianna Fáil won the election with a large majority after a campaign offering a number of attractive – and expensive – inducements to the electorate. Domestic rates and vehicle tax were reduced to zero. The new government's economic plan was based on a green paper, *Development for Full Employment*, and Martin O'Donoghue, a TCD professor of economics, was appointed to the new position of Minister for Economic Planning and Development. Council wrote to O'Donoghue, agreeing with the need for full employment but advising that this should 'only be realised through additional demands for our output' and that government borrowings for current expenditure should be reduced.

The government, however, misjudged the economic situation and increased borrowings on the faulty assumption that government-created employment would in turn stimulate private investment. In fact after a year of synthetic growth there was another oil crisis in 1979 and inflation rose again, massively increasing the interest on government debt and saddling the country with a fiscal problem that endured for almost a decade. By 1980 Chamber's budget submission was expressing disquiet about the high level of government borrowing, high inflation and high wage settlements, all of which were hampering competitiveness. Alas for business, the 1980s were

Early letterhead for Chamber's new premises, 7 Clare Street.

Left: Council held a special gathering in 7 Clare Street on 10 February 1983, exactly two hundred years after a meeting in the Royal Exchange established Dublin Chamber of Commerce. The attendance included many Chamber past presidents.

Seated, front row, are president Declan Lennon; Lord Mayor, Dan Browne; vice-president, Desmond Miller; and Frank Carthy.

Below: An Post agreed to issue a stamp in commemoration of Chamber bicentenary, 23 February 1983, a first-day cover of which was posted to all members. It featured the Ouzel Galley goblet.

characterised by coalition governments unable to come to grips with this mounting national debt.

Having ignored its one-hundred-and-fiftieth anniversary, Chamber began to prepare for its bicentenary as early as 1981. Number 7 Clare Street was renovated and Desmond Miller chaired a bicentenary committee with responsibility for organising the celebratory events. It was decided that Niall Crowley, one of Ireland's leading businessmen and, like Miller, a partner in Stokes Kennedy Crowley, should serve as the bicentenary president (his term ran from April 1983). Crowley was best known to the public as chair of AIB and had for many years been the nominee on Council of the Irish Banks Standing Committee. The year of celebration opened with a Council meeting in Clare Street on 20 February 1983, two hundred years to the day since the founding meeting in the Royal Exchange chaired by Dublin merchant William Colvill. Colvill's great-great granddaughter, Susan Magan (also great-granddaughter of James C. Colvill, the final first captain of the Ouzel Galley Society), presented the original *Ouzel Galley*'s boatswain's whistle to Chamber at a special lunch. (It was deposited in the National Museum for safekeeping.) Chamber had commissioned TCD historian L.M. Cullen to write the history of the chamber and all members received a copy of his book *Princes and Pirates*, as well as a first-day cover of a commemorative 22-pence stamp issued by An Post, incorporating an image of the Ouzel Galley goblet. The Church of Ireland Archbishop of Dublin, Henry McAdoo, led an ecumenical service in Christ Church with representatives from the other Churches, and Chamber president and vice-president gave the readings.

According to Chamber president for 1983, Niall Crowley: '"Opportunity" was the key word of the bicentenary celebrations and is the key word for the future of Chamber.' Opportunity was also the theme of an international business conference that Chamber organised in TCD, with David Rockefeller of Chase Manhattan, Koji Kobayashi of NEC and Tony O'Reilly of Heinz

Niall Crowley.

Niall Crowley (1926-98)

Niall Crowley's father, Vincent, who was also president of Chamber, established the Kennedy Crowley accountancy firm in 1919. Niall was articled to Kennedy Crowley straight from school in Castleknock and qualified as a chartered accountant. With his brothers, Laurence and Conor, he developed the business into one of the largest accountancy practices in the country. In 1969 it amalgamated with Forsyth & Co, then with the old Dublin firm of Stokes Brothers & Pim in 1972. Crowley was a director of Allied Irish Banks, 1968-89, chairman from 1977 and a consultant to Stokes Kennedy Crowley until 1984. One of the foremost businessmen of the time, he held many other directorships, including chairmanship of Irish Life Insurance, and served on Council of Dublin Chamber, 1963-84.

THE BICENTENARY CELEBRATIONS

As well as five receptions for members, a series of events and functions marked the 1983 bicentenary:

10 February	Special Council meeting two hundred years to the day after the 1783 inaugural meeting.
23 February	Issue of bicentennial postage stamp.
5 May	Launch of *Princes and Pirates*, L.M. Cullen's history of Chamber.
21 September	Exhibition of modern art in 7 Clare Street.
29 September	State reception in Dublin Castle.
30 September	'Opportunity' conference in TCD, followed by Lord Mayor's reception in the Mansion House.
1 October	Banquet in the Burlington Hotel.
16 October	Ecumenical Service in Christchurch Cathedral.
2 November	James Galway concert in the National Concert Hall.
1 December	Official unveiling of the fountain in Parkgate Street.
7 December	Reception for members of the Northern Ireland Chamber of Commerce (formerly Belfast. Chamber of Commerce) to mark the bicentenaries of both chambers.
8 December	Symposium in the RDS: 'Dublin's Fair City – True or False'.

Opposite: *The inauguration of Dublin Chamber fountain, 1 December 1983. Front right are city manager, Frank Feely; Chamber vice-president, Desmond Miller; Lord Mayor, Michael Keating; and Chamber president, Niall Crowley.*

Above left: *The top table at a business breakfast during bicentenary year; left to right: John Vaughan, Desmond Miller, David Rockefeller and Niall Crowley.*

Above right: *Niall Crowley addresses the audience and guests at the bicentenary concert in the National Concert Hall, 2 November 1983, at which flautist James Galway performed.*

Left: *Vice-presidents Niall Crowley and Desmond Miller and president (until April 1983) Declan Lennon, holding one of the twenty replicas of the Ouzel Galley goblet made by Waterford Glass at the beginning of Chamber's bicentenary year, 1983.*

Corporation among the speakers. Niall Crowley's keynote address to the conference stressed the advantages of Dublin Chamber as it began its third century: 'Never was there a better time to bring home in our public activity the real benefits of business. It's time to kill the notion that commerce is an exploitative activity. Commerce is creative. It gives people purpose and an outlet for their talent. It puts food on the table. It puts clothes on our children.'

Council agreed that Chamber should make a contribution to the city to mark its bicentenary year and donated £7000 towards a fountain in a new park in Parkgate Street, opposite Frank Sherwin Bridge. The fountain, designed by the corporation, was unveiled by the Lord Mayor, Michael Keating, on 1 December. Alas the fountain has gone the way of most of its ilk, a victim of Dubliners' inability to leave water features alone. It remains in position but without water and has been joined in the park by another victim of Dublin vandalism, Éamonn O'Doherty's Anna Livia statue, which was originally in O'Connell Street but was moved to make way for the Spire.

XIII

THE MODERN ERA

If there is one opportunity to be grasped from all this hard work that went into the success of our bicentenary year, it is to use it to widen and deepen the scope and influence of Chamber in the business life of Dublin.

Niall Crowley's president's report, 1984

Dublin Chamber of Commerce used its 1983 bicentenary as an opportunity to reinvigorate the organisation, with five main aims: to develop a more effective communication between Council and its secretariat and the members; to increase membership in order to make the organisation more representative and provide additional income for improved services; to extend the physical boundaries of Chamber's remit by including the new suburbs of Dublin; to improve the quality of submissions made to government; and to strengthen the management structure. These objectives were achieved between the presidency of Niall Crowley in 1983 and that of Tom Hardiman in 1988.

The current Chamber logo, which no longer has a nautical motif. The castles, spire and bridge all symbolise Dublin.

While the honorary secretaries had driven Chamber's agenda in the 19th century, presidents and Council took a more active role in formulating policy

timeline

1985

Anglo-Irish Agreement.

Former Fianna Fáil minister Des O'Malley founds Progressive Democrats (PDs).

1986

Devaluation of Irish pound by 8 per cent.

1988

Dublin celebrates its millennium.

1989

Fianna Fáil in coalition for the first time, with PDs.

1990

Election of Mary Robinson as Ireland's first woman president.

1993

Further devaluation of Irish pound, by 10 per cent. Maastricht Treaty implemented in EU.

in the 20th century and the job of the secretary was to implement Council's decisions, rather as would the secretary of a government department. The role of the various committees become more directive and Council more managerial. The new role of chief executive was created and in February 1984 Tom Cox was appointed to this position. Justin O'Connell remained as secretary but the post ceased to exist when he retired in 1988.

Tom Cox had worked in the Irish Management Institute (IMI) for twenty-three years and set about modernising the organisation of Chamber along the lines of the IMI. There were other new appointments, a development executive and a membership executive, followed by a marketing executive in 1987. Desmond Miller's president's report for 1984 noted: 'We have since built upon the success of our bicentenary to advance the role of Dublin Chamber. We have in the last year broadened our organisation, increased our manpower resource, reviewed the relevance of our activities and the quality of our services, improved and widened our communications with our members, enlarged and strengthened our committee structure and are putting in place a plan covering the next three years.' Membership had already grown by 12 per cent. The nature of membership also changed significantly as the 20th century progressed. Many more of those joining were employees and the range of companies represented expanded greatly to reflect the gamut of business. Over time Chamber moved from individual membership to company affiliation, with the subscriptions levels dependent on the size of the business in question.

In pursuit of its policy of including Dublin's new suburbs, Chamber helped to establish three local chambers of commerce. Tallaght was first in 1984 (renamed South County Chamber of Commerce in 1995). It had its own council and membership but retained a close relationship with Dublin Chamber; its president and vice-president were ex-officio members of Council. Finglas and District (now North Dublin) Chamber of Commerce was next, in 1986, and finally Swords and District (now Fingal) in 1994. These three chambers are now independent entities.

From the time of its revival in 1820, Chamber had produced reports on various commercial issues, normally brief and factual. After the management reorganisation of the mid-1980s, different committees were tasked with examining a range of topics affecting Dublin as well as Chamber membership and making proposals based on their research. The inclusion of members who were not on Council but who had a particular expertise, as well as outside consultants on occasion, strengthened these committees, as did the employment of a research director in 1988. Reports covered areas such as public transport, tourism, planning development strategy, unemployment and financial issues. Several were long-term strategic documents, including: *Dublin in the Year 2000* (1985); *2010: A Vision of Dublin* (1997); and *Dublin 2020 Vision* (2004). In 1997 alone eleven reports appeared, highlighting issues such as the poor taxi service; inadequate public service and transport networks; the need for a convention centre and new bridges over the Liffey; and the possibility of an elected mayor. Multiple committees evolved into a smaller number of taskforces to tackle issues of more immediate concern. Council still meets ten times a year but an executive committee now augments its work. This comprises the president, vice-president, deputy-vice-president, immediate past president, honorary treasurer, CEO and leaders of Council work programmes.

1994

The IRA announces a ceasefire in Northern Ireland. Other paramilitaries follow suit.

1995

Passing of referendum on divorce.

1996

Breakdown of IRA ceasefire with bombings in London, Manchester and Enniskillen.

1997

Irish government announces a revenue surplus for the first time.

1998

Good Friday agreement signed in Belfast and accepted in countrywide referendum.

2000

Approval of metro system for Dublin.

2002

The Euro replaces the Irish punt.

2008

The Irish government bails out the country's banks.

2010

Europe and the International Monetary Fund (IMF) bail out the Irish government. A 'troika' from these bodies and the World Bank arrive to direct national fiscal policy.

2014

Ireland exits from the bailout.

During the mid-1980s Ireland remained in the doldrums economically as politicians repeatedly failed to tackle the burden of public debt accrued after the 1977 election, successive governments instead adding to it. Unemployment reached an all-time peak of 17.3 per cent in 1985 and emigration remained at a very high level. Chamber reports of the time emphasise the difficulties faced by business: high interest rates and taxes and the constricting effect of debt-servicing on the economy. The 1985 annual report declared: 'It is the consensus of our membership that the single greatest problem holding enterprise back is the crushing burden of the national finances.' This situation persisted until the 'Tallaght Strategy' of 1987 – so called because Fine Gael leader Alan Dukes announced it at a Tallaght Chamber of Commerce event – which committed his party, then in opposition, to supporting the government in any action it took to resolve budgetary difficulties. A number of other policies helped the economy to grow: the development of the financial services sector; a low rate of corporation tax; and social partnership with the trade unions, conceding general wage agreements in return for industrial peace.

Over the years government policy began to show more empathy towards business as it became clear that economic development and national development went hand in hand. Gradually some of the issues of concern to Chamber were resolved. One such was Dublin port. Chamber continued to have four appointees on Dublin Port and Docks Board but the port was not working efficiently or profitably. Chamber set up a port users' committee in 1984, which reported in 1988 that nearly 70 per cent of roll-on/roll-off business from the Republic was passing through Larne. Dublin was losing out because of high charges and archaic and restrictive labour practices. In 1982 the port had set up Cargo Handling Ltd to deal with work practices but after some initial success it too became the victim of labour disputes. It was wound up in 1992, resulting in a seven-month-long industrial dispute that closed the port. Thereafter, stevedoring services passed into private hands. Chamber noted at this point that Dublin's port charges were the highest in Europe. The government proposed that the port be taken over by a commercial semi-state company, a resolution Chamber supported, and in 1997 the Dublin Port Company replaced the Dublin Port and Docks Board, ending Chamber's representation on the port management body.

The authorities also dealt with some of the issues relating to Dublin's infrastructure that Chamber had raised during the preceding years. In 1984 the DART suburban rail system began to operate along Dublin's coastal belt. The East Link Bridge opened the same year, easing traffic along the city's quays. Construction of the M50 orbital motorway began, as well as several bypass routes. Chamber's relationship with Dublin Corporation had become one of partnership rather than conflict and many of its programmes, including a focus on tourism as an economic benefit to Dublin, were carried out in conjunction with the corporation. The theme of Chamber's 1985 conference was *The Future of Dublin* and in 1986 it reported that from a tourism point of

David Manley.

The David Manley Awards

David Manley (1952-2002), who was Chamber president in 2000, worked with accountants Stokes Kennedy Crowley after taking a business degree in TCD. In 1979 he and Gerry O'Reilly set up an accounting practice, Newmarket Partnership, that evolved into Newmarket Consulting, a marketing and business planning company.

Manley was chair and company secretary of Rehab Lotteries and was appointed to the board of the fledgling Railway Procurement Agency just before he died on 15 August 2002. His passion was motor racing: he raced Formula 3 cars throughout Europe. Manley's friends in Dublin Chamber established the David Manley Awards, sponsored by Chamber, which reward emerging entrepreneurship. Swiftxt was the inaugural winner in 2003.

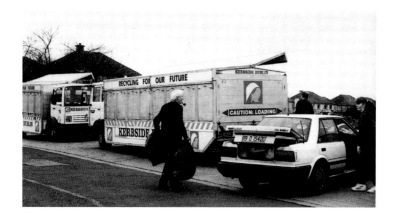

We Recycle
KERBSIDE DUBLIN, UNIT 8, COOKSTOWN INDUSTRIAL ESTATE, DUBLIN 24.

Above: Dublin Chamber set up Kerbside Recycling in 1990 to provide a recycling service, initially for 25,000 houses, The local authorities later took over recycling services.

Below: Kerbside logo.

view 'the breakdown in the fabric of Dublin's inner city in recent decades has been a matter for shame and a source of embarrassment'.

Chamber strongly advocated that a conference centre be built in the city and, as part of its campaign, went so far as to commission an architect, Arthur Gibney, to provide a preliminary concept sketch. It participated in a working party the government set up in 1992 and supported all stages of the initiative until the Convention Centre opened in 2010. Thereafter it held its annual dinner there. Chamber also endorsed the creation of the Irish Financial Services Centre (IFSC) in 1987 and the redevelopment of Temple Bar in 1991, as well as other projects to improve the appearance of the city and promote civic participation. In 1998 it presented to the corporation the *Dublin Environmental Inventory*, an architectural and environmental database that utilised advanced computer technology.

In an effort to encourage businesses to improve the manner in which they presented themselves during the Dublin Millennium, in 1988 the Business Face of Dublin Awards, sponsored by Jurys Hotels, were introduced. In 1993, in conjunction with Guinness, the Living Dublin Awards were established to encourage civic participation in the city's life. Chamber also sponsored a series of advertisements directed at attracting tourists to Dublin from Northern Ireland.

At this time a network of business innovation centres (BICs) were set up throughout the EEC and in 1986 Chamber played an integral role in establishing a BIC in Dublin, with which it is still involved. It was initially housed in Clare Street, subsequently moving to Pearse Street Enterprise Centre.

In 1990 Chamber set up Dublin Kerbside Collection and Recycling Company Ltd, which initially collected recyclables from 25,000 houses, later extending its catchment area. This was a joint initiative with Dublin Corporation/councils, the Department of the Environment and the European Recovery and Recycling Association. Under the chairmanship of George McCullagh, it was the first household recycling service in Dublin and operated until the corporation's own waste management services took over this function.

Another measure that Chamber initiated, in 1994, was the Dublin Schools' Business Partnership, chaired by Brian Duncan, which gave inner-city schools access to business support in association with Ulster Bank and the National College of Industrial Relations (later National College of Ireland). Selected schools could avail of mentoring and internships and the partnership included company visits, mock interviews and work experience, sometimes resulting in employment for pupils.

After the relaxation of relations between the Republic and Northern Ireland, signalled by the cross-border visits of Taoiseach Seán Lemass and Northern Premier Terence O'Neill in 1967, Dublin Chamber was involved in meetings with Belfast, Newry and Dundalk chambers, beginning in 1969. Discussions centred around topics such as customs, communications and infrastructure, which affected commerce between the two states. In 1985 Chamber president, John Vaughan, observed, during a visit to Londonderry Chamber of Commerce: 'Business is a politically neutral activity and is an

Above: A Business Face of Dublin award. Beshoff's Restaurant, O'Connell Street, was the first overall winner.

Below: Part of Chamber's 1985 advertising campaign to attract visitors from Northern Ireland.

ideal vehicle for improving understanding between both parts of Ireland.' Members of Dublin and Northern Ireland Chambers began to attend one another's annual dinners. Dublin Chamber instituted a programme in conjunction with Northern Ireland Chamber, called 'Business Without Borders', which brought business people together at social gatherings in Dublin and Belfast, the first such gathering held in Dublin in 1993. Peter Brook, Northern Ireland Secretary of State, visited Clare Street in 1991 and Baroness Jean Denton, Northern Ireland Minister for the Economy, addressed Chamber in 1995. When an IRA bomb destroyed the Arndale Centre in Manchester in June 1996, Chamber organised a delegation to that city that included Chamber president, Mary Finan, and President Mary Robinson, to show solidarity with Manchester's business community. In 2004 Gerry Adams was invited to speak at a Chamber event and four years later Ian Paisley spoke at the AGM dinner.

In 2001 Chamber initiated a Network and Getwork programme, which gave small and medium (SME) member companies access to the procurement departments of major companies and government institutions. The following year, this was rolled out on a cross-border basis in collaboration with Northern Ireland Chamber and with the support of Intertrade Ireland. SMEs from Dublin and Northern Ireland had the opportunity to pitch to buyers from large companies according to pre-arranged procurement needs, as well as networking among themselves for business development. This programme continued until 2007 and was a significant promoter of cross-border trade. As part of the cooperation, councils of Dublin and Northern Ireland Chamber gathered on a number of occasions for formal meetings, one of which was addressed by the Irish president, Mary McAleese.

Since the 1980s Chamber has become much more proactive in communicating with members. In 1984 it launched a twice-yearly newsletter called *Contact*, which evolved into the monthly *Business Contact* magazine in 1988. Chamber now produces a quarterly, *Business Ireland*. When the organisation first moved to 7 Clare Street some of the space was sublet but it gradually utilised more of the premises, adding a training room in 1985 to provide courses and seminars for members on relevant business and regulation matters; it is now used for a variety of Chamber functions.

From its inauguration Chamber was aware of the importance of communication in business. Communication became increasingly electronic after the rapid development of the internet from the mid-1990s. Chamber set up its first website, www.dubchamber.ie at this time. In 1995 it launched an internet business-to-business service and hosted a conference on the advantages of the internet for business. From 1999 Council included an e-commerce committee, initially under the chairmanship of P.J. Timmins, and Chamber provided the Prism e-commerce course for members, designed to develop an awareness of the advantages of the internet in business. The organisation launched a revamped website in 2000, by which time e-commerce had begun to take off and large multinationals in the information technology field had begun operations in Ireland.

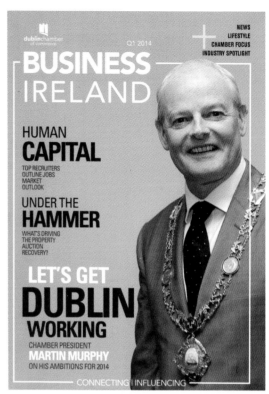

Business Ireland, *Chamber's current quarterly magazine for members.*

Tom Cox (1930-2007), CEO 1984-96

Tom Cox grew up in Kerry, the youngest of twelve children of a Belfast businessman and a Kerry mother. He worked for Guardian Insurance before joining the IMI in 1961, becoming secretary in 1977, responsible for the organisation's annual conference in Killarney. In February 1984 he joined Dublin Chamber as its first chief executive and by the time of his retirement twelve years later had contributed in no small way to its development.

Noel Carroll (1941-88), CEO 1996-8

Noel Carroll was born in Annagassan, County Louth. He joined the Irish army in 1959 and attended Villanova University 1961-5. Well known for his athletics achievements, he represented Ireland in the Tokyo and Mexico Olympics of 1964 and 1968. He worked with IBM and the Eastern Region Tourism Organisation and in 1972 became Dublin Corporation's first PRO. He maintained his interest in athletics and initiated the Dublin City Marathon in 1980. Carroll served as CEO of Dublin Chamber from 1996 until his sudden death in 1998.

Jim Miley, CEO 1999-2000

Jim Miley graduated in agricultural economics in UCD in 1983 and, following a couple of years as a volunteer for Concern, joined RTE as a reporter. From 1995-9 he served as Fine Gael general secretary. He joined Chamber as CEO in April 1999 and left in September 2000, after he co-founded the property website myhome.ie, of which he was CEO 2000-9. He was project leader for the 'Gathering' tourism initiative of 2013 and appointed to the board of directors of *The Irish Times* in 2014.

Gina Quin, CEO from 2000

Gina Quin was born and educated in Dublin and joined Lansdowne Market Research after taking a degree in psychology in UCD. In 1984 she moved to the Irish Trade Board, now Enterprise Ireland, where she worked in market research and business development. She joined the Rehab Group in 1989, becoming CEO of Gandon Enterprises, the group's commercial division. In December 2000 she succeeded Jim Miley as CEO of Dublin Chamber. She was awarded an MBA by UCD Michael Smurfit Business School in 1988, was the UCD Michael Smurfit Graduate Business School Alumna of the Year in 2008 and is a chartered director.

An early innovation on the part of Tom Cox to encourage networking was the introduction of 'Business after Hours', a format he first observed on a visit to chambers of commerce in the US. Chamber now hosts more than one hundred and thirty events annually, with an attendance of 10,000, ranging from its annual dinner in Dublin Convention Centre with sixteen hundred-plus guests, to a business owners' network and 'in-camera' events for senior leaders. Increasingly its events are themed to benefit members' or sectoral interests, for example: Tech Forum, Smart Series, Competitive Edge, Leaders' Series and export-themed events, in keeping with the organisation's mission to deliver inspiring learning and leadership. Chamber provides a significant range of international services, including export documentation, ATA (temporary admission) carnets, visa services and a wide range of supports for exporting companies, most recently through the Enterprise Europe Network, an EU initiative to promote worldwide trade.

Ian Paisley (1926-2014), complete with Union Jack tie, speaking at the AGM dinner in 2008, during Margaret Sweeney's presidency.

Chamber also works with government departments and other key regulatory and institutional bodies and frequently holds briefings for members on significant developments in infrastructure, trade and regulation, ensuring that businesses have the opportunity to maximise knowledge for commercial gain. The organisation surveys members and responds to their commercial concerns. Chamber is the leading voice of business in the Dublin region, bringing submissions to government and other bodies and regularly speaking on behalf of business to the national and international media.

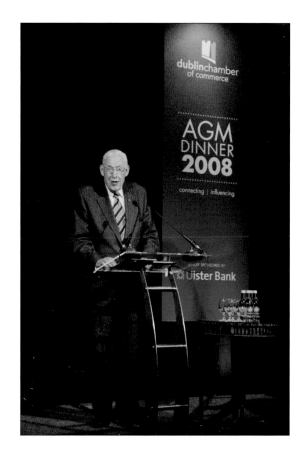

Brochure for Dublin Chamber's eWeek, 26 April-1 May 2004.

In 1986 San Jose, home of Silicon Valley, was twinned with Dublin and there was an exchange of official visits. Dublin Chamber has ongoing links with the Californian city. The twinning of Liverpool with Dublin encouraged the growth of a similar relationship. Chamber also plays its part in foreign trade missions and in International Chamber of Commerce (ICC) meetings.

Government economic policy began to show significant results by the middle of the 1990s. The next five years would see a rapid fall in unemployment, from 12 to 4 per cent. Tom Cox retired as CEO of Chamber in 1996, having presided over considerable change in the organisation. Noel Carroll, former PRO for Dublin Corporation, succeeded him but, unfortunately, on the day after the Chamber annual dinner in 1998 Carroll died unexpectedly. His replacement was Jim Miley, former RTÉ journalist and general secretary of Fine Gael. He left after twenty months to form his own company. Current CEO, Gina Quin, took over the helm in December 2000.

In 2004 Chamber initiated eWeek, 'to assert Ireland's identity as a leader in new communications technologies'. Supported by government, by Enterprise Ireland and by key technology companies, this comprised a week-long series of events, a major conference with EU support and, uniquely, a living experiment, a volunteer who lived virtually, conducting shopping, the ordering of food and all communication from an isolated unit in the window of Clerys in O'Connell Street. eWeek heralded Chamber's commitment to new technologies and opportunities for their commercial exploitation and gained significant media attention for the programme, not least the virtual 'guinea pig'.

The period of economic growth known as the Celtic Tiger came to a shuddering end in 2008 when, as a result of the international downturn and domestic mismanagement, Irish banks faced a liquidity problem. The government announced a bank guarantee on all deposits and was then obliged to provide bailouts to the banks, using borrowed money. In his 2009 presidential address, P.J. Timmins observed: 'Little did I think when I set out upon my presidential journey back in 2005 that our economy was to suffer a stunning reversal of fortune in my year as president of Chamber.'

On 21 November 2010 Taoiseach Brian Cowen announced that Ireland had requested financial support, colloquially known as a 'bailout', from the International Monetary Fund (IMF) and the European Financial Stability Facility. These two bodies, along with the European Central Bank [ECB], formed a 'Troika' that was tasked with managing aspects of Ireland's economy until the country was able to exit from the bailout in 2014. The resulting downturn, which happened relatively quickly, had inevitable knock-on effects on business. The construction sector – the building industry itself and associated professional services – was its most visible

Two Chamber logos from the late 20th century, both with a nautical theme. Above is the logo first introduced in 1986 and below the logo that replaced it in 1992.

victim. Unemployment rose to 15 per cent in 2013 and emigration again became a feature of Irish life. Growth in GDP dropped from a high of 11 per cent in 1997 to a low of -7 per cent in 2009.

In response to the economic crisis, Chamber, in partnership with national government and local authorities, established Activating Dublin, with a clear mandate to drive initiatives to promote Dublin's economic recovery. The partnership spearheaded initiatives including Trading Online, Start-Up Dublin, Activating Youth and Smart City. In partnership with key businesses in the city region, as well as public authorities, it successfully piloted business-expanding learning for companies with little or no online trading experience; promoted Dublin's start-up ecosphere and delivered the appointment of a commissioner for start-ups for Dublin; encouraged a stronger employer interface with employment services, particularly in the area of youth unemployment; continued to activate Dublin as a smart city; and developed a regular economic profiling survey and branding toolkit for the capital.

Chamber is a firm supporter of Chambers Ireland, in which it participates at board level, and of other Chambers throughout Ireland, maintaining strong links on key policy issues for Dublin and for the national economy. Cooperation and alliances with other chambers and business organisations continue to be a key objective for the organisation, as a means of serving businesses and members of the Dublin region. Chamber is committed to the promotion of the economic success of Dublin for Ireland, and a supporter of the concept, acknowledged worldwide, that successful city regions drive successful national economies.

As this book goes to press there is evidence of considerable economic recovery, particularly in Dublin business, and indications for further recovery and growth are positive.

When the Committee of Merchants assembled at the Royal Exchange in 1783 and proposed the formation of a Chamber of Commerce, it was their hope that the new body would help merchants to deal with the impositions and barriers that hindered their trade. In the ensuing two hundred and thirty years Dublin Chamber developed beyond such limited preoccupations, playing a key role in supporting business and planning for the future of the city, in partnership with government and the local authorities.

Chamber continues to have a role representing the interests of business in an ever-developing city and evolving commercial environment, not just on a national level but on the greater stage of Europe and the world. As Ireland is such an open economy it is more necessary than ever for Chamber and its professional team to represent the voice of Irish companies. Genuinely representative of business, industry and the professions, the organisation has learned from history the need to remain flexible in order to deal with any issues that come its way and the development it has undertaken over the past thirty years has prepared it for what the future may bring.

THE REBIRTH OF THE OUZEL GALLEY SOCIETY

It is a great honour – in the real sense of that word – for me to welcome all of you here to this special meeting of the Ouzel Galley Society. Those words have not been heard for a hundred years. It was precisely one hundred years ago that the society decided to wind up its affairs. This historic meeting this evening ensures that that decision a hundred years ago was merely an adjournment.

Opening remarks by Chamber president, Denis Shelly, in his speech
at the Ouzel Galley dinner, 11 February 1988

In the century since the demise of the Ouzel Galley Society, so strongly associated with Dublin Chamber of Commerce, members had from time to time proposed its revival, principally as an arbitration body. But perhaps more successful in rekindling interest in the *Ouzel Galley* was the publication of George A. Little's book in 1940, with financial assistance from Dublin Chamber. It was reprinted in 1953. Little's version became the gold standard for the story. Philip Rooney's radio play, *The Ouzel Galley*, was broadcast on Radio Éireann in 1946 and the following year he published a children's book, *The Golden Coast*, based on the *Ouzel Galley* story.

When Hugh Dolan took over the Bodega licensed premises in Commercial Buildings in 1955 he rechristened it 'The Ouzel Galley'; although Chamber took advice in an effort to prevent him from using the name, legal opinion was that it was not in the organisation's power to do so. In October 1959 a festival called 'Kitchen and Cellar Week' included an reenactment of the *Ouzel Galley* story, complete with ship, on the River Liffey. The *Irish Independent* reported: 'The struggle between the original Dublin crew and the pirates was enacted on a realistically decorated launch below O'Connell Bridge. Thousands lined the river to enact the battle, which was followed by a fireworks display and a recital of sea shanties.' The cast then repaired to the Ouzel Galley Lounge for refreshments.

The celebration of the official millennium of the foundation of Dublin took place in 1988; the same year was the centenary of the demise of the Ouzel Galley Society. Under the direction of the president, Denis Shelly, Chamber took the decision to revive the society. The inaugural meeting was held in the Council room on 11 February 1988, with the ancient painting of the *Ouzel Galley* as backdrop. Present were past presidents of Dublin Chamber. Denis Shelly was host and Susan Magan was guest of honour as the descendant of James Chaigneau Colvill (1814-97), the first lieutenant and highest-

The inaugural dinner of the new Ouzel Galley Society on 11 February 1988. Seated in front of the painting of the Ouzel Galley *is the guest of honour, Susan Magan (holding the boatswain's whistle). Also seated, from left, are James A. Walmsley (president, 1971), Ned Beck (president, 1970), Desmond Miller (president, 1984), the inaugural captain, and J.E. (Jack) Armstrong (president, 1959). Standing, from left, are Roy Donovan (president 1986), Tony Prendergast, (deputy-vice-president), Denis Shelly (president, 1988), Tom Hardiman (vice-president, 1988), Henry Tierney (president 1980) and Declan Lennon (president 1982).*

ranking officer of the society at the time of its demise. The nautical ranks of captain, lieutenant, boatswain, coxswain and bursar were revived and Desmond Miller, the youngest past president, was elected captain. According to its constitution, members of the Society were to include not only past presidents, who were then honorary presidents on Council, but individuals who had made an outstanding contribution to the business affairs of the city or rendered a special service

The larger attendance at the second Ouzel Galley dinner in March 1988, attended by the Lord Mayor, Carmencita Hederman.

The captain's medal with its traditional orange ribbon.

to Chamber. Membership numbers were to be limited to forty, as in the original society. The Society would henceforth meet twice a year for dinner, at which a speaker, either a member or an invited guest, would raise issues 'concerning the promotion of the interests of the capital'. Although they have evolved somewhat since its inception, the functions of the Ouzel Galley Society remain primarily social and charitable. At the end of each year funds in the Society are distributed among three selected charities. The captain, chosen at the autumn meeting, holds office for a year.

The original accoutrements of the Ouzel Galley Society – the glass goblet, the boatswain's whistle and the members' medals – were lodged with the National Museum, so the society uses one of the fourteen replica goblets produced by Waterford Crystal for the bicentenary as the captain's toasting bumper. The captain wears a Galley medal on an orange ribbon as the mark of his position and the boatswain has a replica whistle to call the galley to attention or summon the crew to dinner.

SELECTED BIBLIOGRAPHY

Primary Sources

The National Archives holds minute books for Council of Dublin Chamber 1820-1938 (reference 1064/3/1-19). Chamber wisely placed these documents in the care of the then Public Records Office in 1972. Chamber also recently gave the National Archives the first minute book covering the first two attempts to form a chamber 1783-1807.

Minutes of general meetings of Chamber 1821-1951 are available in two volumes in the National Archives (reference 1064/2/1-2).

The National Archives also has a complete set of reports 1821-1951 – although reports were not printed for several of the earlier years – under reference 1064/1/1-17. In addition the National Library holds an incomplete set of reports 1821-1903 and Dublin City Archive holds some reports.

Chamber itself retains the remaining Council minutes, although some years are not extant, and has an almost complete set of reports, 1889-1990, with some earlier editions.

The minute book and rough minute book of the Committee of Merchants which, between them, cover the years 1764-1783 are in the Royal Irish Academy (reference 12 D 29 and 3 C 25). The Academy also holds two minute books for the Ouzel Galley Society 1748-1882, the minute book for the Society's Council 1853-86, an account book for 1812-69 and three arbitration books 1799-1884 as well as some ephemera, in two boxes (reference 12 F 46 and 12 F 47/48).

Secondary Sources

Bennett, Robert J. *Local Business Voice*. Oxford: OUP, 2011.

Berry, Henry F. 'The Records of the Dublin Gild of Merchants, known as the Gild of the Holy Trinity, 1438-1671', in *The Journal of the Royal Society of Antiquaries of Ireland*, XXX, 1900, pp. 44-68.

Casey, Christine. *The Buildings of Ireland: Dublin*. Yale: Yale University Press, 2005.

Cullen, L.M. *Princes & Pirates, The Dublin Chamber of Commerce 1783-1983*. Dublin: Dublin Chamber of Commerce, 1983.

Corcoran, Michael. 'Through Streets Broad and Narrow: Dublin Trams'. The Sir John T. Gilbert Commemorative Lecture: Dublin City Public Libraries, 2007.

Craig, Maurice. *Dublin 1660-1860: The Shaping of a City*. London, Cresset Press, 1952.

Daly, Mary E. *Dublin, The Deposed Capital: A Social and Economic History, 1860-1914*. Cork: Cork University Press, 1984.

Devine, Francis (ed.). *A Capital in Conflict: Dublin City and the 1913 Lockout*. Dublin: Dublin City Council, 2013.

Dickson, David. *Dublin: The Making of a Capital City*. London: Profile Books, 2014.

Dudley, Rowena. *The Irish Lottery 1780-1801*. Dublin: Four Courts Press, 2005.

Duffy, Hugo. *James Gandon and His Times*. Kinsale, County Cork: Gandon Editions, 1999.

Falkiner, C. Litton. 'Some Illustrations of the Commercial History of Dublin in the 18th Century', in *Proceedings of the Royal Irish Academy*, 1902.

Fagan, Patrick. *Catholics in a Protestant Country*. Dublin: Four Courts Press, 1998.

Farmar, Tony. *Privileged Lives, A Social History of Middle-class Ireland, 1882-1989*. Dublin: A&A Farmar, 2010.

Ferriter, Diarmaid. *The Transformation of Ireland, 1900-2000*. London: Profile Books, 2005.

Foster, R.F. *Luck and the Irish: A Brief History of Change, 1970-2000*: London: Allen Lane, 2007.

Gilligan, H.A. *A History of the Port of Dublin*. Dublin: Gill & Macmillan, 1988.

Griffith, Lisa Marie. 'The Ouzel Galley Society in the 18th century: Arbitration Body or Drinking Club?' in *The Laws and Other Legalities of Ireland*.(Michael Brown and Seán Patrick Donlan eds.) Dublin: Ashgate, 2011.

Haliday, Charles. *The Scandinavian Kingdom of Dublin, with some Notices on the Author's Life by John P. Prendergast*. Dublin: M.H. Gill & Son, 1884.

Lee, J.J. *Ireland, 1912-1985: Politics and Society*. Cambridge: Cambridge University Press, 1989.

Little, George A. 'The *Ouzel Galley*', Old Dublin Society, 1940.

Litton, A.J. 'The Growth and Development of the Irish Telephone System', *Journal of the Statistical and Social Inquiry Society of Ireland*, 1961-2.

Meyler, Walter Thomas. *St Catherine's Bells: an Autobiography* (two volumes). Dublin and London: Simkin Marshall & Company, 1868, 1870.

Morrissey, Thomas J. *William Martin Murphy*. Dublin: UCD Press Life & Times Series, 2011.

O'Brien, Joseph V. *Dear Dirty Dublin: A City in Distress, 1899-1916*. Berkeley: University of California Press, 1982.

Ó Maitiú, Séamus. *Dublin's Suburban Towns, 1834-1930*. Dublin: Four Courts Press, 2003.

Osborough, W.N. *Law and the Emergence of Modern Dublin*. Dublin: Irish Academic Press, 1996.

Prendeville, P.L. *The History of Dublin Chamber of Commerce, 1760-1860*. UCD: Unpublished MComm thesis, 1930.

Royal Commissioners, The. *First Report of the Royal Commission Appointed to Inquire into the Municipal Corporations in Ireland*. London: HMSO, 1835.

Smith, Cornelius F. *The Shipping Murphys*. Dublin: Albany Press, 2004.

Thorpe, Ruth. 'Thomas Cooley before the Dublin Royal Exchange', in *Irish Architectural and Decorative Studies, Journal of the Irish Georgian Society*, VIII, 2005.

Webb, John J. *The Guilds of Dublin*. Dublin: The Sign of the Three Candles, 1929.

Yeates, Pádraig. *Lockout: Dublin 1913*. Dublin: Gill & Macmillan, 2000.

——. *A City in Wartime: Dublin 1914-18*. Dublin: Gill & Macmillan, 2011.

——. *A City in Turmoil: Dublin 1919-21*. Dublin: Gill & Macmillan, 2012.

APPENDIX 1

MEMBERSHIP NUMBERS

Graph of the numbers of individual members of Dublin Chamber 1820-1987. Since 1987 membership has been by company. No membership figures survive from before 1820 with the single exception of the founding year of 1783, when two hundred and ninety-three merchants were admitted. The numbers are taken from the annual report or the attached membership list.

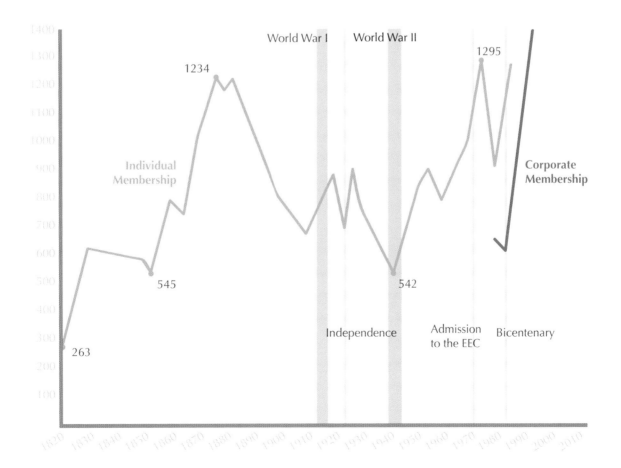

APPENDIX II

CHAMBER PRESIDENTS

The policy of the 1805-7 Chamber was that a Council member would be appointed chairman for three months. The Chamber's list of presidents, accompanying the annual reports, included these chairmen as presidents. However Chamber minutes are not so clear. Joseph Wilson was appointed in 1805, to resign only a week later. Both Nathaniel Hone and John Duncan were in the chair for three months. Randal MacDonnell and Bartholomew Mazière served for six months, George Carleton for eight months and there is no mention of William Hone being appointed although, by tradition, he is on the list. Apart from these chairmen, early presidents remained in office until their death (William Digges La Touche resigned due to ill-health the day before he died); thereafter presidents were generally re-elected and served for two or three years. After the rules changed, in 1914, presidents could not present themselves for re-election until at least a year had lapsed. Today there is an election for the office of deputy-vice-president, the position of vice-president and president following automatically from this.

Term	Name	Place of Birth	Business/ profession	Company	Business Address
1783-8	Travers Hartley (1723-1796)	Dublin	Merchant	Travers & Son	89 Bride St
1789-1804	No president				
1805	Joseph Wilson (?-1809)	Derry?	Merchant	Joseph Wilson & Son	10 Ormond Quay
	Nathaniel Hone (1760-1819)	Dublin	Merchant		79 Fleet St
	John Duncan (1755-1825)	Scotland	Merchant	W. & J. Duncan	6 Granby Row
1806	William Hone (1783-1859)	Dublin	Broker		Commercial Buildings
	Randal MacDonnell (1762-1819)	Spain?	Merchant	Wine importers	Allen's Court
	Bartholomew Mazière (1753-1823)	Dublin	Sugar baker		6 St Mary's Abbey

Term	Name	Place of Birth	Business/ profession	Company	Business Address
1807	George Carleton (1762-1831)	Dublin	Merchant	J. & G. Carleton	12 Eustace St
1808-19	No president				
1820-2	Joshua Pim (1748-1822)	Laois	Merchant		15 Usher's Island
1823-5	Leland Crosthwait (1747-1826)	Dublin	Merchant	L. Crosthwait & Sons	63 Fleet St
1826	No president				
1827-55	Arthur Guinness (1768-1855)	Dublin	Brewer	Arthur Guinness, Sons & Co	St James's Gate
1856	No president				
1857-70	Thomas Crosthwait (1782-1870)	Dublin	Merchant	L. Crosthwait & Sons	63 Fleet St
1871-81	William Digges La Touche (1812-82)	Dublin	Banker	Munster Bank	9 Dame St
1882-4	John Bagot (1812-87)	Dublin	Wine/tea merchant	Bagots Hutton & Co	27-28 William St
1885-7	Sir Richard Martin (1831-1901)	Dublin	Timber/ship merchant	R. Martin & Co	29-33 Sir John Rogerson's Quay
1888-90	John Lloyd Blood (1814-94)	Dublin	Brewer	Mountjoy Brewery	Russell St
1891-3	Michael Murphy (1816-94)	Dublin	Shipping merchant	Palgrave Murphy & Co	17 Eden Quay
1894-6	John R. Wigham (1829-1919)	Scotland	Engineering	Edmundson Ltd	Capel St
1897-9	Sir John E. Barry (1828-1919)	Wexford	Grain/malt merchant	Barry Norton & Co	65 Middle Abbey St
1900-2	Sir J. Malcolm Inglis (1837-1902)	Scotland	Timber/coal merchant	Thomas Heiton & Co	18 Westmoreland St
1903-4	Sir James Murphy (1843-1922)	Dublin	Shipping	Palgrave Murphy & Co	17 Eden Quay
1905-6	Marcus Goodbody (1857-1923)	Offaly	Tobacco merchant	T.P. & R. Goodbody Ltd	Greenville Ave., SCR
1907-8	Laurence Malone (1836-1916)	Dublin	Distiller	DWD Distillery	Jones's Road
1909-11	John Mooney (1842-1923)	Wexford	Baker	Johnston Mooney & O'Brien	Ballsbridge
1912-3	William Martin Murphy (1844-1919)	Cork	Transport	DUTC	Sackville St
1914	Richard K. Gamble (1860-1921)	Dublin	Timber merchant	Brooks Ltd	Sackville Place
1915	Patrick Leonard (1862-1944)	Dublin	Salesmaster	Leonard, Son & Co	17 Lower Dominick St

Term	Name	Place of Birth	Business/ profession	Company	Business Address
1916	Richard W. Booth (1841-1930)	Dublin	Engineering	Booth Bros Ltd	63-65 Upper Stephen's St
1917	Matthew J. Minch (1855-1921)	Kildare	Malting	M.J. Minch & Son	Athy
1918	Edward H. Andrews (1860-1937)		Wine/tea merchant	Andrews Ltd	21-22 Dame St
1919	William Wallace (1843-1923)	Down	Coal merchant	Wallace Bros	23 Westmoreland St
1920	John Good (1866-1941)	Dublin	Builders	J. & P. Good Ltd	55 Great Brunswick St
1921	Andrew Jameson (1855-1941)	Scotland	Distilling	John Jameson & Son Ltd	Bow St
1922	William Hewat (1865-1935)	Dublin	Coal/timber merchant	Thomas Heiton & Co	18 Westmoreland St
1923	James Shanks (1845-1926)	Antrim	Minerals	Walter Brights Ltd	54 Townsend St
1924	W. Lombard Murphy (1877-1943)	Dublin	Newspaper	Irish Independent Ltd	Middle Abbey St
1925	William Crowe (1861-1930)	Leitrim	Timber merchant	W. & L. Crowe Ltd	50-51 South Richmond St
1926	George N. Jacob (1854-1933)	Dublin	Biscuit manufacturer	W. & R. Jacobs & Co Ltd	Bishop St
1927	J.C.M. Eason (1881-1976)	Dublin	Stationery	Eason & Son Ltd	O'Connell St
1928	David Barry (1873-1936)	Antrim	Shipping	B. & I. Steampacket Co	Sir John Rogerson's Quay
1929	Sir Walter Nugent (1865-1955)	Westmeath	Company director	Donore, Westmeath	
1930	W.P. Sherriff (1868-1953)	Scotland	Insurance	Northern Assurance Co	Westmoreland St
1931	James J. Halpin (1880-1948)	Limerick	Provisions	J.J. Halpin Ltd	18-20 Thomas St
1932	D.J. Cogan (1859-1944)	Wicklow	Provisions	D.J. Cogan Ltd	115 Thomas St
1933	H.M. Dockrell (1880-1955)	Dublin	Timber merchant	Dockrell Ltd	South Great Georges St
1934	Edgar Anderson (1883-1959)	Dublin	Company director		Merrion Rd
1935	J. Hubbard Clark (1869-1959)	Scotland	Company director		Iona Rd
1936	John O'Neill (1876-1941)	Carlow	Car assembly	J. O'Neill Ltd	Pleasants St
1937	Frank A. Lowe (1883-1959)	Dublin	Stationery	Hely's Ltd	26-28 Dame St

Term	Name	Place of Birth	Business/ profession	Company	Business Address
1938	Thomas F. Laurie (1894-1981)	England	Petroleum	Esso Petroleum Ltd	1-2 Upper O'Connell St
1939	W. Woods Hill (1875-1951)	Derry	Clothing	Hill & Co (Dublin) Ltd	5 Parliament St
1940	Alfred A. Brunker (1875-1946)	Dublin	Pharmacist	Boileau & Boyd Ltd	90-93 Bride St
1941	Joseph Walker (1885-1953)	Galway	Retail/BDS	Walkers Ltd	27-29 Liffey St
1942	J. Harold Aylward (1881-1949)	Dublin	Insurance	Royal Insurance Co	44-45 Dame St
1943	David Coyle (1896-1968)	Limerick	Tea merchant	Coyle Ltd	30 Upper Abbey St
1944	Ernest E. Benson (1898-1975)	Dublin	Laundry	Dublin Laundry Co	Dartry
1945	G. Brock (1887-1967)	Meath	Accountant	Craig Gardner & Co	39-41 Dame St
1946	John Hawkins (1881-1964)	Wexford	Butcher	Central Meats Products	7a Pim St
1947	A.J. Broughton (1881-1962)	England	Railway	LMS Railway Co	North Wall
1948	Stanley V. Kirkpatrick (1897-1988)	Dublin	Insurance	Insurance Corporation of Ireland	36 Dame St
1949	George Watson (1899-1987)	Dublin	Animal feed	Paul & Vincent Ltd	9-13 Blackhall Place
1950	F.M. Summerfield (1888-1975)	Dublin	Car assembly	F.M. Summerfield Ltd	138 Lower Baggot St
1951	Michael P. Rowan (1892-1961)	Dublin	Seed merchant	M. Rowan & Co	1-3 Westmoreland St
1952	G.H.C. Crampton (1901-76)	Dublin	Builder	G. & T. Crampton Ltd	Ballsbridge
1953	Patrick J. Loughrey (1910-84)	Derry	Food Manufacture	Batchelors & Co Ltd	Cabra
1954	Thomas F. Laurie (1894-1981)	England	Petroleum	Esso Petroleum Ltd	1-2 Upper O'Connell St
1955	Stephen Mackenzie (1891-1967)	Dublin	Coal merchant	Mackenzie & Co Ltd	14 Westmoreland St
1956	Alex O'D. Shiel (1903-66)	Dublin	Radios	Kelly & Sheil Ltd	48 Fleet St
1957	J.W. Gallagher (1894-1974)	Donegal	Insurance	Hibernian Insurance	Dame St
1958	J. Harold Douglas (1912-82)	Dublin	Drapery	John Douglas & Son Ltd	17-19 Wexford St
1959	Lt. Col. J.E. Armstrong (1903-2001)	England	Distiller	John Jameson & Son Ltd	Bow St

Term	Name	Place of Birth	Business/ profession	Company	Business Address
1960	Vincent Crowley (1890-1965)	Cavan	Accountant	Kennedy Crowley & Co	4-5 Westmoreland St
1961	John O'Brien (1910-83)	Dublin	Barrister	Federated Union of Employers	
1962	Philip R. Walker (1915-82)	Dublin	Radios	Walkers Ltd	27-29 Liffey St
1963	Thomas C. Lenehan (1907-79)	Dublin	Hardware	Thomas Lenehan & Co	124-5 Capel St
1964	Thomas F. Laurie (1894-1981)	England	Petroleum	Esso Petroleum Ltd	1-2 Upper O'Connell St
1965	E.C.G. Mulhern (1906-77)	Fermanagh	Stockbroker	Ryan & Dillon	24-5 Anglesea St
1966	J.R. Dick (1910-2000)	Dublin	Minerals	A. & R. Thwaites Ltd	Kylemore Rd
1967	James Boylan (1899-1981)	Dublin	Shoe retailers	Boylan Bros Ltd	43 Upper O'Connell St
1968	R.E.M. Clarke (1906-98)	Dublin	Manager	Arthur Guinness Son & Co Ltd	St James's Gate
1969	Gerald L.M. Wheeler (1908-76)	Dublin	Accountant	Stokes Kennedy Crowley	69-71 St Stephen's Green
1970	Edward W. Beck (1915-93)	Dublin	Corn	Warehousing	11 Burgh Quay
1971	James A. Walmsley (1912-2008)	Dublin	Stationery	Eason & Sons	O'Connell St
1972	Michael W. O'Reilly (1925-72)	Dublin	Stockbroker	M.W. O'Reilly	Aston Place
1972-3	James Gallagher (1920-83)	Sligo	Builders	Abbey Group Ltd	38-40 Upper Mount St
1974	Aleck C. Crichton (b. 1918)	Dublin	Distillery	John Jameson & Son Ltd	Bow St
1975	H.J. Bambrick (1915-98)	Dublin	Engineering	Carthorn Ltd	Commercial Buildings
1976	F.F. Carthy (1934-2001)	Dublin	Accountant	Carthy, O'Neill & Co	20 Earlsfort Tce
1977	Patrick F. Belton (1926-87)	Dublin	Publican	Motels Ltd	
1978	E.J. Kelliher (b. 1920)	Kerry	Stationery	Eason & Sons	O'Connell St
1979	J.A. Lenehan (b. 1940)	Dublin	Hardware	Thomas Lenehan & Co Ltd	124-5 Capel St

Term	Name	Place of Birth	Business/ profession	Company	Business Address
1980	H.C. Tierney (1923-2009)	Dublin	Quantity Surveyor	O'Reilly Hyland Tierney	2 Pembroke St Upper
1981	H. Hannon (b. 1924)	Dublin	Kildare	Arthur Guinness Son & Co Ltd	St James's Gate
1982	Declan Lennon (b. 1932)	Dublin	Insurance	Coyle Hamilton Ltd	7-9 Leinster St
1983	Niall Crowley (1926-98)	Dublin	Accountant	Stokes Kennedy Crowley	69-71 St Stephen's Green
1984	Desmond Miller (b. 1941)	Waterford	Accountant	Stokes Kennedy Crowley	69-71 St Stephen's Green
1985	John A. Vaughan (b. 1936)	Waterford	Petroleum	Esso Teo	Stillorgan Rd
1986	Roy Donovan (1928-2010)	Kerry	Auctioneer	Lisney & Son	23 St Stephen's Green
1987	Denis Shelly (b. 1922)	Dublin	Accountant	Calor Teo	Long Mile Rd
1988	T.P. Hardiman (b. 1928)	Dublin	Company director		
1989	Tony Prendergast (b. 1935)	Sligo	Manager	Arthur Guinness Sons Ltd	St James's Gate
1990	Vincent O'Doherty (b. 1935)	Dublin	Retail	Superquinn Ltd	Sutton Cross
1991	Patrick Loughrey (b. 1934)	Antrim	Food	Cuisine de France	Finglas
1992	Brian Duncan (b. 1935)	Dublin	Insurance	Irish Life	Abbey St
1993	George McCullagh (b. 1936)	Monaghan	Accountant	Brown Thomas	Grafton St
1994	John F. Daly (1930-2010)	Cork	Computing	ICL Ltd	Leopardstown
1995	John Donnelly (b. 1929)	Dublin	Accountant	Deloitte & Touche	
1996	Mary Finan (b. 1945)	Roscommon	Public relations	Wilson Hartnell PR	14 Leeson Park
1997	John McNally (b. 1947)	Kildare	Banker	Ulster Bank	George's Quay
1998	Jim Ruane (b. 1944)	Dublin	Banker	Bank of Ireland	Baggot St
1999	Hugh Governey (b. 1943)	Carlow	Insurance	Coyle Hamilton Ltd	7-9 Leinster St
2000	David Manley (1952-2002)	Dublin	Public Relations	Newmarket Ltd	Fumbally Lane
2001	Alfie Kane (b. 1944)	Derry	CEO	Telecom Eireann	St Stephen's Green
2002	Peter Webster (b. 1943)	Dublin	Manager	Smurfit Ireland	94 St Stephen's Green

Term	Name	Place of Birth	Business/profession	Company	Business Address
2003	Clive Brownlee (b. 1944)	Dublin	Manager	Arthur Guinness Sons Ltd	St James's Gate
2004	David Pierce (b. 1955)	Dublin	Banker	Ulster Bank	George's Quay
2005	Áine Maria Mizzoni (b. 1961)	England	Accountant	Grafton Recruitment	
2006	Eugene McCague (b. 1958)	Monaghan	Solicitor	Arthur Cox	Earlsfort Terrace
2007	Ronan King (b. 1954)	Dublin	Accountant	Amethyst Investments	Clonskeagh
2008	Margaret Sweeney (b. 1960)	Dublin	Accountant	Postbank Ltd	
2009	P.J. Timmins (b. 1962)	Wicklow	Retail	Clerys	O'Connell St
2010	Peter Brennan (b. 1954)	Dublin	Business consultant	EPS Consulting	Sandycove
2011	Imelda Reynolds (b. 1961)	Westmeath	Solicitor	Beauchamps	Sir John Rogerson's Quay
2012	Patrick Coveney (b. 1970)	Cork	CEO	Greencore PLC	Santry
2013	Liam Kavanagh (b. 1958)	Dublin	MD	Irish Times Ltd	Tara St
2014	Martin Murphy (b. 1963)	Louth	CEO	HP Ireland	Leixlip, Kildare

APPENDIX III

CHAMBER STAFF

Secretaries/Assistant Secretaries

Until 1920 the assistant secretary, Chamber's senior employee, was assistant to the unpaid honorary secretary; at this point the job title changed to secretary. The position of chief executive superseded the position of secretary in 1984 and it ceased to exist on the retirement of J.B. O'Connell. Assistant secretaries and secretaries and their years of service are listed in Council minutes and Chamber's annual reports.

Assistant Secretaries 1783-1920

William Shannon	1783-95	Arthur Henry Barlow	1875-1901
Joseph Miller	1805-9	Robert Perry Middleton	1901-11
Lundy Edward Foot	1825-35	Robert King Irvine	1912-21
John Armstrong	1844-74		

Secretaries 1920-88

William Maunsell Calwell	1921-5	P.J. MacDwyer	1948-58
J.J. Crowe	1925-8	Justin B. O'Connell	1958-88
John Robson Clark	1929-48		

Some Secretaries' Assistants 1927-1984

Patrick L. Prendeville	1927-32?	Raphael B. Pares	1950s
Michael McCarthy	1940s-52	J.G. Young	1960s
Justin B. O'Connell	1952-58	Kevin Keehan	1974-84

Chamber Clerks

The revived Chamber of 1820 employed Thomas Jameson, 'register' to Commercial Buildings, as its register. When he retired in 1846 he was replaced by two clerks. It was their job to staff the reading room, accept subscriptions and carry out any secretarial work. Many of the clerks' names appear in Council minutes and annual reports. The last clerk to be employed was P.J. MacDwyer, who later became secretary.

Thomas Jameson	1820-46	Thomas Higginbotham	1880-94
Robert Findlay Heron	1846-50	Louis H. Donne	1894-1921
Augustine Russell	1846-67	Alfred J. McCarthy	1895-1914
Anthony O'Curry	1848-78	J.W. Hall	1922-5?
John W. Pallin	1868-93	P.J. MacDwyer	1925-1948

Chamber Porters

From 1824, Chamber employed a porter in Commercial Buildings, whose job it was to control access to the premises. The position was humble and poorly paid but the porter was provided with a livery and his wife was paid to clean the premises. The early porters also lived in Commercial Buildings. Council minutes contain many entries regarding the porters, who tended to be the cause of some dissatisfaction. The following is a partial list of Chamber porters:

Richard Carr	1824-7	Christopher Byrne	1868-72
Daniel Toohey	1827-35	_____ Creed	?-?
John Holahan	1835-46	_____ Reilly	?-?
John Frew	1849-50	Charles McLaughlin	1918-23
Andrew Keogh	1850-?	R. Lenehan	1923-?
_____ Whelan	1864-8		

The early Chamber had only these three employees: assistant secretary, clerk and porter. From 1824 it also employed a pier-head officer to note the ships coming into Dublin harbour. The harbour master of Kingstown, Captain William Hutchinson RN, was paid a stipend to do the same for Kingstown. From the middle of the 19th century, Chamber employed a boy as a lavatory attendant, with the job of pumping the cisterns with water to facilitate the flushing systems. After the arrival of the first typewriter in 1906 the small staff was augmented by typists, mostly female. An assistant to the secretary was employed 1927-84, as well as a housekeeper and cleaner to maintain the premises. These staffing arrangements remained fundamentally the same after the move to Clare Street, until, in 1984, the organisation was modernised under the management of a CEO. There have been four CEOs to Chamber:

Tom Cox	1984-96	Jim Miley	1998-9
Noel Carroll	1996-8	Gina Quin	from 2000

APPENDIX IV

DUBLIN JUNIOR CHAMBER PRESIDENTS

Those marked with an asterisk were subsequently Presidents of Dublin Chamber of Commerce.

1956-7	James S. Leeson	1978	Derek Sherwin	1998	Martha de Buitléir
1958	John Hegarty	1979	Hugh Cassidy	1999	Niamh Kelly
1959	Charles St. J. Nolan	1980	Brian Crotty	2000	Kevin Hora
1960	Patrick J. Loughrey*		[and Hugh Cassidy]	2001	————
1961	David E. Benson	1981	Alan Benson	2002	————
1962	Sean McMahon	1982	Brendan Herlihy	2003	Raymond Reilly
1963	Owen Coyle	1983	Jerry Cunningham	2004	Raymond Reilly
1964	J.P. Fallon	1984	Claire Shorthall	2005	Kevin Gallagher
1965	Michael W. O'Reilly*	1985	Michael McDonnell	2006	Mark Kelly
1966	Declan Lennon*	1986	John McCann	2007	Peter Butler
1967	Niall McConnell	1987	Gerry Nagle	2008	Kevin Guerin
1968	Frank Carthy*	1988	Tom Kelly	2009	Michelle Daly
1969	Declan Winston	1989	Donal de Buitléir	2010	Laura Borlea
1970	Pat McCabe	1990	Stephen Walsh	2011	Chris Lascor
1971	George McConville	1991	Mary Wrafter	2012	Jani Hirvonen
1972	Brendan Connor	1992	Paula Duffy	2013	Laurynas Binderis
1973	Michael Wright	1993	Dorothy Grey	2014	Julien Gay-de-Montella
1974	Gerry Doyle	1994	Ross McMahon		
1975	Patrick O'Beirne	1995	Helen Twomey		
1976	Thomas J. Sheridan	1996	Yvonne Rohan		
1977	Peter Gibson	1997	Mary Grogan		

INDEX